PREACHING AS A THEOLOGICAL TASK

World, Gospel, Scripture

In Honor of David Buttrick

THOMAS G. LONG and EDWARD FARLEY
editors

Westminster John Knox Press
Louisville, Kentucky

Unless otherwise noted, scripture quotations are from the New Revised Standard Version of the Bible, copyright © 1989 by the Division of Christian Education of the National Council of the Churches of Christ in the U.S.A., and are used by permission.

Book design by Jennifer K. Cox
Cover design by Tony Feltner

First edition

Published by Westminster John Knox Press
Louisville, Kentucky

This book is printed on acid-free paper that meets the American National Standards Institute Z39.48 standard. ♾

PRINTED IN THE UNITED STATES OF AMERICA

96 97 98 99 00 01 02 03 04 05 — 10 9 8 7 6 5 4 3 2 1

Library of Congress Cataloging-in-Publication Data

Preaching as a theological task : World, Gospel, Scripture : in honor
of David Buttrick / Thomas G. Long and Edward Farley, editors — 1st ed.
        p.   cm.
    "A bibliography of works by David G. Buttrick" : p.
    Includes bibliographical references.
    ISBN 0-664-25617-1 (alk. paper)
    1. Preaching.   I. Buttrick, David, date.   II. Long, Thomas G., date.
III. Farley, Edward, date.
BV4211.2.P7344   1996
251—dc20   96-8619

Contents

Foreword   vii
Contributors   ix

1. The Formation of Consciousness   1
    DAVID M. GREENHAW

PART 1:   PREACHING AND THE WORLD   **17**

2. The Search for Public Theology in the United States   19
    VICTOR ANDERSON

3. A Neighborhood as Wide as God's Heart   32
    WILLIAM SLOANE COFFIN

4. A Hearer in the Pew:
    Homiletical Reflections and Suggestions   38
    GIJSBERT D. J. DINGEMANS

5. Twin Covenants in Tension on the
    Eve of the Twenty-first Century   50
    WILLIAM J. CARL III

6. Practical Theology as a Critique of Knowledge   59
    RUDOLF BOHREN

PART 2:   PREACHING AND THE GOSPEL   **71**

7. The Gospel of God   73
    FRED B. CRADDOCK

8. All the King's Men: Constructing Homiletical Meaning   82
    SUSAN KAREN HEDAHL

9. Learning to Speak of Sin   91
    THOMAS G. LONG

10. The Friend We Have in Yahweh   104
    ERNEST T. CAMPBELL

11. To Die and Rise Again:
    Preaching the Gospel for Liberation   112
    MARY LIN HUDSON

12. The Gospel as Empowered Speech
    for Proclamation and Persuasion   122
    DONALD K. MCKIM

PART 3:   PREACHING AND SCRIPTURE   **135**

13. Biblical Studies and Preaching: A Growing Divide?   137
    PAUL SCOTT WILSON

14. Apocalyptic Vocation and Liberation:
    The Foolish Church in the World   150
    L. SUSAN BOND

15. Toward a New Paradigm for Preaching   165
    EDWARD FARLEY

16. Why Preach from Passages in the Bible?   176
    RONALD J. ALLEN

Selected Bibliography of Works by David G. Buttrick   189

Foreword

Over the years of his academic career, David G. Buttrick has challenged, provoked, and invigorated the field of homiletics. He is an original, sometimes controversial, always stimulating interdisciplinary thinker, and homiletics is broader and richer because of his work.

The chapters in this book are intended to honor David Buttrick and his many contributions to preaching, but they also serve to highlight three areas of the homiletical task that have been crucial in Buttrick's own writing and thinking: the world, the gospel, and scripture. The relationships among these three elements of preaching call today for fresh interpretation, analysis, and clarification since the older patterns for negotiating among text, gospel, and context are being challenged, not least of all by David Buttrick himself. How is it that particular situations in the world are interpreted in preaching and how do the gospel and scripture guide those interpretations? These are theological questions, preaching is a theological task, and in this sense, the chapters included here all have a theological character.

"Are you ready to read the fortune of the twenty-first century?" asks Buttrick in *A Captive Voice: The Liberation of Preaching*. "Once more we will have to turn and converse with the secular world. Once more we will have to preach the gospel beyond church walls. Sermons will be more evangelical and, above all, more apologetic. For fifty years . . . there has been some tendency to regard the secular world 'out there' as the enemy of biblical faith. . . . If nothing else, the adversary position lacks courtesy. Once more we must learn to converse with the mind of our age and we must do so with genuine love and respect."

Here, on the brink of the twenty-first century and near the end of David Buttrick's teaching career, sixteen of his colleagues and friends attempt conversations "with the mind of our age." We hope that each of these conversations is accented with the love and respect for the world called for by David Buttrick. It is certain, however, that each of them grows out of love and respect for David himself.

THOMAS G. LONG
EDWARD FARLEY

Contributors

RONALD J. ALLEN, Associate Professor of Preaching and New Testament, Christian Theological Seminary, Indianapolis, Indiana

VICTOR ANDERSON, Assistant Professor of Christian Ethics, The Divinity School, Vanderbilt University, Nashville, Tennessee

RUDOLF BOHREN, Professor Emeritus for Practical Theology, University of Heidelberg, Germany

L. SUSAN BOND, Instructor in Homiletics, The Divinity School, Vanderbilt University, Nashville, Tennessee

ERNEST T. CAMPBELL, former Senior Minister, Riverside Church, New York, New York; Professor of Preaching and Worship, Garrett-Evangelical Theological Seminary/Northwestern University, Evanston, Illinois

WILLIAM J. CARL III, Senior Pastor, First Presbyterian Church, Dallas, Texas; Associate Professor of Homiletics and Worship and Instructor of New Testament Greek, Union Theological Seminary in Virginia, Richmond, Virginia

WILLIAM SLOANE COFFIN, Lecturer and preacher; former President, Peace Action; former pastor, Riverside Church, New York; former chaplain, Williams College, Williamstown, Massachusetts; former chaplain, Yale University, New Haven, Connecticut

FRED B. CRADDOCK, Bandy Distinguished Professor of Preaching and New Testament and Professor Emeritus, Candler School of Theology, Emory University, Atlanta, Georgia

GIJSBERT D. J. DINGEMANS, Professor Emeritus for Practical Theology, Rijksuniversiteit Groningen, Groningen, The Netherlands

EDWARD FARLEY, Drucilla Moore Buffington Professor of Theology, The Divinity School, Vanderbilt University, Nashville, Tennessee

DAVID M. GREENHAW, Dean and Associate Professor of Preaching and Worship, Lancaster Theological Seminary, Lancaster, Pennsylvania

SUSAN KAREN HEDAHL, Pastor, Evangelical Lutheran Church in America; Associate Professor of Homiletics, Lutheran Theological Seminary, Gettysburg, Pennsylvania

MARY LIN HUDSON, Instructor of Homiletics and Liturgics, Memphis Theological Seminary, Memphis, Tennessee

THOMAS G. LONG, Francis Landey Patton Professor of Preaching and Worship, Princeton Theological Seminary, Princeton, New Jersey

DONALD K. McKIM, Academic Dean and Professor of Theology, Memphis Theological Seminary, Memphis, Tennessee

PAUL SCOTT WILSON, Professor of Homiletics, Emmanuel College, Toronto School of Theology, Toronto, Ontario, Canada

1

The Formation of Consciousness

DAVID M. GREENHAW

> Homiletics can emerge from the objective/subjective split in which it has been trapped—either objectively rational or subjectively romantic—by moving toward the notion of consciousness where objective and subjective meet. More, homiletics can find a home in models of revelation that relate to images and symbols in social consciousness.
> —David Buttrick, "On Doing Homiletics Today"

No epigram could more aptly grasp the breadth and depth of David Buttrick's work in homiletics. Liberation from the hold that the objective/subjective split has on homiletics lies at the base of his project. The underlying premise of Buttrick's method is liberation through the "notion of consciousness." Understanding the notion of consciousness, how it overcomes the objective/subjective split, and how it gives homiletics a home in a model of revelation are critical to understanding the work and influence of this homiletician, who is among the most influential of this century.

What Is at Stake

In considering the work of any thinker, it is appropriate to begin by asking what is at stake in the theoretical framework developed. For Buttrick, the questions might be framed: Why be liberated from the objective/subjective split? What is to be gained for preaching, for the church, for the world?

In part, the answer is the recovery of the potency of preaching. This son of a prominent preacher surely desires to rescue and recover an institution that is part of a larger threatened institution. That is, the much ballyhooed decline of mainline Protestantism is paralleled by decline in the influence of the liberal to moderate pulpit. The prominence of liberal pulpiteers at the end of the century pales in comparison to that of mid-century, when the likes of George Buttrick held forth. Although David Buttrick appears to take some perverse pleasure in the decline of mainline Protestantism, as a deserved retribution for cultural accommodation, he is less able to endure the unfaithfulness and collapse of preaching. So, at a perhaps overly psychologized level, what is at stake is something akin to the family profession. But such an explanation is too shallow.

A deeper, more nuanced zeal lies behind Buttrick's project. It is the ancient desire for justice to prevail. An anecdote in *Homiletic: Moves and Structures* is telling:

> Some years ago, around Christmas time, we received two cards in the mail on the same day. One, all pink and blue, showed cradled baby Jesus with a caption reading, "May the Christ Child come to your heart at Christmas." The other card pictured a bloated baby rocking in the dust of Bangladesh with the words "Save the Children!" underneath; the card was an appeal for funds. Our problem can be stated bluntly. If Jesus can do nothing more than to come to our hearts while in the world babies are starving, then he is scarcely the savior of all.[1]

What is at stake in the liberation of preaching from the objective/subjective split is the power to transform a world of profound and pernicious injustice. It is to free the pulpit, or at the very least the American pulpit, from a dangerous ineffectiveness that allows a "nation filled with nice one-to-one Jesus people who will support the most appalling national policies!"[2]

For more than forty years, David Buttrick's professional vocation has been to revive the transformative power of preaching in service to a more just and faithful order. His purpose has been to revive preaching so that it will "once more name God in the world, form faith, address human situations, construct powerful eschatological vision, and indeed, announce God's New Order, what Jesus called 'the kingdom of God.' "[3]

It is a vocation that has taken him from local church ministry to the classroom and again and again into pulpits across the United States. His lifelong effort to fortify the ministry of preaching never ends in the classroom. Former students will well remember hours spent with the large presence of this teacher, sitting at their side, poring over a sermon, considering its moves, rethinking its structure. He worked to establish a graduate homiletics program, to teach future teachers of preaching. Through his writing in recent years, he has entered into countless pastor's studies.

Despite his influence as pastor and teacher, it is as an author that David Buttrick is making his most potent impact. A relative latecomer in the field of publishing, he is now prolific. His first major work, *Homiletic: Moves and Structures*, was published in 1987 and remains the most influential. The book was originally conceived as a work in three parts. However, constraints of the publishing industry restricted it to one volume in two sizable parts. The volume in hard cover is just short of five hundred pages. *Preaching Jesus Christ: An Exercise in Homiletic Theology* followed in 1988, *The Mystery and the Passion: A Homiletic Reading of the Gospel Traditions* in 1992, and in 1994, *A Captive Voice: The Liberation of Preaching*. In the same period, Buttrick has published several articles in books and journals as well as numerous commentaries on the lectionary.[4]

The Notion of Consciousness

Each of Buttrick's published works has provoked comment, but none more than *Homiletic*.[5] There are many favorable reviews, in fact, all the reviews are favorable, expressing an appreciation for the substantial contribution it makes to the field of preaching. Each reviewer, of course, finds an aspect especially worthy of commendation or criticism. Several reviewers, however, express confusion concerning the concept of "consciousness."[6] Indeed, there appear to be diverse and overlapping uses of the term in the massive book. In the epigram quoted above, Buttrick contends that the notion of consciousness is a key to the freeing of homiletics from the trap of the objective/subjective split. He also speaks of preaching as "forming in consciousness," of there being a "communal consciousness," and God being a "consciousness conscious of us."[7]

In part, the lack of clarity reviewers identify is rooted in a specialized use of the term. Consciousness is perhaps the most important word for understanding David Buttrick's perspective on preaching. It is also the most difficult word to understand. By it, he does not mean a mental awareness, as in: "I am now conscious of the pain in my foot." Rather, he refers to a phenomenological understanding of reality, and the peculiarly phenomenological use of the term is key to Buttrick's claim that movement toward the notion of consciousness can free homiletics.

Phenomenology as a Foundation

Many have seen the phenomenological influence on David Buttrick. On occasion, commentators have attributed his attention to the phenomenon of preaching, especially the phenomenon of how sermons are heard, to this influence. It is true that a great strength is his exploration of, as John Melloh states it, "the preaching transaction, that is what is happening in the preaching event."[8] Attending to the phenomenon of preaching is a distinctive mark of Buttrick's work. As Thomas Long has indicated:

> Buttrick's point of departure from the homiletical pack is his
> expressed desire to "describe how sermons happen in conscious-

ness." In other words, he does not want to begin by attempting to describe what a Christian sermon ought to be in and of itself, but rather by asking what *happens* when a preached sermon presses on the keyboard of the listener's mind.[9]

As true as these observations are, the real phenomenological influence on Buttrick is the foundational tie between his work and the philosophical movement loosely described as *phenomenology*. Clearly, attending to the phenomenon of the sermon as it is preached and heard is a dominant feature of Buttrick's work, and might even be the fruit of his familiarity with the methodologies of phenomenology, but it is not the root. The root is found elsewhere.[10]

The casual reader of Buttrick can be fooled by the "chatty" style of his prose into believing that he is an armchair philosopher. Far from it. The bibliography of *Homiletic* is filled with references to the work of Remey Kwant, Maurice Merleau-Ponty, Martin Heidegger, Michel Foucault, and Paul Ricoeur. In addition, Buttrick has enjoyed a long-standing friendship and theological conversation partnership with Edward Farley, perhaps the leading theological interpreter of the phenomenological movement.[11]

The phenomenological movement is a twentieth-century approach to philosophical understanding of reality. It calls into question the "common sense" understanding of what is "real," and proposes a more carefully nuanced approach. In a common sense perspective,[12] there is an object here in front of me, a table, for instance, and there is a subject perceiving the object, me. In a phenomenological perspective, this natural standpoint is set aside, bracketed, and the phenomenon itself is examined more closely. From the phenomenological perspective, the table is there as table through an act of consciousness. That is, through an intentional act it becomes a table for me and not just the bundle of "stuff"—wood, legs, finish, tabletop. It could be construed otherwise, but for me, it is construed as table. In no way is the "actuality" of table called into question; it is not that the table is not really there. It is, rather, that as the bundle of "stuff," it is not necessarily a table. It is a table for me as it is intended as such for me. For instance, if one becomes very tired, bone weary, the very same items that were table for me are now a chair or bed to rest on. They are formed differently by my intention.

A more detailed look at another example of a phenomenological approach to reality will help clarify what Buttrick means by the term "consciousness." The Czech philosopher Erazim Kohak describes seeing a ship in the harbor:

> We speak of "seeing a ship," but that is not what we actually experience. We have to row around it, and what is actually presented is

never a ship as such, but always one side of it—timbers, cordage, canvas—from a particular perspective; and any one of these perspectives could actually be a two-dimensional movie set.[13]

Because we are unable to grasp the ship as a whole in our perception, we must "stitch together" the various aspects experienced sequentially. To use a common metaphor of Buttrick's, we grasp the ship as if through a series of photographic snapshots.[14] The stitching together, the composition of a photo album or a filmstrip, if you will, requires an act of consciousness. That is, the various aspects of our encounter with the ship in the harbor are not whole in themselves but are "built" in consciousness. We do this so naturally, so easily, that we are not aware of the act itself. This is where the phenomenological method comes in; it attends to the phenomenon of experience.

The ship is neither an object "out there" nor simply a subjective experience "in here." What we experience is not the ship as an object in its own right, but the ship as we experience it. This does not make the ship any less real. It is still there as a bundle of entities. It is just that the ship becomes ship through our purposive act. As Kohak puts it,

> Think again of rowing around the ship. What we encounter is a series of exposures as on a filmstrip, each with its characteristics; wooden, real, brown. They are not random. Even if we were to cut up our filmstrip and shuffle the pieces, we could still rearrange them in order, fitting them together in a composite image of a ship. But that bundle of contiguous impressions still is not "the ship" any more than the boards, oakum, cordage, and canvas constitute the ship. The unitary reality, a ship, enters our experience only with our purposive act: I will sail.[15]

Consciousness and a Call to Preach

Forming a ship out of the combination of the perspectival aspects of our perception and our purposive intending of the function of ship, namely to sail, happens in what Buttrick calls *consciousness*. It is not simply that we passively perceive objects in the world or even just aspects of objects. It is rather that through an intentional act, the perception is pulled together into a unitary experience, a lived experience, a formed consciousness. It is not that the ship is formed by our perception; it is that it is formed in consciousness in this way. Consciousness refers to lived experience, not simply an idea or a thought, but the formation of a world out of the various worlds that can be formed. As Kohak says, "The boards, ropes and canvas are there with all their characteristics . . . but the unitary 'thing-in-itself' is there only *in lived experience*, not as a bundle of perceptions but *as a syn-*

thetic unity constituted by my purposive presence."[16] Consciousness is just this lived experience.

The ship, or anything for that matter, is not any less real or substantial because it is formed in consciousness. Nor is consciousness a mere passing state of mind or a simple fancy. It is, instead, the name given to the act of intentionality that "builds" a world we experience. Reality cannot be formed in any other way than in consciousness. Again Kohak: "The point, however, is that the full undenied reality of the ship is a reality *in experience*. It is no less real for it. The ship is real; but the real ship is also experienced, not hidden."[17]

For preaching, the phenomenological perspective becomes more significant when we shift from a ship formed in consciousness and turn to something like God's grace formed in consciousness. Grace is not made any less real simply because it is formed in consciousness. It is not a "mere" fancy. It is a function, however, of human consciousness. The lived experience of grace is the experience of grace formed in consciousness.

This phenomenological understanding of reality poses a danger. It is not that things that matter are less real or merely subjective; instead, the danger is that what is formed in consciousness could be formed otherwise. The ship could be formed otherwise. It could be, in Kohak's words, "a year's supply of firewood."[18] What seems settled and clear can just as easily be recast, re-formed. Because the intentionality of the consciousness into which something is formed plays a role in the formation of the reality, reality can be affected by human intentionality.

If a traditional view of preaching could be characterized as a descriptive presentation of an extant world, then a notion that the world could be recast, re-formed, is indeed dangerous. The making of carefully reasoned homiletical points could easily be threatened by the possibility of construing the world otherwise.

From Buttrick's point of view, it is precisely this possibility—real things can be variously formed in consciousness—that opens the space for, or constitutes the need for, preaching. That the world could be variously constituted forms the clarion call of preaching. Buttrick puts it this way:

> Events, things, inner experiences—all may be variously named. Only the rigid fundamentalist or unreconstructed secularist will insist that there can be only one name for any given happening. As Christians we must never be dismayed by double, triple, or even quadruple naming, for multiple naming is surely the basis of evangelism. Evangelism rests on the open option that anything may be renamed gleefully into a consciousness of God.[19]

If it is possible for "events, things, inner experiences" to be formed differently in consciousness, then it is possible for them to be mistakenly formed. For instance, although it is possible "gleefully" to name God into consciousness, it is also possible to fail to do so. Grace could fail to be formed in consciousness. Hence the call for preaching to take up the challenge of forming the gospel in consciousness is all the more urgent.

Preaching: Forming a Faith World

Formation of a reality in consciousness does not happen solely when persons perceive through their senses. It happens in language. The various aspects of the ship are pulled together into a unitary reality with the word "ship." The reader has some notion of what I mean when I write the words "ship in a harbor" on this page, because language is able to form a reality or image in consciousness. It does so by calling on a shared consciousness. That is, language is not solitary, but communal. As Buttrick puts it, "We do not invent a language out of our secret selves, we inherit a language, in use. When we enter the world we dive into a linguistic pool, a whirling, eddying linguistic pool."[20]

Language shapes a human consciousness that is not a solitary, individual consciousness but a communal consciousness. The shared consciousness of a people, a class, a social group, even a church, can be formed by language. Preaching wields the power of language, which is the power to shape and reshape human communal consciousness. Preaching may alter human intentionality so that what is formed in consciousness is formed differently than it might be were there not preaching. To form a communal consciousness, to change a common cultural mind, is what preaching can do. Preaching shapes worlds in social consciousness.

Buttrick says, "[W]hat preaching may do is to build in consciousness a new 'faith-world' in which we may live and love."[21] Of all the worlds that can be "built" in consciousness, preaching is to build a "faith-world" in which we may live and love. Preaching is to name God in consciousness, and by naming God, to construct the world of the church and the greater social order as a world in which we may live and love. When preaching fails to "build" such a world, it is in part because it is held captive in the trap of the objective/subjective split.

The Objective/Subjective Split

On several occasions, Buttrick refers to the objective/subjective split as a trap.[22] It is an interesting double metaphor—a split that is a trap. The split is between an objective, "out-there" God and a personal, subjective

"in-here" me. The trap springs when homiletics allows the split to be def-
initional for its task. That is, when preaching attempts to overcome the
distance between the "out-there" God and the "in-here" me, it is doomed
because it sets up an artificial task. There is no God who is merely "out-
there" any more than there is a me that is merely "in-here."

God, inasmuch as God is known to us, as God is God as known to us.
The notion of God abstracted from our knowing God, even in itself is
wholly held within our notion of the abstraction. Imagine God, if you can,
as not imagined by humans. It is like the dentist who puts two hands in
your mouth, nearly tickling your tonsil, and says, "Now relax." It is
impossible because the very act of imaging God as not imagined is already
an act of imagining. The subjective me that is "in-here" is not isolatable
from the social milieu in which I have been and continue to be formed as
a person. The me is a me in culture and context, shaped and constituted by
relationships with others and an environment.

Two perspectives Buttrick finds intolerable illustrate his understanding
of the objective/subjective split in contemporary terms. The first is the
biblical theology movement. The second is what Buttrick calls the "triumph of the therapeutic."[23] The first isolates revelation from contact with
human understanding, and the second reduces divine revelation to a
region of the human psyche.

The Biblical Theology Movement

This twentieth-century theological trend, drawn largely from the neo-
Orthodox theologian Karl Barth, has overly objectified revelation. It has
equated revelation with the sources of revelation, namely, the words, stories, and images of the Bible. From Buttrick's perspective, the Bible is a
rich resource for preaching; it is even normative, but it is not revelation.
Revelation is not the words of the Bible or even the words of preaching
but the formation of a faith-world in consciousness. That is, revelation is
something that happens, not something that is reported.

Buttrick opposes preaching as an "end-of-the-line" activity, in which

> God has acted in history; the Bible is a record of the acts of God;
> historical critical research gets at original revelation through scrip-
> ture; preaching preaches recovered revelation to faith.[24]

In such a perspective, revelation is something objective, "out there" or
"back then," and the task of preaching is reduced to the reporting of
this "object" to the contemporary church. This side of the objective/
subjective split results in an aversion to technical considerations of how
preaching is done. It fears too much consideration of the form of preach-

ing. The root of the fear is that revelation, as an object, is fixed; it cannot be tinkered with, added to, or subtracted from.

In part, this emphasis corrects the reduction of revelation to a category of human religiosity or a region of the human psyche. Buttrick shares the interest in overcoming an overly subjective tendency, but he is persuaded that the corrective of the biblical theology movement was too extreme.[25] He says,

> With the dialectical theologians, we may agree that revelation may not be weighed by the measure of our minds, but we must insist that revelation to be revelation must, at least, relate to human understandings.[26]

The Triumph of the Therapeutic

Equation of revelation to the "measure of our minds," narrows preaching's influence to the individual psyche. As Buttrick puts it, "Most sermons from most pulpits, particularly since 1950, seem to have been aimed at an existential self in psychological self-awareness."[27] The split, brought about in the biblical theology movement, between the object of revelation and the receiving subject produced such an arid preaching terrain that preachers sought any sort of relevance or point of contact. The result has been "a pool-gazing Narcissus,"[28] a near obsessive focus on our well-being, sense of "wholeness," "wellness," "inner-child," or any other of a number of faddish "psychologisms." They have filled the vacuum of theological force created when preaching is "trapped" in the "split."

In a lament that demonstrates his grief over the state of things, Buttrick names what is lost:

> How have we read scripture during the height of the twentieth century? We have read the Bible as objective facticity or as a message of personal psychological salvation—"You can be a new person inside of yourself." So, though we have revered the Bible as God's Word, we seem to have ignored both its mythic depth and its social message.[29]

Preaching Finds a Home

"Preaching can find a home in models of revelation that relate to images and symbols in social consciousness."[30] The models of revelation of which Buttrick speaks are models that do not reduce revelation to a past tense event but understand revelation as always eventful and productive. Revelation happens! It forms a particular communal consciousness. Out of a full range of worlds that can be formed, it forms a faith-world in which we can live and love. It announces the good news of the gospel and initiates God's redemptive purposes. In short, whether revelation is happening depends on the character of the world "building" in consciousness.

Again we are brought back to Buttrick's commitment to justice. The relationship between preaching and revelation is founded on preaching's correlation to the redemptive purpose of God's revelation. In Buttrick's words,

> Why is preaching a "Word of God"? Preaching is a word of God only if it serves God's redemptive purposes. Preaching announces good news of the gospel and, in so doing, sets people free for God's new humanity. Preaching is not word of God because it is under church auspices. Preaching is not a word of God because it speaks from a "warmed heart." And preaching is not a word of God because it draws on a biblical passage. No, preaching is only word of God if, instigated by the Spirit, it serves God's redemptive purpose. But please note: The same argument may be transferred to scripture! Is the Bible the Word of God? Yes, the Bible is lofty literature. And, yes, it gathers a noble assembly of religious voices representing thousands of years of faith. But can the Bible be Word of God when it is used to demean women, inflame prejudice, or bash members of the gay/lesbian community? With both scripture and preaching "in use," activity is the test. Neither preaching nor scripture is Word of God per se. The Bible *can be* God's Word because it can speak redemptively.[31]

Buttrick's model of revelation envisions the power of building a world in consciousness, the "being-saved" world in consciousness. The test of whether this world is the gospel's world is its performance of God's redemptive purposes. As Buttrick says, "Activity is the test."[32] The "home" that preaching finds is found by participating in God's redemptive purposes. Such a "home" requires of preaching thoroughgoing theological investigation of what constitutes the redemptive purposes of God.

Although much of Buttrick's project has involved an effort to overcome the near stranglehold Karl Barth has had on preaching, he has not come to this without traversing at least part of the way with Barth. By his own account, he undertook a "determined ploughing through Barth's *Church Dogmatics*."[33] The seriousness with which Barth takes the need to faithfully preach the gospel accords with Buttrick's own desire for preaching to serve God's redemptive purposes. The relationship between theology and preaching that is characteristic of Barth is also central for Buttrick. When Barth's lecture notes on preaching were collected, translated, and issued in an American volume, Buttrick wrote the foreword. There he notes that "Barth linked theology and preaching: He proposed that theology should be 'nothing other than sermon preparation.' "[34] Buttrick concludes his remarks in the foreword by saying, "Barth's thoughtful wrestling with homiletic definitions and issues is still worthy of attention because, to reverse Barth's own claim, sermon preparation after all is nothing other than theology."[35]

Indeed, sermon preparation is theology. And what is more, according to Buttrick, "congregational theology is largely a product of preaching."[36] It is here that Buttrick breaks most radically with the biblical theology movement and makes his most indelible mark on the theory of preaching. How one structures a sermon affects how congregational theology is shaped. Even more, how one structures a sermon affects the formation of the faith-world in consciousness and the resultant redemptive activity. Buttrick recovers a focus on the crafting of sermons, not simply as an ancillary matter but as central to the power and potency of preaching. This is what he is referring to when he says,

> The gospel, in its prophetic power, clearly runs counter to all-American cultural values, so that people may not want to receive the message we preach. Nevertheless, adequately formed language will be heard and will probably not be twisted into other meanings by listeners. Baldly, if preachers preach well, people will hear.[37]

If a sermon is well formed, it will form consciousness. Therefore, the question of which consciousness is formed is critical. Preachers rightly have a "doubled fear of misinterpretation"[38] because how they say what they say matters.

Partnership with Rhetoric

In *Homiletic*, Buttrick undertakes a systematic approach to structuring sermons. He outlines with considerable care many aspects of sermon construction. Relying on social science evidence, he argues the relative merit of various strategies for preaching. Buttrick explores whether preachers should use personal examples, the length of introductions and conclusions, the proper use of alliteration, humor, and doublets, and many other stylistic considerations. Taken as a whole, these reflections amount to a recovery of rhetoric for preaching. A reader of *Homiletic* could easily see that the choice of the singular word "homiletic" rather than the customary plural, "homiletics," suggests the classic rhetorical works simply called *Rhetoric*.[39]

The phenomenological premises of Buttrick's larger project create space for a new relationship between preaching and rhetoric. He is inter-

ested in reestablishing the partnership between preaching and rhetoric.
He puts it this way,

> Nineteenth-century homiletics drew on rhetorical study. In the
> twentieth century, homiletic wisdom was reduced, while at the
> same time the connection between homiletics and rhetoric was
> severed. We decided to preach the Bible, to draw method from the
> Bible, and to turn away from the machinations of secular rhetoric.
> The result: We made biblical noises but in fact we did not preach
> very well. Of course, the black pulpit continued to speak with
> force, the force of a highly sophisticated black rhetorical tradition.
> But note, as theology moves toward philosophy and as biblical
> criticism connects with literary criticism, homiletics must shyly
> make up and relate to rhetoric once again.[40]

The reference to "shyly" making up with rhetoric might have been
advice taken more to heart by Buttrick himself. He has demonstrated a
zeal in his argumentation about what is effective in sermon crafting that
has been anything but shy. For many readers this zeal has been off-
putting. Even more to the point, it has been the basis of criticism of his
work. Perhaps one of his most articulate critics has been Thomas Long,
who doubts whether it is possible to predict what happens in consciousness by any given focus in the homiletical act.

On the one hand, Long appreciates the partnership Buttrick begins
with rhetoric. On the other hand, he expresses disappointment with the
results. He says, "In the nuts and bolts section of his homiletical textbook,
Buttrick seems to assume that each and every hearer is essentially alike."[41]
As Long notes, this leads to a set of highly technical, even technological
rules that are presented as always applicable. This leads Long to quip, "So
many of Buttrick's rules are clearly exaggerations, that one suspects him
at times of winking slyly at the reader, employing hyperbole as a playful
strategy to force the reader to reconsider unchallenged assumptions."
Long concludes that "a potentially exciting conversation between
homiletical theology and rhetoric" begun by Buttrick does not live up to
its potential. It is overcome "by a quasi-technological monologue in which
rhetoric does most of the talking while homiletics takes notes."[42]

Long's criticism strikes a strong chord. There is in Buttrick's prose,
especially in *Homiletic*, a nearly authoritarian style. Although Long's suspicion that Buttrick is "winking slyly" would soften the stylistic blow, it
is probably not the case. Because Buttrick is interested in reestablishing
how a sermon is structured as central to the vocation of preaching, one
must assume he is serious.[43] Long's criticism of Buttrick is compelling.[44]
It is all the more so, because it recognizes much of the genius in Buttrick's
project.

In part the genius of Buttrick's project is the way he puts together the thick formation of a communal consciousness and the cultural apparatus in which it takes place. His familiarity with phenomenology and his attention to the philosophy of language set his work apart. Hardly anyone could claim to have thought through the dynamics of a sermon more carefully than David Buttrick. At the same time, it is his remarkable attention to sermons that is also one of his greatest flaws. He focuses so much attention on the sermon that it begins to overshadow preaching.

Preaching is not a sermon. A homiletic that assumes that any given sermon can make a huge difference credits too much to sermons and not enough to preaching. Preaching unfolds in the long season of a fruitful ministry with a congregation. It is not simply what is said in Sunday installments, but the denouement of a faith-world formed in consciousness week after week, season after season, year after year.

One misses in Buttrick's work the extension of the notion of forming a communal consciousness to preaching more than a sermon, but a season of sermons. If, for instance, a communal consciousness is formed around images and symbols of racial hatred, it is unlikely that any one sermon will effect a genuine shift in communal consciousness. However, it might be possible to reform a communal consciousness by introducing, developing, and instituting enduring images and symbols of racial equity, tolerance, and appreciation. To do so would take more than a sermon, but an equally systematic program of proclamation executed in the course of a preacher's tenure with a congregation.

It is true that there are things in preaching that work, that make a difference, that can be done one way more effectively than another. And David Buttrick is perhaps more capable at naming and identifying those elements than anyone else publishing in preaching today. His lasting contribution will not be measured by the accuracy of his prediction on the effectiveness of a move, a structure, introduction or conclusion. His genuine and lasting contribution is in the loud and long call he has issued to a church grown complacent about how it preaches. His call has amounted to a recovery of rhetoric. But it is more than that. It is a recovery of the awareness that we are shaped rhetorically willy-nilly. The question is not whether the church should utilize rhetoric in its preaching. The question is which rhetoric will the church use and toward what end. We are constantly being shaped and reshaped by rhetoric. We forget it because we call it something else; we call it advertising or public relations or spin control. But it is rhetoric. It is pervasive, not intrinsically evil, but constantly present. We cannot escape rhetoric because it is how worlds are formed in consciousness.

The task of preaching is to form the world in consciousness so that God is named. "We are building a faith-world in congregational consciousness."[45] If we are faithful, we might be able to participate in the shaping of a faith-world that will not simply baptize the dominant culture, but "once more name God in the world, form faith, address human situations, construct powerful eschatological vision, and indeed, announce God's New Order, what Jesus called 'the kingdom of God.' "[46]

A Beggar for Grace

David Buttrick, a preacher who has been willing to provoke the rage of an orthodox establishment, has in his personal life often exhibited the marks of a social courage and conviction. He has withdrawn from systems that he found it impossible to support any longer. He left a teaching post at one stage and withdrew his ordination and changed denominations in another. In a more quiet way, he has been a person of faith, a preacher who sits in the pew not solely with the critical ear of a specialist, but in his own words, as a "beggar for grace."

If it is the case that preachers are judged by whether they practice what they preach, I offer this simple anecdote as a testimony for the congruence of practice and preaching in David Buttrick. On a Thanksgiving Day, my wife, two children, and I were invited to join the Buttrick household for the annual holiday feast. When we arrived at the Buttrick home, we were met by David and Betty Buttrick, Emily the massive Newfoundland family dog, and chaos, utter chaos. The kitchen, living room, family room, were filled with friendly folks of all sorts: students stranded in a strange town without means to return home; fellow faculty members without proximate extended family; neighbors who preferred the chaos of this household to the emptiness of their own; literal strangers who were passing by and welcomed in; and a couple of folks who had been picked up at the homeless shelter. Nearly everyone pitched in to prepare the meal. And when all were gathered, there was a mix around the table that cut across social, political, racial, economic, and international lines. Chaotic yes, but the glorious chaos of an eschatological banquet. It is as host to such a meal that I will always picture David Buttrick, the steward of God's Word, who practices what he preaches in ways humble and brave.

NOTES

1. David Buttrick, *Homiletic: Moves and Structures* (Philadelphia: Fortress Press, 1987), 421.
2. Ibid.
3. Buttrick, "On Doing Homiletics Today," in *Intersections: Post-Critical Studies in Preaching*, ed. Richard L. Eslinger (Grand Rapids: Wm. B. Eerdmans Publishing Co., 1994), 104.

4. For a selected bibliography of Buttrick's works, see pp. 189–91.
5. The 1995 American Theological Library Association's *Religion Database* lists over thirty reviews of Buttrick's *Homiletic* alone.
6. John A. Melloh, "Homiletic: Moves and Structures," *Worship* 62 (May 1988):266; John Riggs, "Homiletic: Moves and Structures," *Journal of Religion* 69 (April 1989):270; Donald K. McKim, "Terror and Gladness," *The Reformed Journal* 38 (January 1988):18.
7. For example, see Buttrick, *Homiletic*, 116ff.
8. John A. Melloh, S.M., "Forum: *Homiletic: Moves and Structures*, Response to David Buttrick," *Worship* 62 (May 1988):266–69.
9. Thomas G. Long, "Homiletic," *Theology Today* 45 (April 1988):108, 110–12.
10. For an account of Buttrick's intellectual movement toward phenomenology, see David Buttrick, "On Preaching a Parable: The Problem of Homiletic Method," *Reformed Liturgy & Music* 17:1 (Winter 1983):16–21.
11. David Buttrick and Edward Farley as young professors served together on the faculty of Pittsburgh Theological Seminary. Buttrick then left Pittsburgh and served for seven years at St. Meinrad School of Theology in St. Meinrad, Indiana. A few years later, Farley went to Vanderbilt University Divinity School where, in 1983, he and Buttrick were reunited on the same faculty. For more on Farley, see Edward Farley, *Ecclesial Man: A Social Phenomenology of Faith and Reality* (Philadelphia: Fortress Press, 1975).
12. Edmund Husserl, among the most prominent theorists in the phenomenological movement, calls the common sense perspective *"natürliche Einstellung,"* or the "natural standpoint" (*Die Idee der Phänomenologie*, ed. Walter Biemel [The Hague: Martinus Nijhoff, 1950]). (E.T., *The Idea of Phenomenology*, tr. W. Alston and G. Nakhinikian [The Hague: Martinus Nijhoff, 1968].)
13. Erazim Kohak, *Idea and Experience* (Chicago: University of Chicago Press, 1978), 51–52.
14. See esp. the description of "point of view" in Buttrick, *Homiletic*, 50–61.
15. Kohak, *Idea and Experience*, 52.
16. Ibid., 53, author's italics.
17. Ibid.
18. Ibid.
19. Buttrick, *Homiletic*, 8.
20. Ibid., 179.
21. Ibid., 17.
22. In addition to the passage that serves as the epigram above, see Buttrick, *Homiletic*, "Of course, turn-of-the-century 'social-gospelers' may have stumbled into the same trap. Social gospel pulpits addressed problems in the world, an objective world 'out there,'. . . . Thus, definitions of preaching seem to be trapped in models of authority that maintain an objective and subjective split" (249).
23. This phrase is one that Buttrick has drawn from Philip Reiff, *The Triumph of the Therapeutic: Uses of Faith after Freud* (New York: Harper & Row, 1966).
24. Buttrick, *Homiletic*, 115.
25. "The biblical theology movement is a strange legacy. We have gained much from a golden age of historical-critical biblical scholarship. But maybe, just maybe, we have lost our homiletical souls—prophetic silence, past-tense faith, and an enlarging tension between the Bible and the good news of the

gospel message" (David Buttrick, *A Captive Voice: The Liberation of Preaching* [Louisville, Ky.: Westminster John Knox Press, 1994], 12).

26. Buttrick, *Homiletic*, 115.
27. Buttrick, *A Captive Voice*, 13.
28. Ibid., 14.
29. Ibid.
30. Buttrick, "On Doing Homiletics Today," 104.
31. Buttrick, *A Captive Voice*, 30–31.
32. Ibid.
33. Buttrick, "On Preaching a Parable," 19.
34. David Buttrick, foreword to *Homiletics*, by Karl Barth, trans. Geoffrey Bromiley and Donald E. Daniels (Louisville, Ky.: Westminster/John Knox Press, 1991), 8.
35. Ibid., 10.
36. Buttrick, *Homiletic*, 19.
37. David Buttrick, "Who's Listening?," in *Listening to the Word: Essays in Honor of Fred B. Craddock*, ed. Thomas G. Long and Gail R. O'Day (Nashville: Abingdon Press, 1993), 204.
38. Buttrick, *Homiletic*, 270.
39. See, for instance, the classic work by Aristotle called *Rhetoric*.
40. Buttrick, *A Captive Voice*, 3.
41. Thomas G. Long, "And How Shall They Hear?" in Long and O'Day, *Listening to the Word*, 183.
42. Ibid., 184.
43. See my note on Buttrick's overemphasis on congregational recall as a criterion for sermon effectiveness, in David Greenhaw, "As One with Authority," in Eslinger, *Intersections*, 120, n. 36.
44. Long is not alone in this assessment of Buttrick's work. See, for instance, Ronald Allen's review of *Homiletic* in *Encounter* 51:1 (Winter 1990):69ff.
45. Buttrick, "Who's Listening?," 206.
46. Buttrick, "On Doing Homiletics Today," 104.

1. PREACHING AND THE WORLD

2

The Search for Public Theology in the United States

VICTOR ANDERSON

> There are voices in the church today that urge the preservation of
> our faith story as the number-one task of the churches. But what
> are we to preserve? Enlightenment Christianity has already crum-
> bled. No, once more we must risk faith's conversation with cul-
> ture. Sometimes, it is called evangelism.
> —David Buttrick, *A Captive Voice*

This chapter on public theology in the United States is based on discussions that have preoccupied David Buttrick and myself for several
years. My intention is not to overromanticize the contributions of various
thinkers to American public theology. Rather, the focus on public theology is my attempt to acknowledge the impact of Buttrick's own commitments to genuine public discourse about social justice, poverty,
homophobia, and sexism. Public theology is a way to situate the paradoxical claims that Buttrick makes for the gospel in *A Captive Voice: The
Liberation of Preaching* (1994) and for his insistence on liberating yet theologically responsible preaching within our postmodern North American
context.

The idea of public theology is not new. However, the idea has gained
recent currency among academic theologians in the United States. The
list of recent contributors includes Protestant as well as American
Catholic thinkers: David Tracy, Joseph William Buckley, Michael Novak,
John Richard Neuhaus, Mary McGlone, Roger Shinn, Ronald Thiemann,
Linell Cady, and Gerald McDermott. Catholic contributors tend to see
exemplary accounts of public theology among such figures as Father
Isaac Hecker, John Courtney Murray, Jacques Maritain, and Yves Simon.
Mary McGlone sees public theology everywhere in the actions of past
saints such as St. Augustine, St. Francis Assisi, St. Thomas Becket, but
particularly in the actions of the sixteenth-century predecessor of Latin
liberation theology, Archbishop Toribio, and Latin liberation theologians. Protestant writers tend to highlight figures such as Martin Luther,

John Calvin, Reinhold Niebuhr, H. Richard Niebuhr, Paul Tillich, and Harvey Cox.

A quick survey of the literature reveals several key meanings of public theology. Public theology is the deliberate use of distinctively theological commitments to influence substantive public debate and policy. It emphasizes the use of "religious resources for discourse about social conflict within the wider society," and through religious symbols and concepts it creates "disclosive and transformative possibilities for public argument and interpretation."[1] According to Roger Shinn, public theology identifies the theologians' responsibility "to enter into the processes of public discussion that determine policy."[2] For Ronald Thiemann, Christian public theology has two goals: "to understand the relation between Christian convictions and the broader social and cultural context within which the Christian community lives" and "to identify the particular places where Christian convictions intersect with the practices that characterize contemporary public life."[3]

Common to these various descriptions of public theology is what Paul Tillich regarded as the paradoxical dimension of theological discourse. This dimension refers to the interdependency of religious activities with other cultural activities. It signals the "interstices" and not only the "intersections" of theology and culture. That is, it reflects on the ways that theological discourse differentiates itself from other cultural activities while always remaining a cultural activity. Tillich's discussion of the paradox of the churches adequately discloses the paradoxical dimension of theological discourse. According to Tillich, "the paradox of the churches is the fact that they participate, on the one hand, in the ambiguities of life in general and of the religious life in particular and, on the other hand, in the unambiguous life of the Spiritual Community."[4]

The churches are entailed in a "secular history with all the disintegrating, destructive, and tragic-demonic elements which make historical life as ambiguous as all other life processes," says Tillich.[5] As a spiritual community, the churches are differentiated from other human organizations by theological doctrines and religious functions that are not transferable to other organizations without a real loss to their religious identities. Therefore, Tillich argues that their content and functions ought not to be internally ambiguous. "A church which is nothing more than a benevolent, socially useful group can be replaced by other groups not claiming to be churches; such a church has no justification for its existence," says Tillich.[6]

Various Views of Public Theology

Public theology reflects on the paradoxical relations that circumscribe the place and functions of religion in public life. Therefore, it does not rest easy with any public/private distinction that might conceptually uncouple theological discourse from public discourse. Public theology recognizes that the internal languages that identify the doctrinal commitments and cultic practices of particular religious communities are, at the same time, cultural languages that render religious communities particular discursive sites for public discourse. That is, religious communities are distinctive locations where moral, social, cultural practices are theologically criticized and legitimized through the apparatuses of doctrine, liturgy, and organization. In these communities of discourse, the public function of theology may be prophetic, calling into question public acts that distort and disrupt effective communication of the common goods that persons require for social equilibrium and cultural fulfillment. However, it may also exercise a priestly function when the rich resources of doctrine, piety, and organization enable the public realm to flourish in peace.

Catholic Public Theology

Sister Mary McGlone sees in Augustine's *City of God* a public theology that is in the service of Christians blamed for the fall of the Roman Empire. She sees it in St. Francis's "public affair" with the life of poverty and his critique of the accumulated wealth of the papacy. McGlone regards St. Thomas Becket's opposition to King Henry II as a public theology that defends ecclesiastical right over monarchial rights. However, it is the Archbishop of Lima, Toribio, whom she regards as the exemplary public theologian:

> Toribio's pastoral priorities eventually put him in direct conflict with established Spanish interests in Peru. His understanding of his mission did not permit him to confine his activities to the sacristy, but moved him to become involved in every aspect of the life of his people. Caring for his people meant that in addition to addressing clerical misconduct, he directed his attention to Spanish civil officials and laypeople as well. Recognizing the deep-seated conflicts between the natives and the Spaniards, Toribio's option for the "integral well-being" of all of them, forced him to take more than one public stand on the temporal well-being of the natives and its connection with the spiritual well-being of the Spaniards. From his perspective, the two were intimately connected.[7]

According to McGlone, Toribio's function as archbishop placed him in a position to represent the right of the church over Catholic mercantilists. This responsibility often placed him in the position of being the public critic of Spanish atrocities and the king's conscience in the New World, says McGlone. "Toribio of Mogrovejo was one of the outstanding public theologians of his era. His continuous mission journeys, his exercise of authority and his public protests flowed from his vision of the vocation of being a shepherd," says McGlone.[8]

Within the United States, American Catholics tend to cite Fathers Isaac Hecker and John Courtney Murray as exemplary figures in Catholic public theology. Both men were separated from each other by a century. Formerly a Protestant who converted to Roman Catholicism, Hecker's pilgrimage is characterized by disenchantment with the schismatic tendencies of Protestantism and the failure of Protestant ecstatic piety to solve the irritation of religious skepticism. Hecker became the founder of the Paulist Fathers. According to Buckley, his mission was to win over Protestant America to the true faith by demonstrating the compatibility of Catholic theology and American liberty. Buckley sees in Hecker's justifications surrounding the American Civil War distinctive features of public theology. "Hecker clearly saw that it was the church's duty to relate the dramatic and unthinkable violent local situation of the civil war to the religious tradition of Roman Catholicism. In doing so, he gave us a valuable and distinctively American nineteenth century public theology," says Buckley.[9]

As Father Hecker was an exemplary public theologian in the nineteenth-century United States, in the twentieth century such a position belongs to Father Murray. Perhaps no greater monument represents his influence on public theology than Vatican II's "Declaration on Religious Freedom." In spirit, the declaration is libertarian. It insists that religious freedom is entailed in the languages of human rights and ought to be conducted uncoerced by external authorities, whether that of the church or the state. Murray's position is balanced by insisting that the exercise of religion is "recognized in the constitutional law whereby society is governed. Thus it is to become a civil right."[10] Insofar as religious freedom is entailed in human rights, civil rights, and the constitutional principles of the United States, Murray argued that it is no threat to the magisterial authority of the church. "The doctrine of the Church that no one is to be coerced into faith has always stood firm," says Murray.[11] He also argued that the state vitiates its legitimate authority if it restrains anyone "from acting in accordance with his own beliefs, whether privately or publicly, whether alone or in association with others, within due limits."[12]

Michael Novak credits Murray as the public theologian who influenced his own public theology. Novak writes of Murray:

> He took something from the American experience and found a way to articulate it in a traditional Catholic language that made it acceptable to the Catholic Church at the Second Vatican

Council—the principle of religious liberty. He took a principle that many traditional Catholics would have argued was counter to the Catholic tradition, and showed how it actually served that tradition, and was a better roadway for the Catholic tradition to follow in the future. You could say that Murray's work represented a distinctively American contribution to the Catholic Tradition.[13]

Among the several Catholic figures introduced above, key theological vocabularies remain stable and effective in their public discourses. According to Buckley, the controlling motifs in Father Hecker's public theology are providence and redemption. "Whatever the 'public' and whatever the 'theology' which helps to form a new 'public theology,' all such efforts are aimed at answering important questions about the ways in which God redeems us as a community," says Buckley.[14] Buckley uses Father Hecker's claim that "God is redeeming us through the civil war" as a possible condition for public theology.[15] Buckley argues that Catholic public theologians can also take "Hecker's fascinating remarks about God's inscrutable providence in history to reflect on how his eschatological symbols can function as a critique of ideologies."[16]

Sister McGlone suggests that the ideas of *santos* and *vocation* are rich with possibilities for public theology. Commenting on Archbishop Toribio, she argues that "his pastoral practice was designed to fulfill the three-fold purpose of protecting the natives, correcting the Spaniards and illuminating the conscience of the king."[17] McGlone unites Toribio's three-fold pastoral purpose with the idea of the saints and finds the effective influences of past saints on contemporary public theologies documented at Medellín, Puebla, and San Domingo.[18] On McGlone's account, *santos* creates an interpretative possibility that sees in the active lives of saints public theologians who "confront us with new and often disturbing ways to believe in, understand and integrate the values of the gospel into the complex societies we call our own."[19]

For Novak, the great contribution of Catholic moral theology to public theology is its emphasis on a substantive tradition of "practical wisdom" that is disseminated didactically to the particular social conduct of church members under the magisterial authority of the church. Novak explains:

> The defence of reason and the grounding of moral life in principles of reason may become another great contribution of the Catholic tradition to American life. I would like to include here the term "prudence" or "wisdom"—as understood in a practical way—as part of the Catholic understanding of reason. . . . This is an important Catholic contribution to American self-understanding."[20]

Protestant Public Theology

The search for public theology in the United States becomes more difficult when discussing Protestant Christianity. The difficulty lies in the inex-
tricable connections between Protestant evangelical Christianity and the
liberal politics that undergirds North American culture. Gerald McDermott
acknowledges that there exists a determinate legacy of Reformation theologies and Puritan influences on North American political culture and that
"the history of American evangelicalism is littered with many theories of
private moralities but very few plans for public action explicitly grounded
in Christian principles."[21] He also recognizes that most attempts to do public theology fall outside of evangelical circles.[22] Nevertheless, three figures
tend to dominate Protestant writings on North American public theology:
Paul Tillich, H. Richard Niebuhr, and Reinhold Niebuhr.

What brought these thinkers to the surface of Protestant public theology in the United States? They were German Americans who wrote out of
the experience of a theological liberalism whose roots lay deep in German
pietism and the social gospel. However, it was their proximity to events
occurring in Europe between the two World Wars that rendered their
voices distinctive, exposing the demonic influences of national socialism
in Germany and criticizing what they perceived as an evangelical complacency and indifference in the United States toward world war intervention. In their attempts to speak prophetically and priestly within their
religious situation, they also challenged theological liberals to provide an
effective mode of religious criticism in the context of a world at war.

These thinkers helped a generation of Americans to understand that
the fascist sickness plaguing Europe was not regionally isolated. Rather,
their theological discourse helped many American intellectuals to understand that the sickness was constitutive of Western mass democracy and
the capitalist impulses that justified it. Walter Lippmann recalls the
American mind, against which Tillich and the Niebuhrs gave prophetic
and priestly guidance. In *The Public Philosophy* (1955), Lippmann writes:

> It did not come easily to one who, like myself, had known the soft
> air of the world before the wars to recognize and acknowledge the
> sickness of the Western liberal democracies. Yet as we were being
> drawn unready and unarmed into the second of the great wars,
> there was no denying, it seemed to me, that there is a deep disor-
> der in our society which comes not from the machinations of our
> enemies and from the adversities of the human condition but from
> within ourselves.[23]

Tillich and the Niebuhrs unmasked American moral and cultural pre-
tensions through their critical, theological analyses of American public

problems. First published in 1932, Tillich's *The Religious Situation* stands as a classic in Protestant public theology in the United States. The publisher's note captures the importance of this book for American public theology:

> The developments of our time have accentuated doubts about the rationality of science and technology. Political and religious forces, their alignments and their hopes, remain astonishingly similar. And Tillich's treatment of the Protestant principle in terms of its power and its fault remains relevant to our religious situation. This is a prophetic book which gives a clue to the history of our time and the ground of cultural renewal.[24]

H. Richard Niebuhr, who translated *Religious Situation* from the German, argued that as the social gospel and theological liberalism (both of which crystallized Protestant public discourse around domestic social reforms) declined with the collapse of liberal public philosophy, Tillich's importance to American theology laid in his demand for a new Protestant public theology.[25] Tillich's critical principle for public theology was "The Protestant Principle."

The Protestant principle is paradoxical. It requires a faith that "protests against the tragic-demonic self-elevation of religion and liberates religion from itself for the other functions of the human spirit, at the same time, liberating these functions from their self-seclusion against the manifestations of the ultimate."[26] The Protestant principle requires a public theology that is rigorously theocentric, relativizing all particulars, while advancing an ethics of radical self-transcendence.[27] Tillich's was a paradoxical theology (a belief-ful realism) that transcends dichotomies between theory and practice, this world and the otherworldly, faith and reality, and the prophetic and the priestly. It would not permit American theologians "to stand aloof as non-participating observers," but they are required to "think and speak about the religious situation of the present with unconditioned, active responsibility."[28]

In his discussion of the Niebuhrs, Sydney Ahlstrom describes them as "involving a whole generation of readers and listeners in their creative reexamination of the [Christian] heritage and in their realistic relating of this heritage to contemporary dilemmas."[29] In *Social Sources of Denominationalism* (1929), Richard Niebuhr drew on the critical sociology of Max Weber and Ernst Troeltsch to criticize what he saw as the compromise of the American churches to the alienating structures of classism, regionalism, and racism. He chided American denominations as "emblems of the victory of the world over the church, of the secularization of Christianity, of the Church's sanction of that divisiveness which the church's gospel condemns."[30]

However, in *The Kingdom of God in America* (1937), Niebuhr turned "inward" to the evangelical roots of American Protestantism in order to isolate the critical principle of Protestant public theology. He suggested that the critical principle that differentiates Catholic and Protestant faith was "the kingdom of God."[31] This critical principle involved three elements: the sovereign rule of God over all creatures, the finitude of all human self-initiatives, and the temporal nearness of the kingdom that calls for moral responsibility. Richard Niebuhr's critical principle led to one of the more powerful indictments of Protestant liberalism in America. He said that it was devoted to "a God without wrath [who] brought men without sin into a kingdom without judgment through the ministrations of a Christ without a cross."[32]

For Richard Niebuhr, the critical principle of Protestant public theology could be derived from no other source than an internal history of Protestants' faith in revelation. This placed a double burden on Protestant public theology. It suggested that Protestant theologians faithfully transmit the internal logic of their theology and that they live faithful to their theology in their interactions with culture. To be sure, as Richard Niebuhr continued to wrestle with the relation of theology and culture, the kingdom of God principle receded into the background as "revelation" ascended as the organizing principle of his public theology. In *The Meaning of Revelation* (1941), he writes:

> Christian theology must begin today with revelation because it knows that men cannot think about God save as historic, communal beings and save as believers. It must ask what revelation means for Christians rather than what it ought to mean for all men, everywhere and at all times. And it can pursue its inquiry only by recalling the story of Christian life and by analyzing what Christians see from their limited point of view in history and faith.[33]

While Tillich and Richard Niebuhr are usually counted among the American public theologians, Reinhold Niebuhr is most cited as the exemplary Protestant public theologian of the twentieth century. Reinhold Niebuhr's *Moral Man and Immoral Society* (1932) remains a classic in Protestant public theology. Ahlstrom regarded it as "the most important book and probably the most disruptive religio-ethical bombshell of domestic construction to be dropped during the entire interwar period—the major document in that 'protestant search for political realism.'"[34] Like Tillich and Richard Niebuhr, Reinhold Niebuhr also wrestled paradoxically with the demanding issues of his times. He structured his arguments between the paradoxes of socialization and morality, coercion and freedom, group determinacy and self-transcendence. The paradoxical flavor of his critical, cultural analysis is pointedly summarized in the following quote:

> The limitations of the human mind and imagination, the inability of human beings to transcend their own interests sufficiently to envisage the interests of their fellowmen as clearly as they do their own makes force an inevitable part of the process of social cohesion. But the same force which guarantees peace also makes for injustice.[35]

Reinhold also states that "as individuals, men believe that they ought to love and serve each other and establish justice between each other. As racial, economic and national groups they take for themselves, whatever their power can command."[36]

For Reinhold Niebuhr, the paradoxical relation between society and the individual always involves the paradox of coercion and freedom. This paradox frames his doctrine of Christian realism. According to Reinhold Niebuhr, a realistic liberal politics acknowledges that persons in society are not likely to take altruism as a determinate value of the moral life without, at the same time, considering its limitation and the necessity of coercion on each person's freedom. And a realistic religious ethics acknowledges that altruism ought to be a free action flowing from the ethical impulses of religious life but it is not likely to be free unless it is also an obligation and responsibility owed to the absolute in the religious life.

For Reinhold Niebuhr, Christian realism requires a theology of radical transcendence. In this regard, his theology is commensurable with that of Tillich and Richard Niebuhr. For Reinhold, the possibilities of radical self-transcendence (individually and socially) lie theologically in his belief that divine transcendence centers both the religious and moral activities of persons. This relationship between self-transcendence and divine transcendence is also paradoxical. Reinhold explains:

> The religious sense of the absolute qualifies the will-to-live and the will-to-power by bringing them under subjection to an absolute will, and by imparting transcendent value to other human beings, whose life and needs thus achieve a higher claim upon the self. That is a moral gain. But religion results also in the absolutizing of the self. It is a sublimation of the will-to-live. Though God is majestic and transcendent he is nevertheless related to man by both his qualities and his interest in man. His qualities are human virtues, raised to the nth degree. . . . In religion man interprets the universe in terms relevant to his life and aspirations. Religion is at one and the same time, humility before the absolute and self-assertion in terms of the absolute.[37]

Reinhold Niebuhr warned that the paradoxes of Christian realism ought not to be taken as a justification for defeatist complacency regarding human incapacities to intervene into world affairs or to ameliorate fully human conflict. Rather, the paradoxes of radical transcendence resist treating the relations between God and the world dualistically, he said.[38] However, he also warned that the principle of radical transcendence justifies neither theological liberals' optimism in human progress nor monistic theologies that identify our moral and social problems with divine opportunities for self-realizing the human spirit and vitalities. In his critique of Protestant liberalism, he writes:

> We have developed a type of religious idealism, which is saturated with sentimentality. In spite of the disillusionment of the World War, the average liberal protestant Christian is still convinced that the kingdom of God is gradually approaching, that the League of Nations is its partial fulfillment and the Kellogg Pact its covenant, that the wealthy will be persuaded by the church to dedicate their power and privilege to the common good and that they are doing so in increasing numbers, that the conversion of individuals is the only safe method of solving the social problem, and that such ethical weaknesses as religion still betrays are due to its theological obscurantism which will be sloughed off by the progress of enlightenment.[39]

The principle of radical transcendence (divine and human self-transcendence) gives warrant for a public theology justified paradoxically in terms of Christian realism. For Reinhold Niebuhr, the paradoxes of Protestant public theology are summarized in what he regarded "the impossible possibility." In a summary passage, Niebuhr explains this grand paradox:

> Society must strive for justice even if it is forced to use means, such as self-assertion, resistance, coercion and perhaps resentment, which cannot gain the moral sanction of the most sensitive moral spirit. The individual must strive to realize his life by losing and finding himself in something greater than himself. . . . [T]he contradiction between them is not absolute. But neither are they easily harmonized.[40]

Conclusion

The search for Catholic public theology in the United States reveals key theological languages that connect Catholic doctrine, piety, and organization with the social problems of American public life. In Buckley's expropriation of providence and redemption, McGlone's exoneration of *santos* and vocation, and Novak's retrieval of a substantive tradition of social teachings and practical wisdom, Catholic public theologians have sought to enact both prophetic and priestly practices in public theology. Protestant public theologians also elicit distinctively religious vocabularies that enlarge the range of discourse applicable to the critique of American cultural practices and appropriate for moral guidance in public debate and policy.

Central to the public theology of Tillich and the Niebuhrs was a paradoxical theology. The paradoxes of their public theologies resist the uncoupling of theological discourse and public discourse and reject private/public and world/church dualisms. At the same time, they reject any easy reduction of the private to the public or the church to the world. Each theologian searched the internal vocabularies of his Protestant heritage for critical principles that expose the tragic-demonic dimensions of American cultural life. Moreover, these principles legitimize dimensions of social experience that not only bring about genuine fulfillment of the basic goods persons require for making life in the United States morally manageable but also bring about as much human flourishing as is possible.

For Tillich and the Niebuhrs, the critical principle of Protestant public theology was radical transcendence. Historian Winthrop Hudson sees four themes unified under this critical principle: a reassertion of the sovereignty of God, a radical stress on the demonic power of sin and a less optimistic evaluation of the human situation, a renewed appreciation for the centrality of biblical faith in divine revelation, and a renewed sense of responsibility that church membership requires.[41] Hudson especially accents the paradoxical character of their public theology by disclosing its tendency to move to the "right" theologically and to the "left" politically.[42] He suggests that Reinhold Niebuhr set the tone when he wrote in his *Reflections on the End of an Era*, "In my opinion, adequate spiritual guidance can come only through more radical political orientation and more conservative religious convictions than are comprehended [at present] in the culture of our era."[43]

In the tradition of these other theologians, Buttrick also takes notice of the cultural shifts that decenter the cultural mainstream by centering difference and multicultures, and he pronounces the end of the Protestant era.[44] He also calls for a new Protestant public theology that engages the postmodern crises that characterize late twentieth-century North American life. He suggests that it is the gospel that Christians are called to preach. "We reach out, past our own defensiveness, to see where God may lead us. And surely we delight in seeking new ways to speak, not fixed on the past, but on the unfolding future of God. In every age, the gospel is good news," says Buttrick.[45] I am not altogether sure just how much work Buttrick's recovery of the "gospel" is supposed to do as the critical principle of public theology in our postmodern culture. What is clear is that the public theology he commends remains within the tradition of the Protestant paradoxical theology that Tillich and the Niebuhrs stamped on the American scene. Like these other thinkers, Buttrick also sees the wrestle of Christian faith with culture as a paradox of the cross and grace. In a summary statement, he adds his own voice to Protestant public theology in the United States. He writes:

> The cross convicts the age, every age, and all humanity by exposing our structures of sin. At the same time, we know the cross is a great gesture of God's love toward the world. Love cuts two ways. The church in its common life must be different, rejecting worldly ways that conflict with love; at the same time, the church must reach out in love, offering God to a wearied world. Perhaps, just perhaps, God's love is the clue.[46]

It is not clear what impact Buttrick's call for a renewed evangelical public theology will have on our present context. Nevertheless, I think that Buttrick rightly sees in the wrestle of public theology with postmodern culture the need for a paradoxical theology of culture and cultural theology.

NOTES

1. William Joseph Buckley, "Public Theologies in an Age of Ethnic Rivalries," *Catholic World*, November–December 1994, 273.
2. Roger Shinn, "The Public Responsibility of Theology," in *America and the Future of Theology*, ed. William A. Beardslee (Philadelphia: Westminster Press, 1967), 179.
3. Ronald F. Thiemann, *Constructing a Public Theology: The Church in a Pluralistic Culture* (Louisville, Ky.: Westminster/John Knox Press, 1991), 21–22.
4. Paul Tillich, *Systematic Theology*, vol. 3 (Chicago: University of Chicago Press, 1967), 165.
5. Ibid.
6. Ibid., 166.
7. Mary M. McGlone, "The King's Conscience," *Catholic World*, November–December 1994, 284.
8. Ibid., 285.
9. Buckley, "Public Theologies," 277.
10. John Courtney Murray, "Religious Liberty," in *A Documentary History of Religion in America since 1865*, ed. Edwin S. Gaustad (Grand Rapids: Wm. B. Eerdmans Publishing Co., 1983), 476.
11. Ibid., 479.
12. Ibid., 476.
13. Michael Novak, "Looking at the World in a Theological Way," interview with Dennis McManus in *Catholic World*, November–December 1994, 268.

14. Buckley, "Public Theologies," 276.
15. Ibid.
16. Ibid., 278.
17. McGlone, "The King's Conscience," 285.
18. Ibid.
19. Ibid.
20. Novak, "Looking at the World," 269.
21. Gerald R. McDermott, "What Can Jonathan Edwards Teach Us about Politics?" *Christianity Today*, July 18, 1994, 32.
22. Ibid.
23. Walter Lippmann, *The Public Philosophy* (New York: New American Library of World Literature, 1955), 12.
24. Paul Tillich, *The Religious Situation* (New York: Meridian Books, 1956), 5–6.
25. Ibid., 22ff.
26. Tillich, *Systematic Theology* 3:245.
27. Ibid., 248.
28. Tillich, *Religious Situation*, 219.
29. Sydney Ahlstrom, *A Religious History of the American People* (New Haven, Conn.: Yale University Press, 1972), 940.
30. H. Richard Niebuhr, *The Social Sources of Denominationalism* (Cleveland: World Publishing Co., 1929), 25.
31. H. Richard Niebuhr, *The Kingdom of God in America* (Middletown, Conn.: Wesleyan University Press, 1988), 20–21.
32. Ibid., 193.
33. H. Richard Niebuhr, *The Meaning of Revelation* (New York: Macmillan Co., 1941), 31.
34. Ahlstrom, *A Religious History*, 941.
35. Reinhold Niebuhr, *Moral Man and Immoral Society* (New York: Charles Scribner's Sons, 1960), 6–7. Reprinted with permission of Scribner, a Division of Simon & Schuster. Copyright © 1932 by Charles Scribner's Sons, Renewed 1960 by Reinhold Niebuhr.
36. Ibid., 9.
37. Ibid., 63–64.
38. Ibid., 78.
39. Ibid., 79–80.
40. Ibid., 257.
41. Winthrop Hudson, *Religion in America*, 3rd ed. (New York: Charles Scribner's Sons, 1981), 383.
42. Ibid.
43. Ibid.
44. David Buttrick, *A Captive Voice: The Liberation of Preaching* (Louisville, Ky.: Westminster John Knox Press, 1994), 72.
45. Ibid., 113.
46. Ibid., 75.

3

A Neighborhood as Wide as God's Heart

WILLIAM SLOANE COFFIN

As a part of this section on the global dimensions of Christianity, I turn to the parable of the Good Samaritan. Better than any other parable, and more lyrically than any nonparabolic statement, this parable makes the point that the love of God and the love of neighbor are absolutely inseparable. It also makes another point, often missed, that when the lawyer asks about neighbor as object—"Who is my neighbor?"—Jesus answers by defining neighbor as subject. At the end of the parable, he asks, "Which proved neighbor to the man?" In other words, the question is not "Who is my neighbor?" but "Are *you* a neighbor?" And the implied truth of the parable is that to be a neighbor you have to be one in a neighborhood as wide as God's heart.

David Buttrick has long preached international equality as the sole basis for Christian community. He has taught that nationalism at the expense of another nation is as evil as racism at the expense of another race. And he recognizes that God not only answers questions but questions our answers—especially those that are parochial or provincial. In fact, he left his beloved Presbyterian Church because its God was becoming too small.

But how are we to affirm an international understanding of community when almost every valley wants to become an independent state and when the whole world is awash with weapons?

A half century after the bombing of Hiroshima, I want to recall my feelings then and compare them to my feelings now. I also want to contend that a nuclear weapon-free world is today not so wild a dream and that, in such a world, it would be infinitely easier to moderate national sovereignty and increase global loyalty.

When the Japanese finally surrendered in August of 1945, I was stationed in Europe, a second lieutenant in the infantry about to begin a two-year stint as a liaison officer with the Red Army, first in Czechoslovakia and then in Germany. I had just turned twenty-one.

It pains me now to recall that the Allied bombings of German cities such as Hamburg, Berlin, and Dresden had troubled me not one bit. The targets to be sure were invariably described as military and the bombings as "precision," but, if any of us had stopped to think, and few of us did, we would have known that the civilian casualties were heavy. Also it was natural for Americans to be more concerned for the safe return of our pilots than for the wholesale destruction of human life that resulted from the success of their missions. And finally, as the Germans had first bombed Rotterdam, Coventry, and London, giving them a taste of their own medicine was to many of us emotionally, if not morally, satisfying. Without question, by war's end Hitler had won a significant victory: his means had become ours. The saturation bombing of cities was accepted as a legitimate means of undermining enemy morale.

That being the case, it was not hard for me to join in the general rejoicing that followed the dropping of the first atomic bomb. It helped that President Truman called Hiroshima "a military base." Also, there was no report of cruel and lingering effects; radiation was not even mentioned. The bomb was certain to shorten, if not end, the war, which, we never forgot, was started by the Japanese at Pearl Harbor and continued with such horrors as the Death March on Bataan. As an invasion of the fortified mainland of Japan would now be unnecessary, it was possible to claim that the bomb preserved more lives than it destroyed—Japanese lives included. In short, the bombing of Hiroshima was, in Winston Churchill's words, "a miracle of deliverance." Not for a moment did I suspect that wise diplomacy could have avoided the carnage.

For a long time I remained uncritical. For one thing, in those days we trusted our leaders. For another, it is always more comfortable not to raise questions. For example, even as I escorted Soviet dignitaries to the Nuremberg trials, it never occurred to me to wonder how only the vanquished in a lost war are tried for crimes. It was the same with the atomic bomb. I resisted all threats to the simple clarity I craved. Together with so many other Americans, I wanted to believe that the decision to drop the bomb on Hiroshima was judiciously conceived, morally tenable, and unquestionably necessary. So, the recollection of my own experience, as well as that of so many others, convinces me now that Robert Lifton and Gregg Mitchell have it right: "From the time of Hiroshima, Americans have assigned themselves the task of finding virtue in the first use of the most murderous device ever created. We have felt the need to avoid at any cost a sense of moral culpability for this act."[1]

That's why no president, while in office, has publicly questioned dropping the bomb. That's why it was inevitable that the proposed Smithsonian exhibit of the *Enola Gay* would cause such an uproar. When it comes to the bombing of Hiroshima, even fifty years later, we Americans want no debate. For most of us the book is closed.

But the book is not closed. More accurately, there are some pages as yet unread. And the importance of studying these pages can hardly be exaggerated if ever we are to rid the world of nuclear weapons. Many Americans resist the idea of abolishing nuclear weapons not only because they are infatuated with their power but also because to condemn them today makes our action fifty years ago morally untenable.

What do these as yet unread pages tell us?

They tell us that, while there were perhaps as many as 40,000 soldiers based in Hiroshima, the bomb was aimed at the center of a city of some 350,000 people. Of the more than 100,000 dead, only about 250 were military personnel.

They tell us that military censorship, lifted only in October 1949, made sure no Americans saw photos of Japanese doctors and nurses at work or any photographs of immolated and radiated bodies. This censorship also helped to prevent publication of John Hersey's *Hiroshima* in Japanese.

Further, these pages disclose that Generals MacArthur and Eisenhower and Air Force commander "Hap" Arnold, Admirals King and Leahy, and Ambassador Grew, among other military and political leaders, either believed at the time or shortly thereafter came to believe that the bomb was not necessary to end the war. The Japanese air force, after all, was finished; likewise the navy. Japanese leaders had put out peace feelers, their only condition for surrender being that the Emperor be retained. The Soviets were about to enter the war, and any planned invasion of Japan was still months away. Incidentally, for this invasion the highest casualty estimates before Hiroshima were 63,000; only afterward, as we walked the treadmill of justification, did they steadily climb to well over a million.

I concur with those who hold that dropping the bomb on Hiroshima did not make America "morally unique—just technologically exceptional." And I am glad that if someone had to discover the bomb it was our scientists as opposed to Nazi scientists. But I also recognize that being grateful that we were the first to get the bomb suggests that its use by a decent people against evil forces was morally acceptable.

To my mind, that use was not acceptable. Never did I think the bombing of Nagasaki was justified. Now I am persuaded that the bomb over Hiroshima should also never have been launched.

One of the most forceful early critics of the Hiroshima bombing was Lewis Mumford. He felt the bomb's power "was too absolute to be entrusted to human beings," and the very fact that we used it proved that human beings are "neither intelligent enough nor morally sound enough to be in charge of this weapon."[2]

I agree. Only God has the authority to end life on this planet. All we have is the power—the power now to turn not only whole cities into crematoria but whole continents into gas chambers.

Deterrence is not a justifiable policy, for deterrence depends on the credible prospect of use. Besides, what is to deter us, those entrusted with the deterrence, when to save American lives apparently excuses any atrocity?

Nuclear proliferation is an enormous threat. There is no way in the world a scientific discovery can long be kept secret. Furthermore, we cannot have it both ways: either the nuclear nations relinquish their right to possess nuclear weapons, or any nation can claim that right, and more and more of them will. The only way to halt nuclear proliferation is through the worldwide abolition of nuclear weapons under the strictest possible international control. The fact that so many Americans cannot see this is, to me, a measure of our madness.

In 1946, a commission of the Federal Council of Churches condemned the saturation bombings of World War II and, especially, the bombings of Hiroshima and Nagasaki. The twenty-two church leaders urged "active penitence," including aid in rebuilding "the two murdered cities." In so doing they recognized "a crucial linkage: to acknowledge the truth of the past can be a first step to altering our approach to the future." The future they envisaged contained no more atom bombs.

I wish that fifty years ago I had shared the remorse of these clear-sighted Christians. Had enough of us done so, we would all be living today in a far saner and safer world.

Turning now to the future, is a safer, saner world a realistic expectation? It is my feeling that a nuclear weapon-free world is neither inevitable nor impossible. At least it is far less the fanciful idea it once was thought to be. Since the close of the cold war the antinuclear movement has gone Main Street; witness the protests against further nuclear testing. As the French writer Dominique Moisi put it, "Now that the threat against which we needed nuclear weapons is no longer clear, all that is clear is the threat of the nuclear weapons themselves—to the environment and to the human race."

More and more military strategists, even a former U.S. Secretary of Defense, have come to embrace the idea of a nuclear weapon-free world, not only as a moral ideal but as a national policy goal. They are now convinced that nuclear weapons diminish rather than enhance the security of nuclear weapon states. The examples of Korea, Vietnam, and Argentina have shown that nonnuclear weapon states have not been deterred from engaging in war with nuclear weapon states. These military experts also see no stability in the lower numbers cited in various doctrines of "minimal deterrence." They point to the analogy of a forest fire. As long as there is any fire at all, a change in the wind can produce a major conflagration. So, too, with nuclear weapons. A change in the international climate can provoke a new and deadly arms race reigniting the danger of global nuclear war. So they want a nuclear weapon-free world (NWFW).

Already a pattern has been set by the Biological Weapons Convention (BWC) and the Chemical Weapons Convention (CWC), both of which call for a total ban.

How to abolish nuclear weapons is not difficult to conceive. The first step would be a global ban on all nuclear tests, followed by a ban on the production of fissile material. These steps should be accompanied by support for an advisory opinion from the International Court of Justice that the threat and the use of nuclear weapons are illegal. A next logical step would be to negotiate an agreement that goes beyond the Strategic Arms Reduction Talks (START) II Treaty and reduces U.S. and Russian arsenals below a thousand warheads each. Then both nations could lead other nuclear weapon states in negotiations to abolish all nuclear weapons and their delivery systems.

It goes without saying that "anytime anyplace" inspections would need to be instituted and countermeasures devised should illegal development of weapons be detected. Technical means for verification are even now, in principle, available.

What Christians, in particular, need to recognize is that human fallibility, sinfulness, and nuclear weapons are a lethal combination. Just as individuals, and on occasion, individual nations exceed their financial means, so nuclear weapon states are presently living beyond their moral means. They must scale back.

Whether they will or not remains to be seen. But we can take heart by recalling an earlier abolitionist movement. Initially the abolition of slavery was an idea ridiculed and resisted, especially by slave owners. But gradually, more and more people came to see that something as fundamentally immoral as slavery cannot in the long run be considered politically prudent. So the ranks of the abolitionists swelled until their pressure produced emancipation worldwide.

Likewise, so immoral is the continued presence in the world of thousands of nuclear warheads, so unspeakably sad, so relentlessly insane, that we have to hope that eventually humanity will refuse to countenance their further existence.

I recognize that to abolish only nuclear, chemical, and biological weapons—these instruments of megadeaths—is to leave the world safe for Vietnams, Afghanistans, Bosnias, and Rwandas. Awash with "conventional" weapons, the world cries out for their elimination too. But wouldn't further disarmament seem all the more reasonable once nuclear weapons were abolished? Clearly if arms reductions are to become more likely and wars less so, new measures will have to be devised for conflict resolution. Mediation must become the order of the day. Nations must abandon their claim to be judges of their own causes. People must become as mindful of international law as they are of domestic law. The concept of common security must replace that of national security, an understanding that the security of countries cannot be imagined separately, for none is really secure until all are secure.

But first things first—the abolition of nuclear weapons. The decision to use them was made in 1945. Whether to keep them is now up to us. That Christians could be of enormous help in ridding the world of nuclear weapons is not in question. The only question is whether they will. How seriously will they take the parable of the Good Samaritan? Will we see ourselves as neighbors in a neighborhood as wide as God's heart?

NOTES

1. Most of the information presented in this chapter can be found in three books: Gar Alperovitz, *Atomic Diplomacy: Hiroshima and Potsdam* (New York: Penguin Books, 1985); Robert Jay Lifton and Gregg Mitchell, *Hiroshima in America: Fifty Years of Denial* (New York: G. P. Putnam's Sons, 1995); Donald W. Shriver, Jr., *An Ethic for Enemies* (New York: Oxford University Press, 1995).
2. Lifton and Mitchell, *Hiroshima in America.*

4

A Hearer in the Pew:
Homiletical Reflections and Suggestions

GIJSBERT D. J. DINGEMANS

From Pulpit to Pew

For more than three decades, I have been a regular preacher in various congregations of the Dutch Reformed Church. In that period, I have learned to see congregations and people in the church from the point of view of the person who stands in the high position of the pulpit and who understands himself fundamentally as an interpreter of or as a witness to the gospel. I felt it as my task to be faithful to the Word of God, and sometimes I had the secret feeling of being a sort of prophet who had to speak the Word of God before the assembled congregation.

But since I attend worship services more often as a hearer and as a "normal" member of the community of believers than as a preacher my mind has been changed. I began to ask myself what the reasons might be that I, as a member of the congregation, go to this kind of worship and what I, as an ordinary churchgoer, really expect from the man or the woman in the pulpit. I discovered that my reasons were that I wished to get some kind of help for my personal faith: something for my mind—an intellectual understanding of God and our world; something for my heart and my personal attitude—a challenge for my faith or for my lifestyle; and something for my relational feelings—I want to belong to a community and particularly to the people of God, and I want to be confirmed in that feeling.

Rhetoric

In my bookcase at home, I found manuals on classic rhetoric,[1] and I was surprised to learn that the old rhetors of Greek and Roman antiquity (Gorgias, Protagoras, Cato, Plotius, Demosthenes, Aristotle, and especially Cicero, *De oratore, libri tres*) in their *ars bene dicendi* make distinctions among different types of speeches. They distinguish *arguments* as a way of dispute giving rational arguments (*rationes, logoi*) and asking for meaning, for instance, for the court of justice and in philosophical or scientific reasoning. They call this way of reasoning *genus judicale*. Second, they speak of speeches that make an *appeal* to the will of the people, for example, in politics, at electoral meetings, or in the assembly of the city to move people toward decisions. They call this way of persuasion *genus deliberativum*. Finally, there is the *eulogy*, the *genus demonstrativum*, that not only means flattery (*laudatio*) but also seeks to establish or to strengthen the relationship between persons and groups. I found that these three types of speeches roughly correspond to my feelings in the church.

In my homiletic work, therefore, I tried to make these insights fruitful for my students.[2] In every sermon there should be three levels: (1) a level of explanation, information, and clarification, in which the meaning of the text is transmitted. The aim is *docere* (teaching)[3] explanation of the historical, sociological, and theological backgrounds of the text and, of course, the transmission of its meaning to the congregation; (2) a level of proclamation, persuasion, and appeal, in which the message and the power of the text is transmitted. The aim is *movere* (moving and persuading): confronting the congregation with the moves, challenges, and the driving powers of the text; and (3) a level of basic trust and relation, in which the credibility and reliability of the text, the church, and the preacher is to be shown. The aim is *delectare* and *conciliare* (pleasing, propitiating, and reconciliation): the consolidation and confirmation of the common faith, if possible in an entertaining and easy way. That is the most difficult task of preaching, the *genus grande*, as the old rhetors said, to transmit the passion, the deepest moves of the faith, without the dangers of superficiality or a false pathos.

The Needs of the Hearer

Sitting in the pew again, I realized that the order of these levels may differ for the various types of persons around me and also for the various moments in my own life. Sometimes I am a modern, individualist, and intellectual person that has a first order interest in a personal clarification and clearness about God and the world on level 1 and sometimes I have the deep human need to belong to a group of like-minded people (Maslow) of level 3: I want to be accepted as a member of the community or as a child of God, without too much reasoning. And I think that most people—and I include myself—sometimes also have desires for fundamental changes in their lives through the working of God's grace, though they are terribly afraid for it at the same time. I learned from the investigations of Hans van der Geest[4] that people actually expect a liberating working of sermons, although they resist changes intensely, at the same time! Van der Geest supposes that changes in human life are possible only on the basis of a real basic trust, for instance, in God's faithfulness, but also on behalf of the preacher's reliability. I think that level 2 only works on the basis of level 3 and/or 1. If I look at my own attitude in the church, I observe a need for clarification and belonging to a group of reliable people, before I am prepared to change my mind, my opinions, or even my style of life! So, if I ask myself what I really expect by attending worship services, I honestly have to answer, "I hope to find a community of faith in which I can breathe and feel accepted with my feelings and thoughts and a worship, including the sermon, in which I can meet God and perhaps change my mind!"

A Double Communication

In my reflections about church services, I also began to realize that all participants of worship already have their own history with God, with the Christian faith, and with the church. The people around me are no more "blank tablets" than I am! Their experiences with God, the Christian faith, and the church may be either positive, negative, or neutral, but all people in the church on Sunday morning do have a kind of relation with God. They may be firm believers or hesitating people or even be full of hatred; they all have a "prejudice" ("Vor-urteil" or "Vor-verständnis"), as Hans-Georg Gadamer[5] says, a primary, reflected, or unreflected relationship or history with God which I call—in this context—a personal communication with God.

My problem in many services is that the preacher is often placed by the church (and sometimes places himself or herself) between the text and me and therefore between God and me. And sometimes I feel that my personal understanding of the gospel or even my relation to God is blocked by the personality, the attitude, the intentions, or the theology of the preacher. That is obviously not his or her purpose! Of course not. But it is often a fact. In a pluralist society—and therefore in a pluralist congregation—the vision and the way of believing of the preacher is not necessarily the same as my personal experiences. From the older books of homiletics I have learned that the preacher is primarily and fundamentally the servant of the Word of God (Barth[6]) and that she or he simply (!) has to explain the gospel in a proper way for the congregation. All these books use, whether they are conscious of it or ignorant, linear schemes of communication that mostly run as follows:

Message → Speaker → Channel (speech) → Hearers

or

God → Bible → Message → Preacher → Sermon → Congregation

The relation between the Word of God and me as a listener in the pew in this model of communication is totally and absolutely mediated by the preacher and his or her theological knowledge, personality, and faith. She or he knows what the text—and what God—has to say to me this morning. And that position most of the time is undergirded by a theological theory of the Christ-representation of the clergy. The pastor (preacher) is the (only) authoritative representative and interpreter of the gospel of Jesus Christ. Thus are the rules and roles in the church: The preacher preaches on behalf of God and the hearer hears and has to obey the Word of God (as interpreted by the preacher). If the hearer does not accept the words of the preacher it often is explained as disobedience to the Word of God!

In my opinion, however, all people in the church have their own relation and communication with God (a "personal communication") and it is the task of the clergy through their pastoral, homiletical, and catechetical communication to help members of the congregation to widen and deepen and sometimes also to improve or to change their personal relation with God. In my homiletical work, I was, therefore, looking for another theory of communication, one that gives more room for the individual hearer and for communication with God. And that at the same time takes into account that preaching belongs to the category of mass media. That means in mass communication people are not able to react personally and immediately in the church in the way as it is possible in catechetical and pastoral conversations.

It is a pity, therefore, that theories of *circular* communication, that indeed give room to word and reply, explanation and reaction in feedback-loops (as used in all kinds of face-to-face conversations) are useless for sermons. There is no real opportunity for spontaneous reactions, serious questions or profound replies in worship, except exclamations, prayers, and songs.

Fortunately, in an article of T. M. Newcomb (1953)[7] that refers to communication through radio and television programs, I found a communication theory that takes into account the personal relation of hearers with a matter (*Sache*, as it is often called in German literature) and the speech-communication of speakers or lecturers that try to help, inform, and instruct people. People actually have their own interpretations, associations, and feelings in seeing television programs, and commentators can only try to reinforce or to correct these interpretations and feelings. Their main activity on level 2 is a kind of communication about the interpretations and feelings of the viewers. Applied to sermons in the church it means that a double communication takes place. God speaks to and with the congregation in the liturgical setting of the worship and the participants react and reply in prayers and songs. And at a given moment the preacher intervenes in this communication with his or her homiletical communication to assist people in their own relationship to God. Preachers should be able to give information on level 1 and they should strengthen and reinforce the feelings of the hearers on level 2. Sometimes they may be able to remove obstacles and to correct obvious misunderstandings on level 1. But it is very hard indeed to change the feelings and interpretations of hearers on level 2 and it surely takes much time and patience!

It looks as follows:

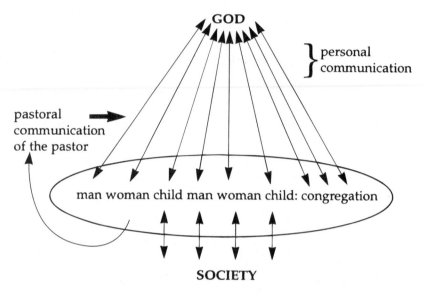

All people in the congregation live in a circle of communication and have the vocation to assist and help their fellow members. Also the pastor, as one of the members of the congregation, is called to the special task of helping his or her fellow members to deepen their communication with God. The pastor in this scheme, therefore, is not put between God and the congregation, but she or he is a member of the congregation and—at the same time—is called to stand next to the people as a helpful assistant. Since everybody—not only the preacher—can become a representative of Christ for his or her fellow members, in my opinion professional pastors have the task to use their knowledge, ability, and tools to help the congregation in a particular way of pastoral communication to understand the gospel, to find their way in the Christian tradition, and to discover a personal and congregational style of life. The congregation as a whole and the individual members finally are characterized in this scheme as instruments or mediators between God and society.

Back in the Pew

As a hearer in the church, I have gradually learned to see the preacher in the pulpit as the man or the woman who should be able to help me understand the gospel, interpret my experience of the faith and the style of my life. But what does that actually mean? Which kind of assistance may I really expect? My manuals on homiletic tell me that the primary task of the preacher is to explain the Word of God—on level 1. Of course! But how? By simply passing over the meaning of a text, leaving the application to the hearer? Is preaching the same as transmitting the results of exegesis to give the hearer room to make his or her own application? I agree: that gives a great freedom to the hearers. But how many hearers in the church can handle that appropriately? And "a bag full of original meaning may not help much in the living of life today."[8] Also the person of the preacher is fully eliminated in this way of preaching. It is not the way I appreciate. The question is, however, whether there is a way for preachers to be personally present in their sermons—with their preferences, beliefs and attitudes— and at the same time to give room to the personal beliefs and attitudes of the hearers. I like nice, personal guides, who have the knowledge and the tools to show me the treasures of the past with enthusiasm, demonstrating that they are touched themselves and giving me the freedom to enjoy the things I see in my way: Look how beautiful this is! Do you feel the power of this sentence? Did you see that Mark gives a different interpretation than John does? And did you notice that Deuteronomy has another theology than Chronicles? It is also interesting to know how things are connected to other things. Preaching is not only exegesis, it is also interpretation, showing connections and backgrounds, with ability, knowledge, and enthusiasm. The shepherd of Psalm 23 brings his flock to the green pastures and he probably shows them where the best grass is to be found—but the sheep have to select, eat, and digest the food themselves.

A Broad Spectrum of Colors

As a young student, I liked to hear various kinds of theological approaches and interpretations from the pulpit because I was seeking my own way in the Christian tradition. I was in the stage that James Fowler describes as the synthetic, or even individuative reflective faith, and preachers should help this category of people to get the proper information and backgrounds to find and select their own ideas and beliefs. Now, as an experienced man, I want assistance for my own way of deepening my faith. I have arrived at the stage of conjunctive and universalizing faith and I expect preachers to help me knit the patchwork of my personal life and personal faith. And I understand that it is very difficult for preachers to give younger people the chance to select an opinion and older people the opportunity to deepen and perhaps to change their opinions! Therefore, preachers should change their objectives and preaching structures from Sunday to

Sunday. Sometimes the accent is to be laid on information, widening the horizon, and sometimes on deepening the faith of the congregation.

Surplus of Meaning

Reading the work of Paul Ricoeur, I understand that many texts have a "surplus of meaning." There is not one meaning or one message in a text, as I learned as a student in former days from Rudolf Bultmann. There are various angles that can be used in approaching texts. Perhaps the preacher could help hearers a little bit to show (and probably to connect) the different layers of interpretation in a text. If I read John 18:15–27 and 21:15–23 from the standpoint of Peter's denial of Jesus, another sermon comes out than if I approach these texts from the angle of Peter's rehabilitation and Jesus' reconciliating attitude in John 21. And it may be possible also to read these passages from the viewpoint of the first congregation dealing with the questions of forgiveness of sins. The preacher also may put Peter's denial over against Judas's betrayal of Jesus. Texts conceal more meanings than one sermon can stand. Sermons should exploit the layers and possibilities of the surplus of meaning in texts as much as possible to help hearers in their various interests and needs, in a way that people can identify themselves with different persons (Peter, the woman in the house of the high priest in 18:17, the other disciples in chapter 21, the first congregation telling these stories to the generations to come).

Access to the Plot of
the Moves and Structures of the Bible

As a professor of homiletics, I often used David Buttrick's fine book *Homiletic* to help my students in their homiletic work. I was impressed by his proposal to replot the biblical plots in a homiletical way. We did many exercises to make new—homiletical—plots for Bible stories to bring the texts to the hearers. After a while I understood, however, that it was also possible to help hearers to get their own access to the plot of the Bible story and to bring the hearers directly into the fascinating stream of power of the text. I believe that most biblical texts have a very strong inner power that comes through immediately, in spite of the centuries of distance. That is the *perspicuitas* of the scripture, as the old Reformation theologians said, or the (first or second) naïveté of understanding texts, as Ricoeur puts it.[9] If there is no possibility for an immediate access to the text, sermons should address the blocks and problems of the hearers to make texts open and accessible. Preachers may help hearers to gain access to the immediate inner power of texts by removing the blockades. It was again David

Buttrick who taught me to pay attention to the congregational blocks that prevent hearers to penetrate into the meaning and power of texts. And I connected his thoughts with the observations of Ernst Lange.

Intellectual and Emotional Blocks

Preachers may be helpful in destroying and breaking down the obstacles and impediments that block the access to texts. They should track these blocks and figure out where people actually have no access to texts. That demands conversation with members of the congregation before the preacher writes down his or her sermon. In the realm of feelings and attitudes as well as in intellectual understanding preachers should help hearers to conquer these obstacles and should pay attention to the problems people have getting an immediate contact with the stream and the power of the text. It was Ernst Lange who pleaded for preaching as a way of "advocating the problems of the hearers before the text." To penetrate into the heart of the hearers, preachers should raise the matters of misunderstanding, unbelief, and impotence of the hearers. "In the beginning of the sermon there is not the text," Lange says. "In the beginning there is a circle of hearers with their own resistance, their own problems, questions, needs, and hopes, with their knowledge of Christian faith and their doubts, a circle of hearers in their *temptation*. And just this temptation . . . is the challenge for the preaching of the church."[10] Preaching is an effort to come to an agreement of understanding ('Verständigungsbemühen'[11]). "I make the situation of the hearers valid over against the text[12] to trace and to name the resistance, the blocks and obstacles." "I have to come to an agreement with the hearers about that, what I have to see as my mission for preaching."[13]

Analogical Bridges

Hearers should have some sort of a common frame of reference with the authors of the Bible to understand what they are speaking about. To have an access to the message of the Bible there must be a minimum basis of recognition and identification. I call this *analogical bridges*, bridges that connect our world with the world of the Bible, so that we are able to recognize the features of that old world. Very often in sermons, personal analogies are used to bridge the world of the Bible and our personal understanding. Most of the time, it is rather easy for me, as a hearer, to recognize the persons of the Bible in their feelings, experiences, faith, doubts, hesitations, unbelief, and temptations. During many centuries of Christian interpretation, personal feelings and experiences had a central position in preaching. Sermons were about "forgiveness of my personal sins," "individual life after death," "living as free persons." These were the frames of reference or the paradigms in which the proclamation of the gospel took place during many centuries.

For the last two centuries, however, a new analogical bridge has been developed as the vision of history changed. In the eighteenth century, feelings of progress for the human species arose. History and humanity were supposed to be on their way to a glorious future! Translated into homiletical language, this meant that many sermons were speaking of the progress of personal and global life, thanks to the grace of God. And people in the pew could understand these feelings, because they felt themselves part of this ongoing and progressing history of God. We shall overcome! We shall overcome, someday! Liberation theology in South America, the model of exodus (Moltmann), and political theology in Europe were twentieth-century exponents of this kind of feelings.

Now, however, hearers in the pew have problems with this rather optimistic analogical bridge. The world did not make so much progress! The promised land is far away. Mighty powers resist peace and liberty all over the world. And, in the last fifty years of our century, injustice, hunger, violence, and cruelty have proved to be very mighty powers. It gives us feelings of impotence and fear because we know that we, ourselves, called down these powers on us. At the same time we have, indeed for the first time in human history, the technical means and tools to change and improve our world, we also have the experience that we are not able to control these powers that we ourselves caused. Apart from all kinds of personal and emotional obstacles and impediments (misunderstandings, educational problems, bad experiences, stupidity, psychological blockings, etc.), the fundamental problem that often blocks the understanding of biblical texts for many contemporary hearers is not individualization or secularization but the (new) feelings of impotence, helplessness, and fear over against the powers of modern society, that we caused ourselves or that we can identify as products of modern society. These modern feelings of ambiguity, however, have no direct analogies in antiquity, because people in those days were feeling absolutely dependent on circumstances, events, rulers, powers, and the help of Almighty God—without any technical tools that could influence the events and developments, except prayers and sacrifices. How can we bridge our feelings of the year 2000 with the experiences of two thousand years ago? What about the insuperable distance[14] of Lessing? Is not our modern, technical, communication-rich world too far remote from the primitive world, including the faith, of the Bible?

This is a problem I want to deal with in the last part of my reflections as an example of homiletic help that preachers may offer to modern hearers in the church, though I am conscious of the fact that not all hearers in the pew will have the same feelings as I have.

The Powers of the World

In his book *Christus en de Machten* ("Christ and the Powers") H. Berkhof stated that the New Testament powers (*dynameis* and *stoicheia*) are to be interpreted as "the superhuman structures of our world."[15] On the one hand, they are the girders or supporting beams of our society, which act as pillars of our world (he calls that the providential function of the structures) but on the other hand, they are inclined to lead a life of their own. In that case they may become satanic powers or even idols. Berkhof is building an analogical bridge by translating the biblical powers into structures of the modern society. And we can understand them as structures that are partly made or caused by human beings and partly by other causes (nature, mutations, fate, chance). We might call them *causae secundae* because they are theologically to be interpreted as structures *between* God and world. They consist of a complicated network of natural laws, accidents, chances, rules, institutes, and human activities that operate as rather independent structures between God and our world. The authors of the Bible had a shorter perspective on the powers than we have, as we have learned to pay much more sophisticated attention to the whole range of these *causae secundae*. We realize their importance and their dangers.

According to the New Testament, however, Christ has dethroned the rebellious powers (1 Cor. 15:24f.), and Berkhof interprets that as Christ "unmasked" and "demythologized" them. Financial systems, for instance, helping our modern society to exchange goods and services in a rational way, tend to become mammon: powers that dominate and submit the world for their own sake. But Christ unmasks them and brings them back to financial systems. Berkhof, in that time, pleaded for a secularization of the powers, so that we—as human beings—can handle and, if necessary, change them. Finally, he says, these powers will be overcome by Christ and his dominion.

At this moment, however, we mistrust these depersonalized structures that nobody is able to control, because nobody is (personally) responsible for them. Berkhof was rather optimistic in his view that these powers have become (nearly) powerless if they are unmasked and that they are under the ultimate control of Christ. We know how strong and severe these depersonalized powers are. And we even doubt whether God is able to bring this world to a good conclusion.

The Power of God

That brings us to the core of the problem: In the Bible, God is often pictured as the glorious and mighty Sovereign, who as a matter of fact evidently is the Lord over the powers, the Victor on the throne, the Controller of the cosmos. In our feelings, however, God does not seem to be matched for the task to control and defeat the atrocious and inhuman powers of injustice and death in our time. In the great world of politics, business, commerce, and increasing technology, we are not able to see the unmasking and healing influence of God. Does that mean that preachers better return to the realm of personal analogies? Is God only a God for the personal life of (weak) people who need God in times of sorrow and pain? And is God's power restricted to the life after this life? Has God nothing to do with the malicious and inhuman powers in our world?

Modern theology has answered these questions with the concept of the "weak God" who was crucified[16] and so conquered the powers. But it does not seem to help me very much. My problem is that I can neither believe in the strong, mighty God of the past, who defeats his enemies and punishes the disobedient people, nor in the weak God who is in extreme solidarity with God's people but has no strength to intervene. I think preachers should try to help hearers in the pew with another type of theology and another idea about God and God's work. Neither the God who rules from a throne in heaven as a monarch nor the God who goes down with the world is the God of love. I believe in a God who gives much room to human activities and failures, to natural laws and deviations, to good powers and bad powers in our world. But at the same time, this God is struggling with the powers of this world through human beings and with the weapons of love. For me God is the inspiring power who is living among us and who is working in, with, and among human beings as a spiritual influence. And I believe in God's ultimate victory. Not as a certain and indisputable fact, but as a matter of real hope and confidence. For as a congregation of believers we have experienced God's love as a real and effective power! And, therefore, we believe that God will ultimately win the struggle, through ups and downs, sometimes cooperating with people and sometimes in opposition to them. God is our Brother or Sister rather than the almighty heavenly Father or Mother: our partner or ally, and not the absolute monarch that rules the world in a sovereign way.

What does that mean for the preacher in the pulpit? Preaching for a congregation, in my opinion, is not primarily proclaiming the Word of God in an absolute way, but opening the texts of the Bible and helping people to discover the power of God's love in the moves and structures of these texts for themselves.

NOTES

1. H. Lemmermann, *Lehrbuch der Rhetorik* (Munich, 1964); H. Geißner, *Rede in der Öffentlichkeit* (Stuttgart, 1969); J. Kopperschmidt, *Allgemeine Rhetorik: Einführung in die Theorie der Persuasiven Kommunikation* (Stuttgart, 1976); W. Eisenhut, *Einführung in die antike Rhetorik und ihre Geschichte* (Darmstadt, 1983, 1990).
2. G.D.J. Dingemans, *Als hoorder onder de hoorders* (Kampen: J. H. Kok, 1991), 159ff. In a similar way R. Zerfaß, *Grundkurs Predigt I* (Düsseldorf: Patmos-Verlag, 1987), 104–11, and C.J.A. Vos, *Die blye tyding* (Pretoria: Raad, 1995), 406ff., tried to use the insights of the old rhetoric for homiletics.
3. It was Augustine who used the word *docere* instead of reasoning especially for sermons. That was adopted by Melanchthon, who introduced the term *genus didacticum* (*Elementa Rhetorica*, ed. 1846, 421).
4. Cf. Hans van der Geest, *Du hast mich angeprochen: die Wirkung von Gottesdienst und Predigt* (Zurich: Theologischer Verlag, 1983), 92.
5. H.-G. Gadamer, *Wahrheit und Methode* (Tübingen: J.C.B. Mohr [Paul Siebeck], 1960), 261ff.
6. K. Barth, *Die Gemeindemäßigkeit der Predigt*, 1935 in *Evangelische Theologie 16*, 1956; *Aufgabe der Predigt* (Darmstadt: Wissenschaftliche Burhgesellschaft, 1971), ed. Gert Hummel; *Homiletik: Wesen und Vorbereitung der Predigt* (Zurich: Theologischer Verlag, 1966). Cf. Wolfgang Trillhaas, *Evangelische Predigtlehre*, 1948, and Rudolf Bohren, *Predigtlehre*, 1971.
7. T. M. Newcomb, "An Approach to the Study of Communication Acts," *Psychological Review* 60 (1953):393–404. Cf. H. Albrecht, *Arbeiter und Symbol*, Soziale Homiletik im Zeitalter des Fernsehens (Munich, 1982), 81–103; Johan Hahn, *Liturgie op televisie of 'televisie-liturgie,'* Grenzen en mogelijkheden van een programmasoort (Amsterdam, 1982), 32; and G.D.J. Dingemans, *Als hoorder onder de hoorders*, 146ff.
8. David Buttrick, *Homiletic: Moves and Structures* (Philadelphia: Fortress Press, 1987), 265.
9. Many texts are so open and straight that people can enter them immediately—in a primary naïveté. For other texts preachers should help hearers to open the doors and remove the obstacles. In that case Ricoeur speaks of a second naïveté: the eyes of the people have to be opened to get a new—enlightened—vision.
10. 'Am Anfang der Predigt ist nicht der Text. Am Anfang ein ist Hörerkreis mit seinem Widerspruch, mit seinen Problemen, Fragen, Nöten, Hoffnungen, mit seinem Vorherwissen vom Christlichen und seinen Zweifeln, ein Hörerkreis in seiner Anfechtung. Und eben diese Anfechtung, vielleicht als solche, nämlich als Bestreitung der Möglichkeit des Glaubens, gar nicht wahrgenommen, ist die Herausforderung der Predigt der Kirche' (E. Lange, "Brief an einen Prediger" in *Predigtstudien III/1*, 1968 S. 12).
11. E. Lange, *Predigtarbeit* 1968, *Edition Ernst Lange* 3, 10, 22, 25f., 34.
12. 'Ich mache die Situation gegen den Text geltend' (*Edition Ernst Lange* 4, 336).
13. 'Ich habe mich mit dem Hörer über das, was ich als meinen Predigtauftrag erarbeitet habe, zu verständigen' (*Edition Ernst Lange* 4, 340).
14. "der garstige breite Graben, über den ich nicht kommen kann."
15. H. Berkhof, *Christus ende Machten* (Nijkerk: Callenbach, 1952).
16. Jürgen Moltmann, *Der gekreuzigte Gott* (Munich: Chr. Kaiser Verlag, 1981).

5

Twin Covenants in Tension on the Eve of the Twenty-first Century

WILLIAM J. CARL III

For a long time now, the church in its preaching has had a lover's quarrel with the world. From Paul on Mars' Hill to modern preachers on Main Street, Christianity has wrestled with creative ways of getting beyond the cloistered walls of academe and the stained-glass comfort of ecclesial ostentation to the hard-edged despair and the "gleeful secularism" of the society that surrounds it. From Augustine to Aquinas, from Calvin to Tillich, from Eurocentric to more praxis-oriented liberation theologies, the homiletic of every age has struggled with the move from polemic to apologetic and from evangelism to social justice ministry.

Throughout much of this century the problem has been ignored by many in the mainline (some call them sideline) churches; but with the end of Christendom as we have known it, from Constantine's conversion to the triumph of the secular and the therapeutic (à la Philip Rieff) in our time, churches find themselves in a very difficult and exciting place at the close of the twentieth century. Baby boomers shop religion the way they look for cars, with no more loyalty to denominations than contemporary consumers in search of a new laptop—"Who cares who made it or where it comes from as long as it works for me?" American pragmatism reigns in church choice these days. The boomers' parents are worn out or have retired to the lake, and their own children, although in some cases the most spiritual of all, may be into New Ageism with their noses in *The Celestine Prophecy* or can be found rocking and rolling on Saturday night to Christian praise songs at the local megachurch, which looks more like a mall than a place of worship, study, or service, with a little something for everyone.

Despite the fact prognosticators suggest that we are entering a more religious era in our world and many are reading one of the pope's books like *Crossing the Threshold of Hope* or Thomas Moore's latest offering, there are still many more who haven't a clue about religion these days. They still see the church as answering questions that no one is asking, questions that are basically irrelevant to their lives. To be sure, people are searching for something deeper in their lives, deeper than what CNN, MTV, or Wall Street can offer. They're asking, "Is this all there is?" Like Nathanael and Cornelius, sitting on the back pew of every church they come asking questions but aren't sure why. In part they are trying to find answers to the "meaning thing."

Then, there are those who come antagonistically. Loren Mead, in his *Once and Future Church*, suggests that today's post-Christendom congregations may find themselves embattled at times, as were the earliest churches. The attack may come from the right as much as from the left, theologically and politically, since both peddle their own forms of fundamentalism. For example, in the early 1990s, First Presbyterian Church of Dallas found the national head of Operation Rescue (a radical antiabortion group) and some of his lieutenants disrupting Sunday morning worship services because the church had allowed Planned Parenthood to hold workshops on responsible decision making with poor, inner-city youth. The pastor in charge that day told the ushers to call the security guards and signaled to the organist, who launched into "A Mighty Fortress Is Our God," which the congregation, after leaping to its feet, sang with a fervor and a volume that surprised everyone including themselves. How appropriate that Luther's *Ein' feste Burg* was summoned for such an occasion as this. In the weeks following, church officers and ushers stood guard at every entry point around the church to keep Operation Rescue out, as a kind of twentieth-century version of reverse evangelism.

Here is a scene from the church at the end of another millennium, more embattled than bored, which means that it is becoming much more like the early church every day. But in a couple of ways, at least, the mainline (or sideline) churches in America are very different from the early church in its preaching and its ministry. Two marks of the early church homiletic and praxis are crucial to the modern church's future as we enter the twenty-first century: *evangelism* and *social ministry*, the twin covenants found throughout the Bible, which have coexisted in a kind of strained civility within religious communities for centuries.

Twin Covenants:
Evangelism and Social Ministry

We see both evangelism and social ministry in the Old and New Testaments in the Abrahamic and Sinaitic covenants. On the one hand, Abram is told by God (Gen. 12:1–3) that he will be the father of a great nation. He is given a promise and a blessing for himself and all his descendants. They will be fruitful and multiply and have land on which to live; their future will be bright and open. "In you all the families of the earth shall be blessed." Here is a very inclusive message, which points to growth and to a building up of the body. The story of the prophet Jonah reminds Israel of its responsibility to be a light to the nations and to spread the word far and wide, even to peoples of different cultures. This Abrahamic message of the promise from God to build up the body and bless all the nations of the earth demonstrates an evangelistic fervor lurking in the Old Testament. Paul highlights the evangelistic side of the Abrahamic covenant by saying, in Gal. 3:7–8, "So, you see, those who believe are the descendants of Abraham. And the scripture, foreseeing that God would justify the Gentiles by faith, *declared the gospel beforehand to Abraham*, saying 'All the Gentiles shall be blessed in you' " (author's italics).

In tension with the Abrahamic covenant in the Old Testament is the Sinaitic covenant, in which the prophetic corpus finds its inspiration and its root. The emphasis of the Sinaitic covenant is not on promise or blessing or building up of the body but on binding the believers to obey the divine commandments under threat of penalty. The Sinaitic covenant (seen in Ex. 20:1–17 and Deut. 6:20–25) stands as a sober corrective to the unconditionally optimistic future spelled out by the Abrahamic covenant. The Sinaitic covenant could be a blessing, but it could also be a curse, depending on the extent of Israel's transgression. Those preachers throughout history who have appealed only to a covenant that talked of Israel's future glory and conquest risked the danger of crying "peace, peace" when there was no peace.

If the Abrahamic covenant described the religious community's more evangelistic approach to the world, the Sinaitic covenant proffered a more prophetic example. The Sinaitic covenant is the one that reflects a moral imperative concerned not only with one's relationship with God but also with one's responsibility for the world as one cares for the widows, the orphans, the strangers, the aliens, the disenfranchised, and the dispossessed. The Sinaitic covenant is the model for social justice in the world, whatever the age may be.

These twin covenants, the Abrahamic and the Sinaitic, are held in tension with each other in the Old Testament, just as evangelism and social ministry are in modern ecclesiastical preaching and practice. They come together in the New Testament in the Luke-Acts tradition, which is the most worldly of the gospels or any of the writings in the New Testament. The Luke-Acts tradition peers out not through stained glass but through plain glass at the worried merchant, the teeming market, the homeless and the hungry, the poor and the poor in spirit, in short, the world that is ever in search of itself or actually something beyond itself.

Luke-Acts is the tradition that emphasizes both evangelism and social ministry and makes little distinction between them. A Luke-Acts homiletic never hides behind cloistered walls but goes to the world with a living Lord, a helping hand, and an honest interest in the world's questions. A Luke-Acts homiletic argues openly for the gospel and presents a Christ who did the same. Luke-Acts is where we find Peter preaching the gospel to those outside the faith. It is where we find Paul on his many journeys, evangelizing wherever he went and whomever he could. But it is also where we find Christ's concern for the widows, the orphans, and the strangers, presented in ways that none of the other Gospel writers do. For example, the Good Samaritan story is found only in Luke. *Evangelism* and *social justice ministry* coalesce in the Luke-Acts tradition. Most of all, they come together in the person and work of Jesus Christ, who never distinguished between the two, never elevated one over the other. In both, those who would minister fully spend themselves as living sacrifices.

The Great Divide

Unfortunately, in the transition from the nineteenth to the twentieth century, a great divide began that separated evangelism and social ministry with the Billy Sundays of the world on the one side and the Walter Rauschenbusches on the other, although Sunday and some who both preceded and followed him in revivalism were concerned with global moral issues, and Rauschenbusch found his social gospel preaching rooted in an evangelicalism that was concerned for the world. The divide widened in America with a Billy Graham on the one side and a Reinhold Niebuhr on the other, a separation that some have seen as the roots of today's Christian right and Christian left. What would a homiletic for the twenty-first century look like that might blend evangelism and social justice ministry?

Two things have to be understood before venturing forth into a new evangelical homiletic that understands social justice ministry as something besides the enemy: (1) one is knowing clearly the meaning of the gospel and its message for the whole person, the whole community, and the whole of creation; (2) the other is being able to reinterpret old metaphors for the gospel into the contexts of new paradigms without losing its real meaning. Two tall orders, to be sure, but very important ones.

An evangelistic homiletic not divorced from social ministry is one that presents the gospel of Jesus Christ to the whole person and to all creation, not merely to individuals. If it is true, as David Buttrick suggests, that the gospel is truth that leads to salvation/wholeness/shalom, that means salvation/wholeness/shalom not only for individual souls but also for the whole person—body/soul/spirit (the more Hebraic way of talking about *nephesh*)—and for the church, the world, indeed all creation. James Gustafson makes this point eloquently when he suggests that we are stewards of the whole of creation, including the environment, and need to be careful about both an anthropocentric theology and an anthropocentric homiletic. Like William Sloane Coffin, Buttrick believes that one cannot talk about the individual without also addressing the corporate community because both are inextricably bound together. According to Buttrick, we should quit retreating into the privatization of religion, which leads to the trivialization of Christianity and seeks to separate *homo religiosus* from *homo politicus*. Twenty-first century preaching needs to keep both in mind as it seeks to do evangelism and social justice ministry together.

Clearly, this "whole" gospel, which is both individually and socially minded, has to be reinterpreted for each new generation, but not without first understanding its essential meaning on its own. For example, one cannot enter into interfaith dialogue with Muslims, Buddhists, or any other adherents of non-Christian religions without all parties understanding as clearly as they can what they believe themselves. Otherwise, the so-called interfaith dialogue turns into an insipid theological mush, which reduces the whole thing to the lowest common theological denominator, where neither party wants to offend and both agree that they believe in some God, whoever that is, and both seem to have some incentive to serve together at the local soup kitchen, but they are not quite sure why. No, each party must dig deep into its own tradition and speak with as clear and articulate a voice as it can what it really believes. Thus, Christian evangelical preaching must present unashamedly the truth claims of the gospel of Jesus Christ, which include not merely the individual's but all of creation's sinfulness and lack of hope for the future without the divine intervention of undeserved grace that brings biblical Word and human longing together in a startlingly incarnational way.

The trouble is, twenty-first century preaching cannot present that gospel with that kind of theological jargon anymore. "The gospel of Jesus Christ" is a nice phrase rich with meaning, but in today's world, what does it mean? No matter how correct one's theology is in any generation, it makes no difference if it is not translated into its own time and cultural perspective. Buttrick, especially, has made this point repeatedly. Atonement, sanctification, Trinity—all fine theological shorthand—must be translated because the twenty-first century world knows not the stories from which they came.

Preaching in the Twenty-first Century

The gospel has to be reinterpreted over and over again. Paul found that out long ago. So have all the major theologians throughout church history, as have missionaries and evangelists. Buttrick understands clearly as we enter the twenty-first century that the white Anglo-European homiletic that has been dominant in the twentieth century in America may be on the way out or on the verge of being altered drastically as African American and Hispanic Christians increasingly become the majority. Preaching in the twenty-first century may have to be very different, more passionate and less propositional, more expressive and less Aristotelian, more metaphorical, musical, worldly, and even political. Radical homiletical paradigm shifts like this may be as hard for mainline Anglo-Christians to swallow as it was for the little Jewish sect and the Galatian Judaizers when Paul wanted to take the word to the Gentiles (that is, outsiders) as the gospel exploded onto the Mediterranean world. As hard as it is to hear, the gospel has never been bound by any time, place, or culture. This means Thomist or Calvinist or Lutheran or Barthian or Tillichian or Niebuhrian or liberationist or feminist or womanist or whatever may come next. Each has something to say, but each, taken by itself, is limited just as one of the four Gospels or one of Paul's letters by itself only presents part of the gospel message and never the whole.

The challenge here is finding a "point of contact" as Brunner used to say, and the hidden danger is "accommodating" too much to culture, as in H. Richard Niebuhr's "of culture" position, where the equal sign often finds itself between Christianity and the best of culture. How do we preach the gospel in culture's language with culture's metaphor without turning our sermons into either Marxist ideology on the one hand or the *Wall Street Journal* on the other? How do we speak to the contemporary, scientific, computer-headed, cyber-spaced, psychologically oriented, and fitness-crazed mind without turning Bill Gates into the new savior and the newest software or the latest feel-good technique into our salvation? Buttrick himself has noted with Crane Brinton that, since the Enlightenment, "the Second Coming turned into Utopia; original sin became environmental corruption or, sometimes, after Darwin, an evolutionary lag; God's covenant turned into natural law; eternal life was reduced to eternal values; and providence gave way to Hegel's historical dialectic."[1]

Evangelical Preaching

Twenty-first century evangelical preaching that addresses the whole person (individual and social) living in the context of community, world, and the whole of creation has to be street-smart and tough-minded enough to know the gospel, the culture it is addressing, along with its worldview and its weaknesses, and how to communicate clearly without selling out and without worrying about the future or the survival of the church as we know it. After all, the whole purpose of the preaching of the gospel, according to Buttrick, is not to build the church bigger and bigger but to liberate humanity. It is not socialization but transformation.

But today's mainline churches are more into surviving as they are than into losing themselves for Christ's sake. No wonder most mainline churches have a hard time with evangelism and social justice ministry; they both mean risk. Buttrick believes that "we are called to preach the gospel in the world and leave the preservation of the church to God's good graces. After all, the commissions in the Bible do *not* say, 'Go out into the world and hold onto yourselves!' "[2] Buttrick believes in what he calls a "churchless kingdom of God," prophesied in Revelation 21–22, where the gospel does not suffer because of competitive Christianity, which finds each denomination trying to keep up with the next.

Social Justice Preaching

Social justice ministry preaching means being able to lose oneself for Christ's sake by making common cause with the poor and the poor in spirit, seeing God at work, and wanting the church to be at work wherever there is suffering and injustice in the world. This means tackling the tough issues of the day because Christ and the prophets did and God expects us to do likewise. One should never tackle these issues as a stricken Elijah, whining and griping, but as one who loves God and people deeply and seeks authentically to bring the biblical word to bear on public life and policy. Social justice preaching that is truly authentic is rooted in the Bible, but is also very savvy about the world. It is a preaching that takes seriously the Johannine phrase, "the Word became flesh and lived among us."

In addition, social justice preaching and action, when done as the early church intended it, leads to real evangelism the way it is modeled in Acts 2, as Buttrick is fond of noting in his lectures and writings. What happens in this scene of the first Pentecost? A revival? An evangelistic crusade with droves marching forward to "Just as I Am, Without One Plea"? Neither. Jews have gathered from all over for the Feast of Weeks, and there is disturbance on the side. Some who follow the one called Christos seem to be excited, a little too religious even for a giant church picnic like this one. They are speaking in tongues! Someone suggests they must be drunk. Up pops Peter (Have sermon will travel!) who says, "No, they can't be drunk. It's only nine o'clock in the morning. But, now that I have your attention, let me tell you about Jesus Christ." And off he goes. Buttrick often uses this story as an example of how the church can be involved in the world in such a way that it attracts the world's attention—a soup kitchen, a free dental clinic for the poor, a march for peace, whatever—and the world looks up and asks, "What's going on here? Why are you doing this?" And the church responds, "Let us tell you about Jesus Christ. That's why we're here." Or if the church is a little timid and wants to be a little less explicit, it can always give the answer that Philip gave to Nathanael when asked about Jesus: "Come and see," which doesn't just mean, "Come and see our neat church" or "Come and hear our great choir or our stirring preacher," or "Come and see our great gymnasium" but "Come and see the Lord who gets us out into the world doing things we'd never do on our own!" In this way social justice ministry becomes evangelism and the two intersect.

There is one thing more, perhaps the most important point of all. Social justice preaching rooted in a deep evangelical faith can never be done fully by the clergy alone. It was never intended to be. God calls every person to evangelism and social justice ministry, not merely pastors, priests, or preachers. The job of the clergy and educators is not only to model both forms of ministry but to train the laity to do both in the world. "Out-church preaching," which is what Buttrick refers to as social justice and evangelical homiletics, is "primarily the task of the laity, those who by Baptism have been ordained to a common, evangelical ministry. If the church is a chosen witness to the resurrection, a servant people with a particular task assigned, namely, preaching good news to the 'end of the age,' then speaking *out* is the church's calling."[3]

Conclusion

The clergy's and educators' calling is to train the laity, to equip the saints for the work of ministry in the world. What does that mean? Church history and theology classes that can go much deeper than Sunday school? Yes. Biblical theology and criticism? Why not? How about Greek and Hebrew for those who would like to give it a try? These classes are being taught in churches today. Liturgy classes to learn more about the meaning of worship. Courses in medical ethics. Absolutely. And finally a preaching class for those who are on the front line of ministry every day of their lives. Buttrick asks, "How many churches have actually designed a lay homiletic course, so as to prepare folks to give an account of themselves with apologetic smarts (instead of pushy triumphalism); or required theological study so that people will know not only whom, but what they are talking about?"[4] Too often all we share is a "vapid, semi-sincere sales pitch for the local parish programs," when we should be introducing people into the presence of the risen Christ, who saves us and challenges us at every turn. Buttrick is right; "out-church preaching," as he calls it, is primarily the work of the laity. It is the task of the whole church. It always has been.

What kind of preaching will emerge more and more as we enter the twenty-first century? One that takes seriously the twin covenants of Abraham and Sinai held in tension in the Old Testament—twin covenants that coalesce in the Luke-Acts tradition, in the person of Jesus Christ, and in the work and ministry of the church in every age. We call them evangelism and social justice ministry—twin covenants that together announce the coming kingdom of God.

NOTES

1. David Buttrick, *A Captive Voice: The Liberation of Preaching* (Louisville, Ky.: Westminster John Knox Press, 1994), 59.
2. Ibid., 107.
3. David Buttrick, *Homiletic: Moves and Structures* (Philadelphia: Fortress Press, 1987), 226.
4. Ibid.

6

Practical Theology
as a Critique of Knowledge

RUDOLF BOHREN

Before there were written texts, there was the Spirit brooding over the waters until a voice spoke. When texts appeared, there came along with them books and libraries, universities and faculties, and a monstrous scholarly apparatus was installed in order to give texts a voice to carry the Spirit. It has been said that theology should be a practical science, but when there is a shortage of practice and the whole apparatus spins its wheels, then there is a need for a critique of knowledge. So, I want to ask a systematic and an exegetical theologian what they do when they work as theologians. For this purpose, I will examine their use of language. Moreover, since a critique of knowledge also implies a critique of oneself, I will ask two theologians who, in my opinion, are standing on the same ground as I am: Gerhard Sauter and Peter Stuhlmacher.

The Role of Knowledge
in the Conflict between Letter and Spirit

As I put on poet's glasses to criticize knowledge, Gregory of Nyssa teaches me, "The newfound things, are always more beautiful than the ones already understood."[1] Thus, I welcome the primary things as those that must be newly found each time. And I learn from Calvin that the eye of faith sees more than the natural senses (see 2 Cor. 4:18). It is essential for the primary point of view to see the invisible and to be astonished at newly found things. Thus, I will try to see more than I would see merely with a poet's glasses. It does not matter whether one has the physical ability to see, but whether one has been given sight by one "who has made us competent to be ministers of a new covenant, not of letter but of spirit; for the letter kills, but the Spirit gives life" (2 Cor. 3:6). A servant of the new covenant will receive eyes that see more than any other optics.

"Divine power" of the new creation is primary, whereas the "human ability" of literary arts is secondary. In order to find out something about the quality of knowledge one must prove its origin. One has to examine its spirit to see whether it represents God's power or human ability or, more precisely, whether knowledge serves life or death.

The opposition between the letter and the Spirit described in 2 Cor. 3:6 is normally explained as the opposition between the law and the gospel, an opposition supported by the next verse, which immediately refers to the Ten Commandments (2 Cor. 3:7). However, the next paragraph talks about reading (2 Cor. 3:12ff.), and it is noteworthy that Paul talks explicitly about the "letter," that is something *read*, and not about the "law." The distinction between the letter and the Spirit points to the two possible ways to read a biblical text: as something to *read* versus life from the Spirit.

I probably put myself on the spot when I quote Paul, because he sanctifies the law at the same time that he sanctifies the opposition between "the letter and the Spirit" (2 Cor. 3:6). After consulting Luther, Calvin, and the contemporary commentaries, I found an inspiring word from Oepke Nordmaans, "Prophecy would not have a ground, it would be like hitting the air, if it did not speak out of the law. But the law would be dead and would kill humanity if it did not always receive living power from prophecy. 'The letter kills but the Spirit gives life.' "[2]

As Hans-Walter Wolff explained in his early work, "Quotations in Prophets," the prophets had first been readers and spoke as those who read. Their writings came only later. The prophetic view is primary—theological speech—and it sees through all that is secondary. Every child can count to two, but theology must learn over and over again to distinguish the secondary from the primary. It has to raise the question of knowledge in the conflict between letter and Spirit. Does knowledge serve death or life? If Gerhard Ebeling is still right that "the theology of modern times did not create a significant new systematic answer to the problem of the Spirit and the letter," then this would be an alarming sign that theology is rarely aware of its effect. Rather, it suffers from a lack of self-critique and is unable to discover beautiful new insights. Maybe novelists are helping us to criticize ourselves, since poetry and prophecy are, according to legend, sisters.

Secondary versus the Primary Point of View

When Guenter Grass received the Grand Prize for Literature from the Bavarian Academy of the Fine Arts on May 5, 1994, his lecture was titled "The Secondary from the Primary Point of View."[3] I admit, this lecture is not a rhetorical masterpiece. Its style is as verbose as his novels. Even worse, like a bad preacher, he fell in love with a verbal idea in his first sentence and followed it blindly: "There is something about presentations."

From that point on, he could not be stopped: "There is something about" everything, involved in the prize ceremony: prizewinners in general and, of course, about Grass himself, the prizewinner in particular; about the expression of thanks; about the literary work; about the book; about the academy. All these things were strutting forward like a potbelly, and there was "something about" all of them.

But then, a quick scene change from "I" to "us." Grass began to say how today the secondary supersedes the primary. "The permanent self-celebration of the secondary is not only determining the spirit of the age, it is embodying it. The secondary appears as the original. It is not the newly published book that is the big event but the reviews of it." Shakespeare the performer takes second place to the staging. In a musical concert "the name of Karajan was printed in an extra large font," while names of the composers appeared "in a very tiny font."

In the "surrounding area of postmodern philosophy," the "dominating secondary" tends to "contemplate itself. Avoiding direct discussion of the primary work at all costs, it points to it only with cross-reference." In the meantime, the secondary has become self-sufficient; "it not only rules but dominates business and multiplies itself like a parasite. I am talking about the hubris of the secondary. My speech is about the sell-out," said Grass. "We are served by the second-hand."

The "hubris of the secondary" and its "sell-out" of literature are obvious to Grass when, for example, critics attempt to "find out—sometimes speculating, sometimes puzzling—how to prove Thomas Mann's homosexuality through characters" in his books. Then, they analyzed his diaries. "Now he is ours," they exclaimed. "We know him completely. We do not have to read him any longer." Grass names Uwe Johnson as "another case of a secondary appropriation." One must be afraid that his work "is darkened by creaming off the private delicacies before it has reached the reader and delighted him."

After this broadside, the prizewinner and his readers are left behind: "Because the one, who is reading, is dealing with a primary event—an event without parallels. Nothing can replace the process of reading." In Grass's imagination the reader is idealistic, maybe too idealistic. He makes his statement very courageously: "In a world of the surrogate, the reader has to act in an extraordinary way. Nothing comes between him and the book, much like a talkative speaker on TV. In his imagination, he creates what is written abstractly. He is alone with the book," like the author has been alone with the manuscript. "It is the reader who is reanimating a story that has been declared dead, completing it through his imagination and sometimes even enriching it. He is using the book, sometimes even as a mirror."

It is surprising that a politically engaged author like Grass points out the so-to-speak pastoral effect of literature. He points to letters from readers in a hospital that confirmed that his book *Der Butt* was very helpful in the healing process. I know that the telling of a story can be a primary medical service. And I also know that our world, if it will ever come to consciousness, will not regain health with the secondary. The primary "makes" the world "happy" and heals it, whereas the secondary can be considered as a foreign rule. It establishes itself as "a glittering second-hand shop," in which deception is essential.

A Theological Critique of Knowledge

Now, a slow *scene change* from literature to theological literature and all that it has to do with. But changing the backdrop already causes me trouble. It is all right for Guenter Grass to talk, because he, as a prizewinner, already has the primary view. He is not dependent on nuances that are rightly required from a critique of knowledge.

Let us start again. Theological books bear the same burden as every other form of literature: One must learn how to read and how to write; the sequence cannot be altered if one wants to preserve what has been learned. Reading gives letters a voice, and it is the *voice* that counts. In certain respects, this is the condition and the aim of theological work. It is essential that one learn how to deal with a primary event—"an event without parallel"—not in regard to just any book but in regard to the book of books. A theological critique of knowledge will inquire about the relation between knowledge and this primary event. So, it is essential to keep the elementary order of reading and writing, not just when knowledge becomes practical through preaching but even during the performance of its work. Theology has to prove itself by keeping this order, because, otherwise, we theologians write without seeing, tasting, touching, and listening to what we have written; therefore we are against life.

One example: The first part of Gerhard Sauter's article "The Art of Reading the Bible" is subtitled with a suggestive question, "An art known by everybody?"[4] What everybody knows is not necessarily an art. For this reason, the author is compelled to raise a second question, indeed Philip's question to the Ethiopian eunuch: "Do you understand what you are reading?" Eventually, he moves to the third suggestive question: "Do *we* understand . . .?" But, when two people ask the same question they do not necessarily mean the same thing. Philip asks his question as a pedestrian, from below, getting into the chariot. The movement of Sauter's three questions, however, shows one who is already on a high level and asking from above.

Although Sauter quotes 2 Cor. 3:6, "the letter kills, but the Spirit gives life," this is not a primary experience. If he had truly heard and read the message of the text, he could not have continued: "This does *not*—as it was often misunderstood—refer to the opposition between the dead letter and the vivid spirit." Immediately, the correctness of the "secondary" comes into the scene and calms all fears. The dangerous life that the word of the apostle wants to signal to the reader of the Bible is displaced. It is not a big deal to say what a text does not want to say.

Later comes Sauter's main sentence: "The difference between the letter and the Spirit has to do with *God's freedom when he speaks*." But immediately, he uses a negation: "God is *not* free in regard to the words that he has spoken." In the sentence that follows there appears a word that makes us helpless: "In this regard, the difference between the letter and the Spirit *should* guide each reading of the Bible." This is a program instead of an illustration. It does not help me as a reader of the Bible when Sauter says at the end of his article that the distinctions between "the Spirit and the letter, the law and the gospel, promise and fulfillment" have been proved as "reading instructions." I ask whether he is not mixing "the art of reading the Bible" with theology itself.

It is remarkable that features of legalistic speech dominate Sauter's article. (It would be easy to prove this in a thorough analysis.) Legalism places its hope in human ability, not in God's power, therefore, the "to be" fails because of the "ought to be." Probably the biggest temptation of theology, as scholarly knowledge, is the pressure to justify itself. This serves the letter, not the Spirit. The secondary reflex becomes the main event and prophecy does not exist.

Sauter's article is just one example. Many other cases could be cited of wise men and good theologians serving secondhand knowledge. Although I can agree with much of what Sauter is saying, it is practically good-for-nothing.

When we serve the secondhand, as Sauter does, there is inevitably a clerical tendency implied. In clericalism, the secondary wins over the primary, the letter displaces the Spirit. No secondary negations take their shine from "the primary work." They create a negative aura that hardly motivates serving the Spirit. Such negations protest against errors and demonstrate correctness, but they are not able to liberate. Something that is correct is not always necessarily good. Correctness stands grounded and closed off, but it is not open and inclusive.

A note from Franz Overbeck becomes a general truth for theology during this sad self-celebration of the secondary in which the reading of the Bible does not become and remain a primary experience: "Modern research is, in regard to the Gospel of John, dependent upon light food: it has to become satiated by licking its own paws."[5]

Servant of the letter or of the new covenant? In this regard, the wise man of the First Psalm provides the tape measure for every theology. Through reading and rereading, a text begins to sing and through singing, the soul enters the text. This is the reason why it can be compared to a tree "planted by streams of water." A miracle happens and the reader is changed into the word. This is also what Sauter is talking about, but he does not explain it.

I learned from Karl Barth that theology is obedient worship.[6] Only one who has a vision, who has received something, who is able to "read," can truly worship. In that sense, Anselm of Canterbury "is talking about God by talking to him." Prayer is a part of theological reading and theological writing. There is no service of the Spirit that is not also prayer. The reason for this is that the mover of all things wants to be moved himself, and obedient worship sees itself involved in an event, in a history—a history that is not restricted to the history of theology because we must speak a universal worship. This idea of a universal worship will characterize theology in the house of knowledge. In present academic activities, theology figures as a late-coming messenger. Theology is eating fast food as an inconspicuous backbencher at university. Instead, theology should lead the path of knowledge and know that the opposition between the letter and the Spirit—in an age, where life is threatened, this obviously appears in a glaring light—is binding for all knowledge and that every knowledge discovers its goal in worshiping.

Before his execution, the Jesuit Alfred Delp wrote, with his hands bound, meditations called "Characters around Christmas." He was thinking of all the characters "who were unsung, who were not powerful, rich, scholarly."[7] In this context, he targets "scholarly knowledge" and its permanent self-celebration of the secondary. "Scholarly knowledge forgot how to worship a very long time ago," he writes. "It is bewitched and drunk with its own ideas, captured in its own constructions of the world and its agenda." Delp demonstrates how the letter still kills.

Let us take yet another example: medicine. During my occasional walks through the local vineyards, I meet from time to time medical historian Heinrich Schipperges. We experience no difficulty in talking critically about our subjects, and I will never forget how he summarized a lecture on Hildegard von Bingen. He ended it by naming two subjects very important to her, indeed they were the heart of her worldview: knowledge of how to cure and how to save. "Both ways of knowledge," he said, "will probably shape the coming millennium."

The stage is slowly getting darker. As far as I know, academic activities at our faculties have hardly changed since the golden twenties. Despite all the talk about new paradigms, it is impossible to face the increasing problems of the church. In fact, I see in the bureaucratic manner of our churches a dominance of the secondary similar to that evident in our faculties. And what is sauce for the goose is sauce at the pulpit. "Talk about God is falling into danger through banality as much as through heresy. Indeed, banality is probably the most malicious form of heresy." I read this sentence by Albrecht Groezinger.[8] "Banal" is something the feudal lord gives to his vassal so that he can use it. The texts of the Holy Scripture consist of banal words, and through the kind of language that preachers use they become very easily banal in the common sense. The preacher uses letters and words, but the Spirit cannot use the preacher.

My question is, How is it that our scholarly practice not only allows but in all probability cultivates a practice of preaching that tempts many preachers to say banalities and creates a total vacuum in churches? The crisis of the sermon—although it already became flagrantly a crisis of the church—still remains a task that goes beyond exegesis. We will gain a lot by serving the Spirit if we understand the practice of the church as a critical inquiry of academic theology. In this sense, we as teachers have to take responsibility for the pupils. Therefore, I have to make my issue more precise: not practical theology but the practice of the church is criticizing ipso facto scholarly knowledge. But this knowledge will quietly remain in its dreadful state as long as the practical character of theology does not want to prophesy; it will lose not only its practical but also its theological character. This will happen when academic theology does research and teaches without paying attention to the shape of the congregations.

Spiritual Exegesis and the Participation of the Spirit

My comments remain at the secondary level as long as I do not present the theological roots of the present misery. Today's new dogmatism is due to an insufficient teaching about the Holy Spirit and due, therefore, to the failure to discern the difference between the Spirit and the letter, to an insufficient reflection of the humanity of the Spirit. We stress the divinity of the Spirit and do not see how closely it is related to the flesh. We claim something that we do not have power over, and do not realize how quickly it dissolves. We have a strong method to serve the letter, but we have not done enough to serve the Spirit theoretically, practically, and methodologically. This could only happen because we forgot that the Holy Spirit is also dedicated to us. When Paul has plans to travel to Rome, he believes in the company of the Spirit, and he writes, "I know that when I come to you, I will come in the fullness of the blessing" (Rom. 15:29).

It is well known that it was difficult for the early church to know Christ as a real human being, because they wanted to think of him and to pray to him as a real God. They did not like his humiliation and talked about an imaginary body. But the New Testament already includes opposition to such a position. 1 John 4:2b confesses, "Every spirit that confesses that Jesus Christ has come in the flesh is from God." Later, it was Origen who was against a separation between the human and the divine in the fleshly *logos*. "I do not separate Jesus from Christ."

The word has become flesh in a unique, unrepeatable historical event. The effusion of the Holy Spirit over every flesh was not an event that happened once and forever, but continually occurs in an unending history, that has not come to an end yet. When the time was ripe, God became a human being. Now, God is coming as a Spirit, bringing Jesus Christ to our consciousness and even more to our unconscious, to the heart.

The theological fathers stressed the divinity of the Spirit—at the expense of its mixture with the flesh. When Karl Barth noted, in response to question 53 of the *Heidelberg Catechism*, that "this is the inestimable, central statement of the third article—God is within me. *Deus in nobis*," then this statement has been unmeasured. Then, in fact, we did the same with the Spirit as Origen did not want to do with the son of God. We did— metaphorically speaking—separate Jesus from Christ and we treated the texts with atheistic methods by saying that we would serve the Spirit. But we did not realize that this brought us closer to the real existent atheism in the church. One can hardly say that, in this way, an inestimable, central statement dominates the church. The Spirit is brooding in lonely fashion over a stretch of superficial water. The fatal situation can also be shown in the work of the theologian who honestly tries to replace the fast-food meal through "a feast of rich food" (Isa. 25:6).

Peter Stuhlmacher puts a question mark in the title of his article "Spiritual Exegesis?"[9] This could be a sign that this way of understanding the scripture does not correspond to the theological consensus. We have to rejoice that he writes about an issue that does not automatically give him credits among his professional colleagues. First, Stuhlmacher passes the word to his professional colleague in Old Testament, Hartmut Gese, who suggests that, exegetically, "We have to understand texts as they want to be understood," because "biblical texts themselves require appropriate interpretation."[10] But Gese has come under the cross fire of critique. Nowadays, biblical exegesis that tries to correspond to the hermeneutical originality of the texts finds itself blockaded by "scholarly reserve, clerical fear of the Holy Scripture, and lack of theological knowledge."[11] Thus, Stuhlmacher accepts the advice of a systematic theologian, "that the biblical texts still make themselves understandable and invite a certain way of understanding."[12] In a short survey, he strives to show "that the New Testament has definitely its own ideas of how to interpret the Holy

Scriptures of the Old Testament and the testimony of the New Testament."[13] If I understand Stuhlmacher correctly, he wants to find a method of interpretation in the scripture itself. In this way, the texts should "be interpreted from Christ to Christ in the name of the Spirit. This should be done by interpreters who have been given part of the very same Spirit that blows through the biblical books." But "in the most decisive parts," the Spirit "takes itself away from every method." The reproach to the scholars still remains that "critical Protestant exegesis" has rejected "for a long time the hermeneutical connections" that Stuhlmacher outlines.

In accord with the title of his article, one major sentence contains a negation and proves the apologetical interest of the present scholarly practice: Exegesis recommends itself as something that is "spiritually reflected, and methodologically ordered." Whereas later, "spiritual exegesis" is understood as a part of the *oratio, meditatio, and tentatio*, which follows an "exegesis that is done according to clear rules."[14] Reading 2 Tim. 3:16, Stuhlmacher is *not* convinced "that there is a meaningful opposition between the two ways of exegesis."[15] Apparently he does not realize that he is doing exactly the same thing as those who separate Jesus from Christ. He adds what one truly cannot add.

There is a strange linguistic imbalance between exegesis and the participation of the Spirit. On the one hand, a "spiritually reflected, methodologically ordered exegesis" dominates, that is "done according to clear rules," but on the other hand, the spiritual exegesis "is withdrawing itself in the most decisive parts from the methodological grasp" and "is ruled by the action of God who cannot be taken over by humans."[16] The result is that we are helpless and alone like after a legalistic sermon together with Luther, Hamann, Schlatter and the *oratio, meditatio, and tentatio*. The question is, How can the claim of the texts "of having an interpretation in itself" be fulfilled? Is this the method where both ways of interpretation can be reconciled in the face of the imbalanced separation? As long as scholarly exegesis uses colorful adjectives whereas spiritual interpretation is missing words, there is something wrong with the language. The Holy Spirit remains at the other end of the flesh. When something is wrong with language there is a question, whether the language is conformed to the one Word that was in the beginning or whether the linguistic inconsistency reveals a theological one. Thus, language shows the justification of the secondary, and the inestimable statements of the third article do not get a voice. A question mark replaces the exclamation mark.

Through analyzing sermons, we discovered the word of the "unconscious dogmatic" that guides the preacher and forms language. The old Adam wants to speak through negations, modal verbs, and colorful adjectives. A theological critique of scholarly knowledge tries to point out this unconscious dogmatic that may be based on an unresolved conflict within the author himself. I ask, Do negations become necessary for a systematic theologian because he displays an erudition that inevitably gets sucked into a spirit of constant denial? This is what deeply frightens me when I read this theologically well done article. I also ask if the language of an exegetical theologian gets imbalanced because he stresses the pull of the traditional critique of scholarly knowledge and takes no account of the Spirit in which there was the Yes. One would only have to compare the style of the quoted articles with Bonhoeffer's statements in order to know the domination by the secondary.

In homiletic seminars, I have wondered over and again about how unproductive the effects of being interested in communication with the listener can be. I think that theology as obedient worship is blocked by showing off scholarly knowledge. This is only possible because the Holy Spirit is not related to the flesh and practically separated from the scholarly practice.

What Manfred Josuttis writes about the church is also true for theology and historical critique: "The church is, regarding the methods of psychology, sociology, and communication, up to date in various aspects. It was the concern of the church to reflect and to control the contact between humans. But at the same time the church is helpless, almost infantile: regarding its own field, the contact with the Holy, is methodologically under-developed."[17] One question that Josuttis raises is, "How can I pray?" And, of course, this is related to the question, How can I encounter the holy in the scriptures? That means, can we now read the scripture in the light of the Spirit? I think that Stuhlmacher is an example of how the scholarly approach to the holy remains and will remain underdeveloped as long as the scholars prefer secondary material and do not count methodologically on the humanity of the Spirit.

When one looks carefully, talk about "grasp" and about "unavailability" is revealed as a myth of everyday academic life. It seems to be correct, terribly correct, when one prefers secondary sources to primary ones. Service of the letter goes off course compared to the service of the Spirit. If there is any change through the Spirit, the Spirit wants to be the guide, the leader, and Lord of the changing person. Then one has to think once again of how to do theological work in the power of the holy. We have to develop a method that opens every door and window to the Spirit in the house of knowledge, a method that teaches us how to pray for this event, that appeals for wind coming down from heaven. This is not possible as long as the secondary has the primary right and the Spirit is banned to the prompt box.

I once postulated asceticism as a field of practical theology, and I have lectured—for my own sake—over and over again about prayer. Now, I want to withdraw what I once argued. Practical theology cannot do alone what theology must do as a whole: to teach and to live obedient worship. We have to rediscover not only the Bible but also monasticism, the church fathers, and the Reformed theologians as places of critical ferment for the art of interpretation. And who knows if then the eagerness to prophesy (1 Cor. 14:1, 39) will replace discussion about hermeneutics and if a word of Novalis will enlighten studies and lecture halls: "The true historical understanding is the prophetical one."[18]

Conclusion

When Israel Chalfen asked the poet Paul Celan for an interpretation of one of his poems, Celan answered, "Read! Always read. Understanding comes without saying."[19] Obviously, the reading of the Torah in Psalm 1 stands as a model for the reading of a poem. Understanding that comes without saying would therefore be primary. Through reading and repeating, a text starts to sing and the soul enters the text; the reader is stimulated and stimulates the text.

The insight of Stuhlmacher that "biblical texts make themselves understandable and invite a certain way of understanding"[20] makes the advice of the poet understandable, even for the reader of the Bible: "Read! Always read. Understanding comes without saying." Understanding always comes without saying, like faith itself, even when an angel has to send Philippus to the street that leads from Jerusalem to Gaza.

Maybe, we have turned the mill for too long, but when we look for the pillar with staggering steps, we become blind and instead of growing hair, we become bald. But, who knows, maybe once again a sterile woman will become pregnant and deliver a Samson who will make Israel free from the Philistinian dominance. Until these events happen, I ask for your help to ensure that theology does not any longer serve church and society secondhand, but becomes perceptive.

NOTES

1. Gregory of Nyssa, *Der Versiegelte Quell* (1984), 98.
2. Oepke Nordmaans, *Das Evangelism des Geistes* (1960), 50.
3. *Neue Zuercher Zeitung* 107 (May 9, 1994): 17.
4. *Evangelische Theologie* 52 (1992): 347–57.
5. Franz Overbeck, *Das Johannesevangelium: Studien zur Kritik Seiner Erforschung* (Tübingen: J.C.B. Mohr [Paul Siebeck], 1911), 79.
6. Karl Barth, *Anselms Beweis der Existenz Gottes* (Zollikon: Evangelischer Verlag, 1958), 144.
7. (Rome: Università Gregoriana, 1948), 82.

8. *Predigen zum Weitersagen* no. 24, 6.
9. Peter Stuhlmacher, "Spiritual Exegesis?" in *Einfach von Gott reden: Ein Theologischer Diskurs* (Stuttgart: W. Kohlhammer, 1994), 67ff.
10. Ibid., 68.
11. Ibid.
12. Ibid.
13. Ibid., 71f.
14. Ibid., 80.
15. Ibid., 73.
16. Ibid., 80.
17. Manfred Josuttis, *Petrus, die Kirche und die Verdammte Macht* (Stuttgart: Krevz-Verlag, 1993), 196.
18. Schr. 3 (1968): 601.
19. *Neue Zuercher Zeitung,* 235 (October 8/9, 1994): 69.
20. Stuhlmacher, "Spiritual Exegesis?" 68.

2. PREACHING AND THE GOSPEL

7

The Gospel of God

FRED B. CRADDOCK

To the Christians in Rome, to whom he wrote his most extended and perhaps most deliberately constructed statement of the Christian faith, Paul introduced himself as one "set apart for the gospel of God" (Rom. 1:1). Surprised by the phrase "of God" rather than the expected "of Christ," students of Romans have argued over Paul's precise meaning. Is the genitive objective; that is, is the gospel *about* God? Or, is the genitive subjective; that is, is God the *source* of the gospel? At the risk of seeming indecisive, let me suggest that yes is the answer to both questions. The gospel is about God. Even though Paul goes on to say that the gospel is "concerning God's Son" (v. 3), the message reveals something true of God. For example, Paul himself states that it was the gospel which brought him to a crucial understanding of God, that "God shows no partiality" (2:11). Likewise, the phrase "gospel of God" reminds the reader that God is the author of the gospel. Christ is decisive content but not the origin of the gospel.

The Origin of the Gospel

With the same language, David Buttrick could introduce himself to his readers; in fact, he has. Theocentricity has characterized his work with remarkable consistency. In a 1988 volume titled, interestingly enough, *Preaching Jesus Christ*, he wrote, "All we have to do is leaf our Bibles to discover that the story of Jesus Christ is set within a larger story, a story of God with Israel."[1] He then goes on to say, "Of course, the story of Christ, set within the story of Israel, is located within a still larger story, a story of God and humanity."[2] And in that story, who is Jesus Christ? He is "the image of God's own intending toward us; here is God-with-us."[3] And again, "When we preach, we hold Christ up before our congregations and through him speak of the mystery of God."[4] Later, in the Macleod Lectures at Princeton Theological Seminary,[5] Buttrick responds to his own question, How can preaching recover theological meaning? He suggests that we again preach what Jesus preached: the gospel of God. Drawing on Mark 1:14–15, which describes Jesus' ministry in Galilee as proclaiming the gospel of God, the drawing near of God's kingdom, and calling for repentance and faith in this good news, Buttrick urges preachers, "Once more let us announce the coming of God's new order."[6]

Buttrick's insistence is the insistence of scripture, that it is God who creates, God who provides, God who redeems, God who sent Jesus Christ, God who sends the Holy Spirit. But his words have been prophetic in a time when those who sit before pulpits have been given a steady diet of Jesus Christ without a context in theology. A listener might get the impression that faith in Christ had replaced faith in God or that faith in Christ had been added to faith in God as though an increase in the number of items in one's faith meant an increase in salvific effect. No doubt some hearers of such sermons, lacking any acquaintance with the larger narrative of God's dealing with humanity, have an experience similar to entering a theater after the movie has started. Information vital and essential to understanding must have been revealed early in the film, and it has been missed.

This is not to imply that David Buttrick has been a lone voice for theocentricity; from time to time similar notes have appeared in the margins of biblical interpretation and biblical theology. In a significant, but inadequately noticed, 1975 essay, Nils Dahl of Yale wrote, "For more than a generation, the majority of New Testament scholars have not only eliminated direct references to God in their works but have also neglected detailed and comprehensive investigations of statements about God. Whereas a number of major works and monographs deal with the Christology (or ecclesiology, eschatology, etc.) of the New Testament, it is hard to find any comprehensive or penetrating study of the theme 'God in the New Testament.' "[7] Dahl understood, of course, that God as presented in the Old Testament could be taken for granted by most writers and readers in the early church, but he understood also that New Testament Christology can be treated properly only if it is related to faith in God. After all, faith in God shaped thinking about the life and passion of Jesus just as the life and passion of Jesus shaped faith in God.[8]

A decade earlier, E. C. Colwell, in the Cole Lectures at Vanderbilt, sounded a similar note while developing a different theme. Colwell's thesis is clear and straightforward: "Jesus' mission in history was to make God known and available."[9] His contention, however, is that the church has not accepted Jesus as a revelation of God; on the contrary, the church has used its doctrines about God to characterize Jesus. In other words, says Colwell, the church has taken Jesus' words, "Whoever has seen me has seen the Father" (John 14:9) and reversed them: "Whoever has seen the Father has seen me."[10] The result, of course, is a very high *Christ*ology, but *theo*logy suffers as an almost disposable commodity. Some in the Christian community seem content to supplant theology with Christology, but perhaps unaware of the immense price: the dislodging of Christ from salvation history, the loss of continuity with Israel's faith, the separation of creation from redemption (opening the door to every other-worldly heresy hovering around the church), and the reduction of the first item of the Christian creed to the role of preface.

Back of all this discussion stands the figure of Rudolf Bultmann. Those who contend that Christian theology is consumed without remainder in Christology are fond of quoting Bultmann's statement, "The proclaimer became the proclaimed."[11] This is to say, Jesus came preaching God but the early church preached Jesus Christ. Those who cite this passage and stop should read on. Bultmann goes on to say, "Christian missionary preaching to the Gentile world could not be simply the christological kerygma; rather it had to begin with the proclamation of the one God."[12] In support of this conclusion he cites not only Luke's account of Paul's preaching in Athens (Acts 17:22–31) but also abundant passages in Paul's letters (1 Cor. 8:4–6; 2 Cor. 2:14; 1 Thess. 1:9; et al.). In fact, he reminds us that, to the Galatian churches, Paul spoke of conversion as turning from not knowing God to knowing God (Gal. 4:8–9). Bultmann then continued to speak of God in the New Testament in terms of titles used, among them Creator, Savior, and Judge.[13]

Bultmann's discussion of God in the New Testament in terms of titles is paralleled by Robert Brawley's attention to verbs in his investigation of God as the central character in the narrative of Luke-Acts. God creates, promises, guides, calls, gives, and so on. The entire narrative, says Brawley, is theocentric; in fact, the Christology of Luke-Acts is structured theocentrically. "Jesus' call to follow, then, always carries with it submission to the consummate plan of God."[14]

Enough has been said to make the point. Granted, the New Testament devotes major attention to Jesus Christ. After all, the crucifixion alone pushed the disciples to the polemical wall, and the interpretation of that event, not to mention Jesus' life, demanded full energies of mind and heart. However, it is not fair to lay the blame for neglect of the subject of God at the feet of New Testament writers. There is ample evidence to the contrary, especially if one keeps in mind a fundamental canon of preaching: appropriateness to one's audience.

Content of Contemporary Preaching

What, then, in observance of this fundamental canon, would be proper subject matter for today's pulpit? The gospel of God, in both senses of the phrase: the good news about God and the good news from God. We are not here engaged in semantics, taking much too seriously differences between the words "God" and "Christ." The two words represent two very different frames of reference, very different worlds of understanding and being. Neither are we discussing preferences among believers, some being more comfortable with God-talk, others with Jesus-talk, and yet others with Spirit-talk. Jesus-talk or Spirit-talk, unless rooted in and informed by faith in God, can easily sink into sectarianism or float away in sentimentalism. To say that Christian preaching is or should be a proclamation about God is to say something central to who we are, what we are about, and how we regard the world in which we live out our faith, the world God created and loves. To spell out in particular how this is so is the burden of the remainder of this chapter.

Preaching the Gospel of God

First, let us address the obvious: to preach the gospel of God is to honor the whole Bible. Not all the Marcionites are dead, but they have lost the battle over the canon; the Bible consists of both the Hebrew and the Christian scriptures. Together they tell in many-splendored variety the story in which God is the central character. Paul expressed it as he concluded the principal argument of Romans: "O the depth of the riches and wisdom and knowledge of God! How unsearchable are his judgments and how inscrutable his ways! . . . For from him and through him and to him are all things. To him be the glory forever. Amen" (Rom. 11:33, 36). The writer of Hebrews offers a similar word in a more historical form: "Long ago God spoke to our ancestors in many and various ways by the prophets, but in these last days he has spoken to us by a Son" (Heb. 1:1–2). No one should claim to be a biblical preacher while confining herself or himself to only a portion of the canon.

Second, clarity and meaning can be served only if preaching begins, not with the resurrection or the crucifixion or the life or even the birth of Jesus Christ, but with God's overtures of love and grace toward humanity. Bultmann is right, preaching to Gentiles must begin with proclamation of the one true God, and most audiences today are Gentiles in the theological sense. Just because one's hearers are in a sanctuary does not mean that they know Abraham and Sarah or Moses and Miriam. They recognize the names Peter, Paul, and Mary but not from the biblical story. Many attending worship these days are not products of Sunday school or confirmation classes. They have been hanging out on the church porch trying to decide whether to go inside. Those churches that print in the order of worship the words to the Doxology, the Gloria, the Apostles'

Creed, and the Lord's Prayer are sensitive to the needs of a new generation of worshipers, but that step is hardly enough. There is a need for sermons with a wide-angle lens, sermons that elaborate on Paul's phrase,
"But when the fullness of time had come, God sent his Son" (Gal. 4:4), sermons that attend to both *chronos* and *kairos*. To preach Jesus Christ, however forcefully and sincerely, apart from the larger story of God's
engagement with the world is either to create a Jesus cult apart from faith
in God or to send listeners away feeling they must have missed the first
part of the movie. And if there is anything worse than feeling ignorant it
is feeling you are the only one in the house who is. The result is inevitable:
"This place is not for me; I will go to one of those large auditorium
churches where you just pay your money and watch the show." By no
means is this to urge exchanging sermons for lectures and converting
sanctuaries into lecture halls. More education is needed, to be sure, but
not in any pedantic sense. It is amazing how much learning takes place
when hearers are let in on the plot of God's gracious activity from Eden
until now. Then when the preacher arrives at the chapter titled "But in
these last days God has spoken in a Son" the "ahas" will be audible all
over the sanctuary.

Third, if the church is to address a society quite secular, increasingly
cynical, and impatiently skeptical, even if it still carries a residue of rever-
ence without belief, then it must speak of God. We will, of course, introduce Jesus Christ, but not yet. There are always a few who will meet you
at the club for lunch and discuss the relative merits of Jesus as guru as
compared to Muhammad or Gandhi. It could make for a nice afternoon,
but a thousand such afternoons would not address the fundamental questions of whence and whither. Is there any meaning to life other than the
small disconnected pieces we find or create now and then? Is life a series
of coincidences, chance meetings, accidents, snatches of luck good and
bad, and isolated episodes without theme, thread, or sense? As some post-
moderns would pose it, Is there a metanarrative, some overarching pur-
poseful direction to the life of the world, a beginning of things and an end
of things? James Crenshaw of Duke Divinity School has described life for
such seekers as one huge Easter egg hunt. Everyone rushes out in the
morning with an empty basket, searches frantically, grows discouraged,
hears now and then someone shout "I found one!" and renews the search,
but in the end goes home with an empty basket. Cynicism is not new; it
rose to question ancient pulpits: "Where is the promise of his coming? For
ever since our ancestors died, all things continue as they were from the
beginning of creation!" (2 Pet. 3:4).

But the fact is, whether asked in hardened cynicism or in open inquiry,
the question hangs in the air before the pulpit, waiting for a word. The

preacher need not panic and begin scrambling for proofs. Proofs are neither available nor necessary; a witness will do. And one's witness will
contain clues, hints, and intimations, will point to clouds no larger than a
human hand, to green shoots on a dead stump, and will pause in rever-
ence before the mystery of God. This is no time for manufactured certainty, giving the impression we had walked all the way around God and
taken pictures. An unpretentious witness will suffice. Before that testimony to God's gracious presence in the world for us many will sit in quiet
respect, and later a few will say to each other, "Come, let us go to
Bethlehem and see for ourselves this manger child."

A fourth and final reason for preaching today the good news of God
lies both in scripture and in our present circumstance. The subject here is
creational theology or perhaps more commonly referred to as natural
theology. Those of us still living in the shadow of Karl Barth whisper the
subject, anxious that his ghost may rise to threaten us. So long has revelation through history controlled the conversation that creational theology has seemed a banished topic, sent from the room with the liberal
Protestantism of another generation. But the fact is, God as creator, active
in and revealed through what has been made, is a consideration too
deeply imbedded in scripture to be easily dismissed. The subject is much
more substantive than popular lyrics such as "Every time I hear a new-
born baby cry or touch a leaf or see the sky, then I know why I believe."
The creation story of Genesis undergirds the entire wisdom tradition, not
only in the Old Testament but in the New, found heavily in the Letter of
James as well as the teaching of Jesus, especially in Matthew. God as creator is not only sung by the psalmist, it is integral to the weighty argument
of Romans (1:18–25). As for historical events, the exodus and the crucifixion hold central place, no question, but if "Maker of heaven and earth" is
lost from the church's conversation or from the pulpit, then some doctrine
of the beginning, the ending, and the meaning of the world would have to
be constructed by some imaginative theologians. But the subject will not
go away, as James Barr's recent book testifies.[15]

We pause here to hear two possible objections. First, does not the Fall of
Genesis 3 remove creation from the agenda of topics worthy of the pulpit
and the classroom, except, of course, in expressions of the hope that all
creation will share in the full redemption of the children of God (Rom.
8:18–25)? After all, the created order shared with humankind the corruption and decay following alienation from God. Quite true, and the story of
the Bible is a running account of God's gracious efforts to achieve that har-
monious symmetry in which the End will be as the Beginning. But that
story assumes that all was not lost at the Fall; something of Genesis 1 sur-
vived the crash of Genesis 3. Among humankind the image of God has

become so distorted and misguided that at times one hardly recognizes it, in oneself or in our society. Even so, there remains, not a relationship with God, but the capacity, as Luke puts it, to "search for God and perhaps grope for him and find him—though indeed he is not far from each one of us" (Acts 17:27). Our seeking God does not diminish the gift of God's self-revelation.

The second possible objection to creational theology may be christological. Those who would confine the sermon to Christ alone remind us that New Testament Christology includes creation, and it is true that quite early the church appropriated from late Judaism and Hellenism categories that enabled the development of a cosmic Christology. The New Testament amply testifies to this Christ whose activity extends to all creation (John 1; Heb. 1; Col. 1; Phil. 2; et al.). But preaching Jesus alone, even when the subject is creation, does not address the scriptural insistence that all things were made "through him" or "in him"; that is, God created through the agency of the Word, which is Christ. Nor does it recall Paul's instruction that when all creation is finally subject to Christ, "then the Son himself will also be subjected to the one who put all things in subjection under him, so that God may be all in all" (1 Cor. 15:28). Again, Christology not set within theology is both unscriptural and inadequate.

We return, then, to the subject of the good news of God as creator. What is urgent here for the pulpit in our time? The mind is flooded with important matters, which flow from this subject, but only three will receive our attention. First, creational theology provides the place to stand when addressing the duty of caring for the earth and stewardship of the environment. Dealing with these critically urgent issues from a base of ecclesiology or eschatology or Christology, even when full of fervor and passion, puts the preacher in quite a homiletical stretch, and an unnecessary one. God as creator is the firm and natural ground for such appeals, relieving the sermon of non sequiturs and awkward throat clearings. Second, the gospel of God as creator provides the theological resources to nourish conversation and implement initiatives in the area of human rights. Efforts in this vast and complex area will falter if supported by nothing more than generic speeches on pluralism and fluffy accommodations to each other's habits and peculiarities. The question, On what grounds? must be tackled, and the pulpit can speak of God as creator of us all, the God who "has no favorites" (Rom 2:11 REB). It was here that Vaclav Havel stood when he called for the surrender of all claims of privilege and exclusiveness in a speech at Lehigh University in 1992: "No member of a single race, a single nation, a single sex, a single religion may be endowed with basic rights that are any different from anyone else's."[16]

Third, and in a related vein, the gospel of God as creator is vitally appropriate for conversations on peace, especially in areas where religious differences hinder progress, most notably in the Middle East. In June 1995, an Interfaith Peace and Tolerance Conference was held at the House of Hope, International Peace Center in Shefar' Am, Israel. Jewish, Muslim, Druze, and Christian delegates participated. No one was asked to be silent about the particular items of anyone's creed. Christians spoke freely of Jesus. There was no attempt to work toward a lowest common denominator, on the contrary, every delegate was expected to bring a religious contribution to the discussion of peace. Appropriate texts from the various sacred writings were presented and collected in a booklet, *Wisdom for World Peace*. The conference was hosted by Elias Jabbour, an Arab Christian, but the tone was set by a Jewish rabbi who offered from his tradition (and ours) Mal. 2:10: "Have we not all one father? Has not one God created us? Why then are we faithless to one another, profaning the covenant of our ancestors?" Christian delegates could say "Amen," not with the sense of having swallowed in silence any conviction of their own for the sake of the conference, but with unrestrained joy at hearing one of their own faith statements expressed with such passion by another. Anyone who cannot celebrate that has misunderstood Jesus.

Conclusion

This chapter has proceeded in the firm belief that both Paul and Mark chose carefully and used purposefully the phrase "the gospel of God." The gospel we preach is about God and from God. Perhaps some of the implications of their choice of terms are a bit clearer. And this chapter has proceeded in the belief that David Buttrick has, not indifferently but quite deliberately, called the pulpit to greater theocentricity. And is the price we pay a lower Christology? By no means! Rather such preaching places Jesus Christ in context, a context that Buttrick calls "a still larger story, a story of God and humanity." After all, the question before us is not, Is there a God? An answer to that question, whether affirmative or negative, probably makes no more difference than one's answer to the question, Are there galaxies yet undiscovered? Neither is the question, Do we believe in God? Although that is a question of far greater importance for our life together. The real question is, In what kind of God do we believe? Does the God in whom we believe fuel a life of cruelty and privilege and exclusion or does that God call us to kindness, to justice, and to inclusion? Now enter Jesus Christ. The God in whom we believe is the God revealed in the ministry, death, and resurrection of Jesus, who is, in David Buttrick's words, "the image of God's own intending toward us."

NOTES

1. David Buttrick, *Preaching Jesus Christ: An Exercise in Homiletic Theology* (Philadelphia: Fortress Press, 1988), 70.
2. Ibid.
3. Ibid., 74.
4. Ibid., 75.
5. David Buttrick, *A Captive Voice: The Liberation of Preaching* (Louisville, Ky.: Westminster John Knox Press, 1994).
6. Ibid., 49.
7. Nils Dahl, "The Neglected Factor in New Testament Theology," in *Jesus the Christ*, ed. Donald Juel (Minneapolis: Augsburg Fortress, 1991), 154.
8. Ibid., 179.
9. E. C. Colwell, *Jesus and the Gospel* (New York: Oxford University Press, 1963), 42.
10. Ibid., 49.
11. Rudolf Bultmann, *Theology of the New Testament*, vol. 1, trans. K. Grobel (New York: Charles Scribner's Sons, 1951), 33.
12. Ibid., 65.
13. Ibid., 67ff.
14. Robert L. Brawley, *Centering on God: Method and Message in Luke-Acts* (Louisville, Ky.: Westminster/John Knox Press, 1990), 29.
15. James Barr, *Biblical Faith and Natural Theology* (Oxford: Clarendon Press, 1993).
16. *The New York Times*, July 26, 1992, sec. 4, p. 7. I am indebted to my colleague Hendrikus Boers for this quotation. *The Justification of the Gentiles* (Peabody, Mass.: Hendrickson Publishers, 1994), xvii.

8

All The King's Men: Constructing Homiletical Meaning

SUSAN KAREN HEDAHL

"The question is," said Alice, "whether you *can* make words mean so many different things."

"The question is," said Humpty Dumpty, "which is to be master—that's all."

—Lewis Carroll, *Through the Looking-Glass*

"Preaching the Word of God is the Word of God." Over the centuries, this lofty Reformation statement about preaching and God's Word continues to draw its authority and meaning from several historical sources: the church's imprimatur upon the preaching office, concepts of the sacred, proclamation's derivative nature from scriptural texts, the affective responses preaching can generate, and the human beings who simply assert that the statement is true.

Complicating the import of the statement is the fact that "Word of God" bears a variety of definitions: Christ, the Bible, the preached Word, the general themes of Christ's life (the gospel), the words of Jesus, and those words used in conjunction with sacraments.

However, all these sources share one potential problem. They may have little to do with the reality or the truth of the gospel. In other words, the question of theological meaning may be absent from the discussion. Indeed, the uses of preaching, the meanings attached to it, and the claims made on its behalf now elicit numerous challenges to traditional views of the Word's heritage. David Buttrick's works have engaged this troublesome legacy from the starting point of *meaning*-making in the pulpit. Can we do it? Do we do it? What is at stake here?

I will not engage the question, What is meant by preaching the Word of God? Here the answers are available historically. Instead, the question addressed is, How is homiletical meaning constructed in preaching the gospel in the contemporary context?

The directions and probes I will provide in response are provisional, in keeping with a rhetorically contextualized view of homiletics, and will focus on three areas: the role of the imagination in homiletical meaning-making, the need for a rhetorical vision/version of homiletics, and an examination of the loving, vigorous challenges against traditional forms of the Word. All these areas are interdependent and necessary in creating theologically meaningful preaching.

First, however, it is necessary to address the two realities that Buttrick holds in tension in his demands for an operative homiletical theology: the role of authority and the making of meaning. The issue of homiletical *meaning* can only begin with an assessment of the role of homiletical *authority* in the creation of such meaning.

Authority—Says Who?

What are the "authorities of meaning" in the pulpit today? The various proclamatory authorities to which preachers and listeners consider themselves beholden reveal, on closer examination, both legitimate and inappropriate directives for constituting theological meaning.

Historical assessment of the Word demonstrates clearly that proclamatory authority in any of its forms can supplant, eclipse, or be collapsed into the matter of meaning. Of course, we may get precisely what we think we are getting or we may not, after all, be dealing with what we supposed we were. The question Who says so? must be asked before Say what?

Proclamation, rhetorically defined, shows what role authority may play in the creation or distortion of meaning in preaching. Traditionally, since homiletics is a neo-Aristotelian discourse venture, the elements contributing to pulpit authority are what they always have been: the speaker, the word, listeners, and (additionally) a context.

What is running loose here, however, is the question of *how* the combination of these dynamics creates meaning. In the crucibles of our faith communities, authoritative choices are made, for good or ill. Here, too, the historical accrual of newer ways of rhetorically viewing homiletics adds to our sense that the authorities bear watching!

Which authorities are problematic today for the issue of constructing a healthy, a meaning-full, homiletical theology that preaches the gospel so that it may be heard?

At the center, Buttrick's most recent challenges, on behalf and against the pulpit, deal with the ancient intermediary of preaching: scriptural texts. It is this cache of words that bears most preaching. It is the collection of writings that inescapably sits at the heart of all homiletical meaning-making, explicitly or implicitly. It is the perennial intercessor and mediator of any further meanings preachers want to proclaim. It is these words that carry the signification of "gospel" for most people.

Among what interstices, then, does meaning-making become problematic in Buttrick's estimation? It is through the formation of these texts into the secondary and kaleidoscopic patterns of the liturgically sensitive lectionary system. It is here that I will focus my own reflections with the caveat that, however such systems are formed, the lectionary presents a perpetually shifting set of homiletical tectonics for both adherents and critics.

Before the gospel can even come to voice, the lectionary's determinative presence has set forth a band of choices that already have made certain theological directions for many preachers. Ironically, it sets in motion a kind of textual schizophrenia. Of whose canon are we speaking, and how much of it is there?

Sadly, the use of lectionary readings has become a stranglehold on the life of many parishes rather than a vector of homiletical possibilities. Recent revisions have still left much unchanged. Some of the problem areas include those biblical books not listed in the cycles, the absence of rhetorically sound choices of units of discourse for reading and preaching, the absence of Hebrew Scripture passages that do not fall into the prophetic promise/fulfillment model, the mixed-language messages produced by following the readings but using inaccurate translations of scripture, the paucity of scriptural readings related to women, and, certainly, the question of the current three-year cycle itself. (The partial burial of the Gospel of John throughout the current cycle is a primary example of this.)

However, the issue of lectionary authority begins to shift more precipitously when denominational and interdenominational uniformity of text selection reveals that it has little to do, if anything, with the parish-by-parish choices made in relationship to it each Sunday. Instead, it simply raises the more elusive problem of what each preacher finds meaningful for herself and the congregation. What enforces such meanings and the standards used to evaluate whether or not the gospel is effective in the lives of the listeners?

Lectionary choices also create another divide, which Buttrick and many others find problematic. That has to do with the *types* of preaching that lectionary text selections produce. There is little breathing room for occasional preaching, sustained evangelism, or outreach preaching to church communities predominantly composed of seekers, or a consistent use of *lectio continua*. Lectionary guilt, if not public outcry, occurs in places where such departures are evident, thus making the lectionary a potential adversary of the gospel, its evangelistic purposes, and the need to present alternative meaning-making places from the pulpit.

Furthermore, Buttrick has alerted lectionary users to the reality that the "pure Word of God" is *always* a mediated reality; the lectionary system is prima facie evidence of that. While this gives rightful place to the lectionary as a source of Christian and pulpit unity, it has also driven many panicked individuals and groups toward, among other things, the certitude of mistaking the lectionary for the Bible rather than freeing communities to engage hermeneutically in effective life-giving proclamation.

The question of making meaning in preaching is inextricably linked with the future of the lectionary. This is not simply a task of the preacher but all communities of faith wherever and however they constitute themselves. It is also not a future that should be committed alone to the maintenance of traditional lectionary committee structures. Serious questions have yet to be formulated through effective committee and parish gatherings that raise such questions as, Who makes decisions about lectionary formation? Why? On what basis? And how do these choices create meaningful preaching?

Are there other ways biblically, liturgically, and homiletically to focus parishioner- and seeker-theologies concerning the paradigm of our faith? The life-death-resurrection of Jesus Christ? Education is sadly lacking in this area, not only for sermon listeners but for pastors and ministers as well.

The resulting confusion about the power of homiletical authorities, true or false, has consequently confused the efforts to construct meaning-full sermons. Unless this basic lectionary problematic is first addressed (as only one of several issues), current and future preaching of the gospel in the contemporary forum will remain clouded.

Issues of Meaning

A Proposal

The issue of homiletical meaning, once the preacher is clear about the authorities with which to contend, has yet much business to do with the integrating the reality of *experience*. In one theological school recently, a synodical officer raised the question of meaning in a reflective way when he said, "I wish students could differentiate between having a religious experience and receiving a call to study theology at the seminary." While this differentiation is vital to the student's well-being, the more difficult but necessary project remains as to how to preach well to both windows on reality.

Avoiding the frankly experiential in the preaching event at the end of the twentieth century sidesteps a primary force field of theological meaning for both seekers and believers. Many contemporary sermons suffer from an inability to accept and probe the role of the believer/seeker's experiences and how these relate to the role of the rationality of faith.

From another place and time, Phillips Brooks defines such a balanced relationship well in his sermon "The Mind's Love of God," "Love is I take to be the delighted perception of the excellence of things . . . worse than any blunder or mistakes which any man may make in his religious thinking is the abandonment of religious thought altogether, and the consignment of the infinite interests of man to the mere region of feeling and emotion."[1]

Buttrick's recent discussions of preaching show clearly that homiletical theology must throw out the net in a wider fashion, including those existential areas that have been absent from pulpit discourse, with or without the formative influence of the lectionary.

Such a blending of thought and emotion is central to Buttrick's proposal for a proper yoking of authority and meaning in the pulpit in service of the gospel. This, then, makes the key question, What authority does God's Word have for parishioners' experienced meanings and preached by preachers who think theologically?

If meanings are formed with a view to both experience and thought, what foci draw together meaning and authority in the pulpit, particularly with the current text structures with which preachers now contend? It is a question I answer by starting with autobiography.

A Homiletical Topography

As an ordained female of twenty years in the Lutheran tradition, a feminist and seminary instructor, my own perspectives keep me in constant dialogue with the forces that have formed me. The strength of the Lutheran tradition is a scripturally based heritage that views the phrase "Word of God" as the central mantra of all other meanings. However, many of its assumptions of homiletically produced meaning are relatively unchallenged.

Several elements of personal interest, education, and classroom instruction draw me to consider Buttrick's contentions with authority and the ways these can produce a more critical view of homiletical meaning. Three foci form my critique and response.

First, increasingly, the creation and function of meaning in the pulpit must square its existence with the role of the *imagination* in preaching. What can we honestly claim for our words in this age in connection with the "Word of God"? What of our ethics, our poetry, and our prose? Our dreams and delights, our creative justice, as meaning-full ways of proclaiming the good news? And how does our experience of them image itself in conjunction with our preaching of the biblical texts?

There is a crucial issue at stake here, for in using the word "our" I refer not simply to the work of the preacher. The work of the preacher must begin with knowledge of that cache of images that already resides in the individual and corporate psyches of our parishioners. Do we have any idea which images buttress or destructively engage their views of life? Putting these images together, can we, like writer James Hopewell in his book, *Congregations*,[2] identify the kinds of myths, epics, sagas, and stories that keep our people going, angry, happy, or together?

Tragically, the preacher's identification of parishioners' experiences in creating homiletical meaning stops short of much knowledge of how parishioners' imaginative faith-lives function. If we are unable to move with much homiletical energy or interest through the shared metaphors, stories, jokes, and even the existential "horror flicks" out of which our people construct their lives, we have missed their meanings—and our own. It remains for us as preachers to dispel the ghosts of a certain type of rational authority, which dismisses such ventures as irrelevant to the creation of homiletical meaning.

And we have yet to sort out adequately and homiletically the ties among imagination, inspiration, and theological meaning-making, taking into consideration the authoritative play of the Spirit as the governing voice of proclamation, always decentering the abuses of authority, creating more effective meaning-making.

Second, I deem it necessary to maintain a *rhetorical vision* of homiletical theology. This is one that does not confuse homiletics with rhetoric nor assume that rhetoric is theology. Rather, it presents a dynamic view of reality that lives through the conditional, the provisional, the experiential, and the rational, with a view toward locating the "Word of God" in whichever persuasive context best serves God's redemptive purposes. It is, ultimately, a view of the "Word of God" that allows, even demands, surprise rather than certitude.

This rhetorical vision of homiletics contains a number of key elements that contribute to the process of homiletical meaning-making.

First of all, a genuine rhetorical sense of preaching demands a thorough knowledge of the audience. Who are these people? How many subgroups form their seeming unity? What concerns address and concern them? (These are not necessarily one in the same.) From a theological perspective, the rhetorical view of preaching inescapably focuses on the multifaceted matter of theological anthropology. In other words, how is the preacher describing the human condition and reality? What images of God does a given group hold, and how are they connected with their views of what it means to be human and godly? What words and images are used to do this? Do they apply to all present?

Many authorities of preaching have depended on particular views of the human informed by scripture and tradition, often at the expense of ignoring new learnings in other fields, including the undeniable witnesses of poetry, fiction, and various other media.

As an example, the perennial, contentious factor of the gender divide, signified by Valerie Saiving's pioneering work in 1960, has only begun to surface in the last few years in a significant way in the *pulpit*. The emphasis here is crucial. While the fields of systematic theology, scriptural studies, and pastoral theology have flourished for a number of years in examining gender issues, such contributions are only heard now in a few pulpits. Assessments of these are almost nonexistent for our understanding of what is happening to our homiletical meanings. Homiletics is at the far end of the academic and spiritual time zone. Much pioneering work remains to be written, circulated, and allowed to have its impact on our proclamation of the gospel.

Finally, the very concept and dynamic of the "Word of God" has heard questions of meaning raised against traditions of word and texts from several areas of discourse: feminist, ethnic, generational, and engendered.

These varied voices ask the most important question of all, Why? It is these voices that lead to Rebecca Chopp's demand that the creation of our homiletical meanings be couched in language that is "multivocal, open, practical, anticipatory: rich, embodied, full of connections and of differences . . . [constituting] an open possibility for transformation."[3] It is only within this atmosphere that our "Word of God" will find meaning and a hearing.

It is this painful, interesting possibility of transformation that prompts one feminist poet to note,

> They have given you the key
> to the wrong door, the one marked
> "sins of the fathers."
>   (Source unknown)

Two factors are significant in the area of those engaged in joyful battles from within the gospel. The first is the area of scriptural hermeneutics, and the other is pulpit ethos.

First, scriptural hermeneutics, via the works of Fiorenza, Trible, Ruether, and others, has demonstrated how our loss of an iconic view of scripture has resulted in misplaced and damaging views of meaning. It is clear that the displacement of the tradition through such writers is having an impact on a positive, constructive re-creation of meaning, although pulpits are dying sadly more from atrophied meaning rather than the arresting challenges of its displacement.

While these hermeneutical changes have affected language usage and an exploration of alternative metaphors of God and the human through scriptural translations and preachers' word choices, the arduous work that lies ahead is allowing the changing and shifting views of scriptural reality to inform the preacher's and parishioners' homiletical projects. Changing individual words is simply not enough, as many have learned painfully. Language inclusivity does not necessarily change the settings at the dinner table of community and ecclesial relationships. Whether the incorporation of these newer directions in theology will inform our pulpit meanings sufficiently to produce new, life-giving meanings and new views of authority in our presentation of the gospel remains to be seen.

Second, the voices against the traditional interpretations of the texts (spoken and written) have been forced to return to a reappraisal of the ancient concept of ethos. That is, What impact and function does the preacher have in the community of faith? Contemporary media have only heightened the awareness of who and how meaning competes in the current religious marketplace, vis-à-vis the personality and persona of the preacher.

To avoid the excesses of a focus on the individual preacher, however, it is necessary to combine this older meaning with the current usage of "ethos" as the general sense and texture of a community. In other words, understanding ethos individually and corporately realigns the locus responsible for creating homiletical meaning. We are *all* responsible, both preachers and listeners, for deciding what we mean through the preaching event. A necessary homiletical cycle must be established— preaching, responding, assessing—that serves as a check on our homiletical theologies.

Here we have yet to develop adequate models of interactive preaching that make the construal of meaning more significantly a matter of the entire faith community rather than a preacher's homiletical responsibility. Communities must be drawn into the acts of sharing the creation of meaning.

Conclusion

If authority and meaning-making are the horns of our homiletical dilemma, the question still stands: Just whose calf is being gored here? That is, how might we make our peace, our survival, and our flourishing incumbent on these given homiletical realities without sacrificing either?

In the works of ethicist Sharon Daloz Parks, there is an invitation and a path toward answering this question. She urges the cultivation of the metahabit of imagination as the "habitus" of true living and the source of creating new meanings. The description accords well with Buttrick's own project of homiletical meaning-making.

In comparing the process of meaning-making to being shipwrecked, Parks notes:

> Such experiences may suddenly rip apart our fabric of life, or they may more slowly but surely dissolve the meanings that have served as the home of the soul. . . . The loss of an earlier meaning is irretrievable and must be grieved and mourned. But the gladness of discovery that life continues to unfold with meaning, with connections of significance and delight . . . a primal, elemental force of promise . . . carrying us, sometimes against our resistance, into a new meaning, a new faith, a new ultimacy.[4]

The primacy of imagination and the roles of rhetoric and competing theologies, I have proposed, offer a matrix through which we can attend to the agenda Buttrick offers in the deconstruction and reconstruction of homiletical meaning. Most important, they provide a means for proclaiming the omnipresence of scriptural text from a dynamic rather than a static perspective. While the lectionary system has created, in some quarters, a definite rigor mortis of homiletic authority and meaning, it also provides the place to begin asking how else scripture and sermon might be reconfigured by preacher and listener alike.

David Buttrick's critique of the pulpit in terms of our views of scripture underscores the necessity for attending to homiletical authority and meaning. It is here that his contribution continues to provoke, challenge, and bless both the individual and corporate efforts of God's people!

NOTES

1. Phillips Brooks, "The Mind's Love of God," in *Sermons Preached in English Churches* (New York: E. P. Dutton, 1883), 24, 33.
2. James Hopewell, *Congregations: Stories and Structures* (Philadelphia: Fortress Press, 1987). Thomas Dorsey has also recently written a book, *Congregation: The Journey Back to the Church* (New York: Viking Press, 1995), which acknowledges Hopewell's work and focuses on one congregation in New England. Its strength is the blending in of the author's own faith journey as he is met with the various politics and images of the faith.
3. Rebecca S. Chopp, *The Power to Speak the Word: Feminism Language and God* (New York: Crossroad, 1991), 126.
4. Sharon Parks, *The Critical Years: The Young Adult Search for a Faith to Live By* (New York: Harper & Row, 1986), 24–25. Laurent Parks Daloz, Cheryl H. Keen, James P. Keen and Sharon Daloz Parks will focus on this theme of the imagination in *Common Fire: Lives of Commitment in a Complex World* (Boston: Beacon Press, 1996).

9

Learning to Speak of Sin

THOMAS G. LONG

"When was the last time," the headline wondered, "you had a good conversation about sin?"

Curiously, this question did not appear in a theological journal, but in the *New York Times*.[1] Cast in bold type in an advertisement, it was clearly intended to startle, if not shock, the presumably sophisticated and secular readership of America's leading daily. "When was the last time you had a good conversation about sin?" it demanded to know, confident that the answer would be, "Not lately, thank you."

Even more curious were the origins of this ad. It was placed not by Zondervan Publishing House or the local Catholic diocese or the Christian Coalition but by, of all people, the editors of the *Wall Street Journal*. Unexpectedly, the nation's leading voice of mammon was calling for a seminar on the doctrine of sin. The body of the ad consisted of a reprint of a sharply worded *Journal* editorial that prowled through some of the sleazier recent moral escapades of American celebrities on its way toward a requiem for a lost piety, a longing for a forgotten theological language:

> Sin isn't something that many people, including most churches, have spent much time talking about or worrying about through the years of the [sexual] revolution. But we will say this for sin; it at least offered a frame of reference for personal behavior. When the frame was dismantled, guilt wasn't the only thing that fell away; we also lost the guidewire of personal responsibility.[2]

There was irony here, since, for all its pleading on the public platform for a restoration of the communal conversation about sin, the *Journal* editorial was itself a manifestation of the problem it sought to address. "Sin" for the editors turned out to be a fairly small term, a word almost exclusively about individual moral choices, especially sexual ones, about right and wrong only on the personal scale. In the diminished theological glossary of the *Journal*, sin is more about Magic Johnson catting around after

NBA games than about the whole media machinery that makes glitzy heroes out of sports figures while ignoring inner-city schoolteachers; sin is William Kennedy Smith casually picking up a woman at a trendy bar in Palm Beach and not so much the economic forces that generate staggering wealth for the few in Palm Beach and grinding poverty for so many. The editorial had its finger on sin, all right, but it was only its little finger.

Even so, the editorial was moving in the right direction, grasping for something more than it could name, greater than it could see. The editors sensed a sickness in the land deeper than a malaise in the bond market, and they were appealing for a vocabulary large enough to encompass it. Indeed, they were yearning for a *theological* conversation, and one way to hear their plea was as a cry to the church to get back into the dialogue. To be sure, the *Journal*'s vocabulary was too small, but one could argue that their religious imagination was reduced to the calibration of personal piety precisely because of the veil of silence around the concept of sin in the moderate and liberal churches.

So, the question is worth pondering. How long has it been since we had a good conversation about sin? How long has it been since those of us who stand in the pulpits of polite and educated mainline churches have stimulated such a conversation in our sermons? How long has it been since those of us who preach to educators and merchants, lawyers and teachers, assembly-line workers and computer programmers, janitors and newspaper editors taken up the task of talking coherently about sin?

At the very beginning of the gospel story, the angel told Joseph that the child was to be given the name "Jesus" (which is derived from the Hebrew for "God saves") because "he will save his people from their sins" (Matt. 1:21). From the outset, then, the gospel of Jesus Christ has to do with salvation and with sin. Knowing about one requires knowledge of the other. The gospel is not an abstraction; it is news for and about the human condition, and understanding the human condition takes us, whether we want to go there or not, through the valley called "sin."

The Loss of the Language of Sin

"The awareness of sin," writes Cornelius Plantinga, Jr., "used to be our shadow. Christians hated sin, feared it, fled from it, grieved over it. . . . But the shadow has dimmed. Nowadays the accusation *you have sinned* is often said with a grin, and with a tone that signals an inside joke."[3] The word "sin," as sociologist James Davidson Hunter has observed, exists less now in church and more on dessert menus: "Peanut Butter Temptation" and "Chocolate Sin."[4]

Admittedly, "sin" as a serious concept is not a term that rolls easily off our tongues, in the pulpit or elsewhere, but, despite the protestations and encouragements of the *Wall Street Journal*, there are a number of very good reasons why. First, almost every intelligent theological conversation in America is haunted by fundamentalist ghosts. Somehow the minority of Christians on the far right have won the tug-of-war over theological language and managed to expropriate scores of powerful theological terms. Consequently, phrases like "the blood of the Lamb," "the hope of glory," "believing in the Lord Jesus Christ," and "receiving the Holy Spirit" no longer arrive carrying the treasure they once held in the New Testament but rather come empty-handed and scarred by decades of abuse and malnourishment. Sin is one of these violated words, and most thinking Christians, embarrassed over the rather crude ways that the vocabulary of sin has been treated by its right-wing kidnappers, would prefer to find other words.

Second, in our search for alternative language, there seems indeed to be a workable replacement for "sin." For most people in our culture, the vocabulary of sin has been eclipsed—sometimes helpfully and sometimes not—by therapeutic language. In everyday discourse, it would not occur to most of us to call ourselves or anyone else a "sinner"; to do so appears not only heavy-handed and condemnatory, it also seems to beg more questions than it answers. Is being hooked on alcohol, for example, a sin with a moral and theological remedy, or a disease with a medical and psychological treatment? To say that someone is addicted to a substance or acting out the consequences of childhood abuse or codependent or a dissociative personality seems, to contemporary tastes, far more nuanced, more fully explanatory than simply pointing to "sin" as the problem. In short, the language of therapy is not merely a more trendy pattern of speech than the terminology of sin; it genuinely seems to most people to make more sense of the broken places in their lives and the lives of others. The narrator in one of Peter DeVries's novels quipped that there used to be a time when people dreaded being caught doing something sinful in front of their ministers but now we dread being caught doing something immature in front of our therapists.

Third, the way the church has traditionally spoken of sin has been properly challenged by many feminist theologians. Indeed, one of the earliest projects of American feminist theology was to expose the ways that the dominant male theologians, such as Reinhold Niebuhr, somehow always managed to define sin in virile terms like pride, power, and willful rebellion. As early as 1960, Valerie Saiving noted that

> the temptations of woman *as woman* are not the same as the temptations of man *as man*, and the specifically feminine forms of sin . . . have a quality which can never be encompassed by such terms as

"pride" and "will to power." They are better suggested as . . . underdevelopment or negation of the self.[5]

What was at stake here is not simply the charge that male theologians are methodological imperialists, defining the whole of the human species by the life experience of one sex. The deeper allegation is that, when sin is understood only as prideful strutting and the misuse of power, the end result is not that the proud are brought low but that the low are brought lower, that those without power are "kept in their place." Ironically, then, the accusation of many feminists is that the male-dominated theological establishment has used the doctrine and the language of sin—well, sinfully. It is one thing to warn a Bill Gates about arrogance, pride, and power; it is quite another thing to admonish someone huddled in fear in a shelter for battered women about being too prideful and rebellious and to allow the language of shame to worm its way into her soul.[6]

There are many treatments, scholarly and more popular, of this matter in feminist writing,[7] but probably no presentation is more compelling than Roberta Bondi's autobiographical essay *Memories of God*, where she describes the roots of her own long-term depression:

> In the "badness" of my childhood depression, I was teeth-rattlingly lonely. . . . The . . . Christianity of my childhood offered me no way out of my unhappiness. Rather, with its emphasis on sin, on the thorough badness of all people, and Jesus' death for it, it gave me an explanation for why I ought to be depressed. Sin was what religion was about. If you had asked me in the fourth grade, "Why was Jesus born?" I would have been glad to answer, "It was because of sin. . . ." If you had pushed me about what it took to get our sins forgiven, I would have told you, "We have to repent of our sins." If you had pushed me a little further to ask, "And what does it mean to repent?" I would have said, "To feel really, really bad about what a sinful person you are."[8]

Speaking of Sin: Why Bother?

Given, then, that the term "sin" has been co-opted by the fundamentalists, replaced by the therapists, excoriated by feminists, and used as a club to keep some people down to the benefit of others, why attempt to recover it? When the *Wall Street Journal* wants to start a good conversation about sin, why not simply respond, "No thank you. Been there. Done that"?

There are many excellent reasons that could be advanced for the recovery of "sin" as a term in the active vocabulary of the church—among them, the prominence of evil and sin as concepts in the New Testament and the truth that the gospel itself presupposes a coherent understanding of the human need for grace and salvation. Roberta Bondi makes a telling existential point about the potential depressing effect of claiming that Jesus was born because of my sin, but, as a matter of theological conviction, the Christian tradition has, in fact, understood something quite like that claim, that the incarnation was indeed about human sin.

But these traditional and methodological concerns are not what most impel me here. I am interested in preachers trying to start a "good conversation about sin" precisely because I sense that the culture, like the editors of the *Wall Street Journal*, is aware that it needs and wants such a discussion and, that the culture, if we can rightly read the social signals, is here and there pleading for it. It is as if there is a growing public awareness that there is a set of missing words in the vocabulary we need as a people to make sense of life, and that without a working theological language of sin, people are left either silent or foundering in the shallows.

I cite two examples of what I mean. First, in his recent book *The Death of Satan: How Americans Have Lost the Sense of Evil*, Andrew Delbanco notes the astonishing difference between the public analysis of two great disasters: the sinking of the *Titanic* in 1912 and the explosion of the space shuttle *Challenger* in 1986. When the *Titanic* went down, Delbanco says, "press coverage of the disaster tended to recount it as a 'lesson . . . written in searing lines on ice-floe and curling wave-crest.' The lesson was scriptural: 'Whosoever exalteth himself shall be abased and he that humbleth himself shall be exalted.' "

In other words, the language used to describe "when that great ship went down" was the vocabulary of sin. By contrast, says Delbanco, "when the *Challenger* spacecraft blew up before the eyes of millions . . ., one of the television anchor men . . . groped for words. He literally had nothing to say. When at last he came up with something, it was by turning to the closest thing to metaphysical language he could find, the language of the cold war. He looked at the hastily assembled experts who had joined him around the anchor desk, and asked, 'Does this mean that the Russians are ahead?' "[9]

Somewhere between 1912 and 1986, the whole society suffered cultural aphasia, and the result, argues Delbanco, is that "we have no language for connecting our inner lives with the horrors that pass before our eyes in the outer world."[10]

As a second example, Ron Rosenbaum, in an essay on the emerging interest in evil in our culture,[11] notes his perplexity that many of the public responses of the prominent citizens of Oklahoma to the bombing of the federal building were inexplicably chipper and upbeat, immediately claiming that the whole tragic episode was really about good, not evil.

Governor Frank Keating boasted to a newspaper reporter that Oklahoma had emerged "from this muscular, attractive, and lionized. . . . The good-will generated by this tragedy," he went on to say, "is a door-opening opportunity for us and one we fully wish to enjoy."

Muscular? Attractive? Lionized? It was, Rosenbaum comments, as if "the bombing made the state a sexy celebrity." Rosenbaum goes on to observe that "the Mayor of Oklahoma City was even more effusive. 'This has given the city an opportunity to expand its horizons. It's a terrible way to do it,' he conceded, 'but we do end up getting a real opportunity.' " Wired to the chain link fence around the bomb site, there were scores of teddy bears and colorful letters from children. Rosenbaum admits initial bewilderment:

> It was puzzling to me at first, this repeated insistence that the real meaning of the whole murderous episode was how it was really about good, about the manifestation of the goodness of Oklahoma to the world, almost as if this balanced out the hundreds of dead and injured. . . . But in a sense, it is about . . . those who have to go on living with the knowledge of the presence of evil . . . the diffi-culty we all have in staring too directly into the heart of the heart of darkness. . . . Rather than allowing a space for the contempla-tion of evil, experiencing rage, pain, a moment of doubt about our-selves or the kind of world we're confined in, victory, triumph over evil must be declared instantly. It's an unfortunate tribute to the power, to the fear of evil that its potency has to be denied or erased rather than faced.[12]

Somewhere down deep, the people of Oklahoma City know that teddy bears and chamber of commerce cheers do not describe what they experi-enced on that terrible day. The quick optimism is but linguistic wallpaper pasted over the gaping holes in our cultural vocabulary. Lacking an ade-quate language of sin and evil, all we can do is scream that it really did not happen, but, if it did, it is not all that tragic.

This crevice between what people sense about their lives and what they know how to say about them is a fruitful place for preachers to work. One of our tasks is to help people acquire the vocabulary they are grasping for but cannot quite reach. I realize, incidentally, that, by saying this, I am swinging on a thin vine over a raging methodological river. I am not sug-gesting that the purpose of preaching is primarily to scratch where people already itch or to give names to what the culture already knows and feels. Indeed, I subscribe entirely to that strand of the Christian tradition that maintains that sin can be fully known only as a theological category and not just as an anthropological one; I affirm with Barth that grace precedes repentance, with Luther who said that he could not even know that he is a sinner unless the Holy Spirit taught it to him, with the claim that the lan-

guage of sin makes sense finally only to those who understand it in light
of the gift of redemption. As theologian Christopher Morse states:

> Few New Testament assertions regarding what grace saves us
> from pass muster as common sense. While it takes no great argu-
> ment to admit that we all from time to time have made our share
> of mistakes, suffered our defeats, failed to live up to our full poten-
> tial, even felt guilty for things neglected, and ashamed for things
> committed, the blunt [biblical] announcement that we were dead,
> having in effect taken our own life, renders these admissions quite
> tame in comparison. Yet nothing less radical than this is what
> hearers of the gospel message are told. Whatever sense it all makes
> surely is most uncommon indeed.[13]

Morse goes on to say, "The New Testament confession that 'we were
dead' in sin comes only, it should be noted, from those who confess to
having been made alive in relation to what happens with Jesus. . . . [T]he
only sin we actually know is the opposition that is overcome by God's
being for us."[14]

So, while respecting the theological, ontological, and noetic priority of
redemption, I nonetheless want to suggest that we do not preach at the
methodological starting point; we preach in the middle of a conversation
with the culture. In one sense I want to advocate what New Testament
scholar Daniel Patte once suggested was the preaching method of the
apostle Paul. Carrying the strange categories of a Jewish apocalyptic
gospel into a Hellenistic culture, Paul had to make a decision about how
to put the two together. He could have insisted that the culture stop
speaking in Greek categories and begin immediately to speak the language of Zion, but this was not his choice. Nor did he attempt to translate
the gospel into Hellenisms so that the culture could grasp it on its own
terms. What Paul did, Patte claims, is to look at the Hellenistic culture
through the lens of the gospel, through the frame of the kerygma, and to
spot cross-resurrection places where God was at work and then to
announce those to his Hellenistic hearers. For those who, in God's own
mysterious providence, responded to this proclamation, he taught them,
as a second order matter, the Jewish apocalyptic categories that he, himself, had used to see what he saw.[15]

It is an encouraging development that contemporary systematic theologians are forging discussions of human sin not by translating the
Christian doctrinal tradition into existential or therapeutic categories
(which, as Peter Berger once said, is like "playing poker with the house")
but rather by describing what they see when they look at today's culture
through the conceptual framework of the gospel.[16]

God Be Merciful
to Us Sinners

So what do we see when we look at the world through the Christian claims about "sin"? Many things—too many to describe here—after all, a "good conversation" takes time and requires listening as well as speaking. But let us make a beginning by naming two aspects of sin that, to discuss honestly and coherently, could prove illuminating, useful, healing, and finally "good news" to our culture: sin as tragedy and sin as destructiveness.

Sin as Tragedy

In his brilliant new book on the doctrine of sin, Cornelius Plantinga, Jr., defines sin as "any agential evil for which some person (or group of persons) is to blame. In short, sin is culpable shalom-breaking."[17] In most ways, this is quite a helpful definition. It enables him to focus on human actions (rather than on hurricanes and earthquakes) and to show that sin is blamable human vandalism of what God has designed for human life.

Even so, there is something missing from this definition. Before we employ the language of sin to describe corrupt actions, "agential evil," violations of the rules of the game, we need to use it to describe the flawed nature of the game itself. Sinful actions are culpable, to be sure, but there is also a sense in which people are aware of the fact that, as the polite version of the bumper sticker would have it, "Stuff Happens." Sin happens, even when we are striving mightily to do the right thing, and part of our experience of sin is being caught up in the tragedy of it all. This is part of what the Calvinistic tradition has meant by the much misunderstood idea of "total depravity," which means not that every human being is totally void of good, but that no aspect of human life, not even our noblest motives and deeds, is free from sin's tragic taint.

Not long ago, I was the visiting preacher at a university chapel, and I was walking across campus with the university chaplain. I noticed a tall, very modern building that stood out architecturally from all the others, and I asked him what building that might be. He smiled and said that the building was a monument to a failed vision. The story was that a world-famous sociologist on the faculty had persuaded the university to construct this office building in order to bring together under a single roof the several departments of the human sciences: sociology, anthropology, psychology, and so on. The idea was that the building would house an ongoing conversation among the world's finest experts in human social engineering that would eventually and inevitably lead to wisdom for an improved society. Thus, everything about the interior of the building was designed to emphasize free and open interaction; ample lounges and a common dining room were provided to facilitate this high-level interdisciplinary discussion.

However, instead of a brave new world, the residents of the building soon erupted in turf battles; jealousies over office space, salaries, and secretarial help seethed. The free and open corridors were soon boarded up to keep the disciplines separate. The whole place, said the chaplain, became a cold war zone. Various explanations and excuses were advanced for what had gone wrong, but the best came from a member of the sociology department who had a theological vocabulary. "We lacked," he said, "a proper doctrine of sin."

Another testimony to the tragic aspect of sin has emerged as information has come out regarding the shooting down of Korean Airlines' flight KE007 on September 1, 1983. KE007 was, it may be recalled, a regular commercial flight from New York to Seoul that drifted into Soviet airspace and was ultimately brought down by a Russian fighter plane, costing 269 human lives and considerably heating up of the Cold War. At the time, the Soviets charged that the plane was a decoy and was actually on an espionage mission. The United States, for its part, claimed that the Russians were simply covering up the cold-blooded murder of nearly three hundred innocent people.

What happened? A major report on the incident, based on documents and radio tapes recently released from the former Soviet Union, was compiled by Murray Sayle for the *New Yorker*.[18] The truth of the matter was that KE007 was no spy plane, but a plane under the command of a sleepy crew who were going strictly by the book in navigating their plane. But a couple of ground navigational problems, combined with an auto-pilot switch left too long in the "on" position and an amber warning light they did not notice, merged in an improbable collection of circumstances and errors to allow the plane to stray off course and into Soviet airspace.

As for the Soviets, they had been monitoring the activities of an American surveillance plane. Nothing illegal or dangerous, but something to keep a watchful eye on. That plane faded from the radar scope only to be replaced by the mysterious blip from KE007. Unlike the other plane, KE007 wasn't behaving like a military aircraft, but the framework of military thinking had already been established. A fighter pilot, Major Gennady Osipovich, was sent up in an SU-15 to get a firsthand look.

It was a moonless and dark night, but even in the gloom, Osipovich could see the navigational lights of the Korean airliner, a firm clue that this was not a spy flight. Radio transmission from the ground revealed that Osipovich's superiors were also unsure, hesitant, but finally, when the airliner did not respond to signals or warnings, they decided themselves to go by their rule book; they gave the order to shoot it down.

In other words, both the crew of the airliner and the Soviet military were going by the book, both trapped in systems not of their own making, which would bring them, through no design or intention of their own, to fatal and tragic crossroads. Gennady Osipovich is today a potato farmer, and he still cannot bring himself to accept the fact that he destroyed an airliner and with it over 250 human lives. In fact, he was not originally scheduled to be on duty at all that fateful night, but he had volunteered for the night shift so that earlier that day he could give a talk on peace at his children's school.

This incident is both an example of and a metaphor for the tragic dimension of sin. Welfare programs go awry, therapies end up harming instead of helping, bureaucracies stifle instead of support. People go by the book—even by the Good Book—and other people, innocent people, suffer and die. Who is culpable? No one, every one, both at the same time, caught in the web of sin's tragedy.

Sin as Destructiveness

In her recent commencement address at Vassar College, Meryl Streep told the graduates, "Today you will graduate from college and go out into the real world. Do not expect the real world to be like college. It's actually more like high school."

Indeed, we have all known since high school about the petty jealousies, vanities, and cruelties that lie deep within our hearts and that infect the social fabric as well. When all the various psychological and sociological theories of human behavior have been given their say, there is still a surplus of cussedness in each of us and in all of us that remains unaccounted for. The novelist Thomas Harris in his chilling *The Silence of the Lambs* makes this very point. An FBI agent, Officer Starling, is visiting the jail cell of Harris's arch villain, a mad psychiatrist who bites his victims to death and then cannibalizes them. How could such a monster be created, Officer Starling wonders, and she asks the madman what happened to him. "Nothing happened to me, Officer Starling," he replies. "*I* happened. You can't reduce me to a set of influences. You've given up good and evil for behaviorism, Officer Starling. You've got everybody in moral dignity pants—nothing is ever anybody's fault. Look at me, Officer Starling. Can you stand to say I'm evil?"[19]

Can we stand to say of ourselves, "We are evil"? Somewhere we know it is the truth—the God's truth—about us. In *Lost in the Cosmos: The Last Self-Help Book*, Walker Percy conducts a number of "thought experi-

ments," each designed to show the moral ambiguities and violent capabil-
ities of the self. In one such experiment, readers are asked to check which
of the following statements applies to them:

1. You are extraordinarily generous, ecstatically loving of the
    right person, supremely knowledgeable about what is
    wrong with the country, about people, capable of moments
    of insight unsurpassed by any scientist or artist or writer in
    the country. You possess an infinite potentiality.

2. You are of all people in the world probably the most self-
    ish, hateful, envious (e.g., you take pleasure in reading
    death notices in the newspaper and in hearing of an
    acquaintance's heart attack), the most treacherous, the
    most frightened, and above all the phoniest.

Which would you choose? According to Percy, 60 percent of all respon-
dents chose both.[20] We know the truth about ourselves and we tell fearful
lies about ourselves, and we cannot always discern the difference. When
preachers name human destructiveness, they tell the truth, but pulling the
mask off humanity and telling the unvarnished truth about the grimier
side of human motivation is not the primary goal.

In a provocative essay many years ago, William H. Poteat noted that
"on hundreds of American campuses there are buildings upon which
have been engraved . . . the words, 'You shall know the truth and the truth
shall make you free.' Upon seeing them," Poteat says, "my natural rejoin-
der is: 'The Hell it does.'"[21] Poteat then goes on to exegete three primary
myths of human culture—Adam and Eve, Oedipus, and Faust—to show
that in each case knowing the truth led to tragedy. It was Jesus who said,
"You will know the truth, and the truth will make you free," and only in
the embrace of God's love as found in the ministry of Jesus is this claim
true. The truth alone cannot save or liberate us, only a forgiving God.
Only in the context of grave can we stand to hear and claim the truth
about our destructiveness. As Poteat maintains near the end of his essay:

> The Christian declares that Jesus Christ has overcome sin and
> death. What . . . can this mean?
>   . . . In the posture of this faith . . . one will be able to say with St.
> Paul: "I am persuaded that neither communism nor fascism;
> Freudianism nor Jungianism; Einsteinianism nor the theory of an
> ever-expanding universe; neither historicism nor impressionism,
> existentialism and logical positivism; the theory of deficit finance
> nor the principle of complementarity can separate me from the
> love of God in Christ Jesus."[22]

The Good News about Sin

The news that we are sinners, that we are caught in tragic circumstances and potentially destructive toward ourselves and others is finally good news. Knowing the common human situation is a means to overcome the victim-oppressor dichotomy and the soil in which true compassion grows. Moreover, to know the human condition is to know the holiness of the divine condition and the depths of grace.

One morning while leaving preaching class, a student asked if she could discuss a matter with me. We grabbed a cup of coffee and sat down to talk. Her problem, she said, was that she was working on a sermon based on a biblical text about God's judgment on sin, and she was having a struggle. "I can preach love and I can preach hope and grace," she said, "but I cannot bring myself to preach about sin and judgment. There are already too many bad messages out there in people's lives, and I don't want to add one more burden."

We talked this matter over for a few minutes, aiming at no particular resolution and arriving at none. Then she changed the subject. Her teenage son, she told me, was giving her family problems. He had gotten hooked on drugs, had been suspended from school, and was terrorizing the whole family. He came and went as he pleased, commandeering the car, taking money where he could find it, threatening his parents with his abusive speech. My student told me that her husband's response to this was to retreat into depression. She began to cry, thinking about the situation.

"Last night," she said, "I finally broke down. My son blew into the house and after hurling angry words at his dad and me, slammed the door to his room. I decided that enough was enough, and I went back there. I admit I am afraid of him. My son is over six feet tall and big, and I was unsure of what he might do physically. But I opened the door, stood in the doorway, looked him directly in the eye, and said with all the firmness in my being, "I love you so much I will not allow you to do this to yourself or to us anymore."

We sat there for a moment, her words of the night before still hanging in the air. "I think I have just heard," I finally said, "a powerful and faithful gospel sermon on sin and judgment."

NOTES

1. "Review and Outlook: The Joy of What?" an advertisement in *The New York Times*, January 8, 1992.
2. Ibid.
3. Cornelius Plantinga, Jr., *Not the Way It's Supposed to Be: A Breviary of Sin* (Grand Rapids: Wm. B. Eerdmans Publishing Co., 1995), ix.

4. Ibid., x.
5. Valerie Saiving, "The Human Situation: A Feminine View," reprinted in *Womanspirit Rising: A Feminist Reader in Religion*, ed. Carol P. Christ and Judith Plaskow (San Francisco: Harper & Row, 1979), 37.
6. There is also the notion, popularized by such writers as Matthew Fox, that traditional doctrines of sin and the fall of humanity repress passions and human creativity and lead inevitably to the loss of self-esteem. See *Original Blessing* (Santa Fe, N. Mex.: Bear & Co., 1983), esp. appendix B, 316–19.
7. See, for example, Judith Plaskow, *Sin, Sex, and Grace: Women's Experience and the Theologies of Reinhold Niebuhr and Paul Tillich* (Lanham, Md.: University Press of America, 1980).
8. Roberta C. Bondi, *Memories of God: Theological Reflections on a Life* (Nashville: Abingdon Press, 1995), 153–54.
9. Andrew Delbanco, *The Death of Satan: How Americans Have Lost the Sense of Evil* (New York: Farrar, Straus & Giroux, 1995), 12–13.
10. Ibid., 3.
11. Ron Rosenbaum, "Staring into the Heart of the Heart of Darkness," *The New York Times Magazine*, June 4, 1995, 36–72.
12. Ibid., 61.
13. Christopher Morse, *Not Every Spirit: A Dogmatics of Christian Disbelief* (Valley Forge, Pa.: Trinity Press International, 1994), 237.
14. Ibid., 238.
15. See Daniel Patte, *Preaching Paul* (Philadelphia: Fortress Press, 1984).
16. See, for example, the superb use of the list of "seven deadly sins" to produce a more dynamic anatomy of the development of sin from anxiety through unfaith, pride, concupiscence, self-justification, and cruelty, on to blasphemy in Ted Peters, *God—The World's Future: Systematic Theology for a Postmodern Era* (Minneapolis: Fortress Press, 1992), 155–68.
17. Plantinga, *Not the Way It's Supposed to Be*, 14.
18. Murray Sayle, "Closing the File on Flight 007," *The New Yorker* 49:42 (December 13, 1993): 90–101.
19. Thomas Harris, *The Silence of the Lambs* (New York: St. Martin's Press, 1988), 21, as quoted in Delbanco, *Death of Satan*, 19.
20. Walker Percy, *Lost in the Cosmos: The Last Self-Help Book* (New York: Pocket Books, 1983), 13.
21. William H. Poteat, "Anxiety, Courage, and Truth," *The Duke Divinity School Review* 31:3 (autumn 1966): 205.
22. Ibid., 210–11.

10

The Friend We Have in Yahweh

ERNEST T. CAMPBELL

I confess to being a serious fan of the television show *Jeopardy!* I don't answer the phone or go to the door while the show is on. I enjoy matching knowledge with the contestants and usually come off humbled by my little and their much. The unique aspect of *Jeopardy!* is a format that gives the contestants answers to which they must provide the question. Borrowing on that procedure, I want to get into the subject at hand by asking "What is the question to which the gospel is the answer?"

A hand goes up, a contestant speaks, "What is 'How shall we be saved from our sins?' " There can be no disputing the fact that the overwhelming majority of believing Christian people would hold that the gospel has to do primarily with how we stumbling sinners can find forgiveness. If this be the fundamental question that the gospel answers, then the focus will fall on Jesus. Not just his life in general but on the final week of his life. And not just the final week, but the final day. And not just the final day, but the final hours—between twelve and three when he gave up the ghost.

I have trouble with this way of going at it for several reasons. First, it seems a rather cavalier dismissal of the greatest life ever lived to toss out thirty or thirty-three years just to get to the salvific part. The Apostles' Creed reduces Jesus' earthly life to a comma: "born of the Virgin Mary, suffered under Pontius Pilate." In this view Jesus is hardly more than a pawn, a movable piece on the chessboard of a game that pits cosmic forces of good and evil against each other. An air of unreality surrounds this Jesus. What he accomplished in his life represents more an endowment than an achievement. It was not that he was able not to sin (an achievement) but that he was not able to sin (an endowment).

Second, I have difficulty with the view that the gospel is an answer to the sin question because I think the church has magnified the gravity of sin out of reasonable proportions. God willed our freedom. God took the risk and we get the blame! There is surely some culpability on God's part for having staged this enterprise called history in the first place. The psalmist was right: "He knows how we were made; he remembers that we are dust." In the Garden of Eden after the forbidden fruit was eaten, it was not God who ran but Adam. His holiness did not drive him to abandon the scene. The creation was pronounced good by the Lord. The story begins with a bang not with a fall. Hence the revealing title of one of Matthew Fox's books, *Original Blessing*.

Elie Wiesel contends that the Fall is foreign to Jewish thought. The episode in the garden is viewed by Jewish scholars as a graduation from innocence to responsibility. How then did the church come to such a heavy interpretation of human frailty and weakness? The matter can be traced to four persons: David, Paul, Augustine, and Luther.

I

David could announce that he was "born in sin and shapen in iniquity" because his soul was weighted down with an overriding sense of deserved guilt. To march another man off to the battlefront in order to take his wife is as reprehensible as it gets. Reprehensible, yes, but not typical of the species or normative.

Paul went on and on about his guilt before God and saw himself as the chief of sinners. And well he might have. Had he not tried to shut down the early church—possibly by violent means? He held the clothes when Stephen was being stoned and didn't lift a finger or a voice in protest. Again, reprehensible, but not normative or typical.

And then there was Augustine, a man whose early years were marked by moral profligacy of the most venal kind. No woman's honor was safe in his presence. He seemed terminally aroused. His view of human nature was the lowest of all possible lows. It was the later-to-be bishop of Hippo who once observed that we are born between urine and feces. His mother's prayers were answered, and he was soundly converted to the faith. But his rehabilitation by grace did not keep him from seeing life through the lens of former years. Sin was big to him, forgiven or not.

Martin Luther completes the line. Erik Erikson and others have investigated this man's psyche only to conclude that the reformer was pathologically consumed by a sense of guilt. His relationship with God he saw as a merit-demerit arrangement. His conscience was chronically overwhelmed by a sense of evils committed and good undone.

It takes nothing away from the achievements of David, Paul, Augustine, and Luther to identify their inordinate stress on sin. But the mournful bleatings of their consciences must not be the measure by which we judge ourselves. Jesus used the word "sin" but seven times. We may be obsessed by our transgressions, but Jesus was not. Sin matters, to be sure, but it does not matter most or only. A lapsed stanza of the ecumenical hymn "There's a Wideness in God's Mercy" puts it well:

> But we make His love too narrow
>   by false limits of our own;
> And we magnify his strictness
>   with a zeal He will not own.

Third, I have trouble with the view that the gospel deals only or primarily with the proclamation of forgiveness because of the flawed ways in which Jesus' death is interpreted and applied. This gets us into atonement theory. The church has been plagued in its theology and liturgies by the belief that what happened on the cross was a transaction of one kind or other that involved principalities and powers in high places. The Ultimate One took satisfaction from the death of the Sinless One and thus was now free to forgive. The dreadful tension in God between the need to be pure and the urge to pardon had been transcended. Jesus gave what God wanted so that God could give us what we need. Such a position impugns the very character of God!

I have serious problems with the idea that God needed gore to be good; that until God saw blood flow that day, God could not dispense mercy to any. It is alarming how this notion of vicarious sacrifice dominates our Communion liturgies. A few examples:

Methodist
Almighty God, who of thy tender mercy didst give thine only Son Jesus Christ to suffer death upon the cross for our redemption, who made there, by the one offering of himself, a full, perfect, and sufficient sacrifice for the sins of the world.

Episcopalian
All glory be to thee, Almighty God our Heavenly Father, for that thou, of thy tender mercy, didst give thine only Son Jesus Christ to suffer death upon the Cross for our redemption; who made there (by his one oblation of himself once offered) a full, perfect, and sufficient sacrifice, oblation, and satisfaction, for the sins of the whole world.

Presbyterian
Thanksgiving to Thee, Almighty God, our Heavenly Father, for that Thou of Thy great mercy, didst give Thine only Son Jesus Christ to take our nature upon Him, and to suffer death upon the cross for our redemption; who made there a full, perfect, and sufficient sacrifice for the sins of the whole world.

A Roman cleric friend confided that the mass as understood in his tradition is more a sacrifice than a sacrament.

Paul got off in a large way about how, juridically speaking, one could take the heat for another. That one life could be said to "justify" another. This is a hard sell in the world we know today. A couple speeds along in their car. Red lights flash and a siren sounds. Caught. The driver, aware that additional points on his driver's license will spell suspension, fears the worst. But not to worry. The wife at his side has a spotless record and will volunteer to have this present infraction of highway law charged to her account. The strategy does not stand a chance, nor should it. It violates both justice and common sense. There is no such thing as third-party exoneration.

II

What if it be true that the gospel is the good news that God is for us. The gospel is "the gospel of God." (See Rom. 15:16; 1 Pet. 4:17; 1 Thess. 2:2, 9.) The question that the gospel answers is not in the first instance, How can we be forgiven? but, How is God disposed toward us? The ringing affirmation of the scriptures is that God's banner over us is love. The imagined enmity of the warrior's bow has been transmuted into the many-splendored mercies of the rainbow. Saint Hildegard was right, God never began to love us.

What happened on the cross, then, was not a transaction but an unarguable illustration of a love that is without beginning or end. The cross was not for God's sake, as if the All-merciful One needed to be placated or appeased. Jesus did not die to save us from God! "In Christ God was reconciling the world to himself." How could we have gotten it so wrong? The cross was not for God's sake but for ours. What was always true became not truer but more believable on that awful day that we call Good Friday.

The word I call on here is the word "absorb." The cross is a demonstration in time of what is always going on within the heart of the Eternal. God is forever absorbing, taking into the divine being our manifold transgressions. And this because love is not something God *does* but something God *is*. And when it dawns on human consciousness that this is so it moves the soul to penitence and faith. This is anything but cheap grace. When we look on him whom we have pierced, we are summoned to serious reflection on the distance that exists between what we have made of life and what we could have made and still could make. A down-home illustration puts the matter fairly: The family was the proud possessor of a valued vase that had come down through several generations. It stood in the living room as a prized artifact. The young son was admonished never to roughhouse in that room, out of respect for the vase. One afternoon he and one of his friends began tossing a ball around in that room. The unwanted happened. The ball hit the vase and toppled it into an irreparable mass of worthless chips. The father arrived home first. Seeing his son convulsed in tears, he summoned his compassion and said, "It doesn't matter, it's all right." The lad was not consoled. A short time later his mother entered the room, put her arms around the boy's neck, and said, "It matters, but it's all right."

The gospel is the good news that God is for us. God does not need the "once offering up of his Son" to forgive. God's love does not require mediation. God forgave long before Jesus came. (What a friend we have in Yahweh!) God forgives in lands and cultures where Christ has not yet come.

The parable of the prodigal son is the ultimate illustration of the love that absorbs without sacrifice or mediation. The wastrel son returns laden with remorse and strapped with a sense of failure. He blurts out, "Father, I have sinned against heaven and before you; I am no longer worthy to be called your son." The father, a stand-in for God, responds with a welcoming embrace and joyfully receives him back.

Had Paul been telling this story (and I find it hard seeing him in the role of storyteller) he may have written it this way:

> When he was yet a great way off his father saw him. And being of unblemished righteousness and too pure of eye to look on sin he commanded that the returning vagrant go first to the temple to offer there a sacrificial lamb so that he might be cleansed. For it is written: The pure have dealings only with the pure.

Or perhaps the apostle would have put it this way:

> And the father said, You are caught dead to rights by your own admission, but I know one whose record is clean and I will have my bookkeeper transfer his balance to your account. Then we will be able to sit down and have a meal together.

There is no third son in the story! No third-party exoneration. No mediation. It is enough that the boy is back. The father will do the rest because it is his nature so to do. Richard Niebuhr once noted that most of our troubles come upon us because we do not believe that God is as good as Jesus said He is. It is to the proclamation of this unfailing goodness that we are called.

III

Finally, I want to argue that, by giving up the centrality of atonement in our understanding of the gospel, good things can happen to our faith. Wise pastors have learned never to take away a cherished conviction without giving their people something better in return. What are the better somethings here?

For one thing, we get a more relevant and compelling Christology. In vicarious atonement theory the life Jesus lived is overshadowed by the death he died. About all that is at stake regarding the earthly life of Jesus is the need to shore up and defend its perfection. Unless the sacrifice is without blemish it will not do. Forget Galilee and focus on Calvary. Scenes from his life are just the disposable backdrop for the only truth that matters: Jesus died for our sins. The question then becomes, Do you believe? and not, Will you follow?

The traditional creeds of the Christian faith leave us with a disproportionate Trinity. Take for example the Apostles' Creed, which runs to 102 words. Within this statement: six words are devoted to the Holy Spirit; eight to God; and sixty-six to Jesus! The same imbalance can be found in the Nicene Creed. Granted, there may have been historical reasons for this christomonism, but the imbalance does not serve us well. Even conceding the need for centering in Jesus, how can we defend the short shrift given to Jesus earthly life? In an age that has many celebrities and few heroes we can ill afford to reduce the life of Jesus to a punctuation mark.

Jesus' life is relevant to us today in at least the following ways:

1. His utter dependence on God and total independence from all that is not God. His composure before Pilate and his courage in facing down the religious establishment are cases in point.

2. The simplicity of his lifestyle and his sustained indifference toward wealth and ostentation. His last meal was not a power lunch but a modest supper!

3. His attentiveness to people and his ability to see past outward appearances to the self within.

4. His familiarity with scripture.

5. His reliance on prayer for the funding of his life, a habit that enabled him to live from the inside out.

By making Jesus a Superman or a drop-in Deity from another realm, we rob Jesus' achievements of their integrity and we rob ourselves of the power of his example. A high Christology has the effect of excusing ourselves from trying. But John A. T. Robinson was right in noting that unless Jesus were an ordinary man Jesus' deeds cannot be considered extraordinary! Jesus had no more going for him than we do. It is just that Jesus made more faithful use of those means of grace available to us all. If Jesus differed from us, it was a difference not of kind but of degree.

Another benefit that accrues to those who can see the gospel as extending beyond the announcement of sins forgiven is that the kingdom of God can become a reality in our lives. Alas, the kingdom of God is not mentioned in the Apostles' Creed. This is a cardinal omission because the kingdom was the fundamental all-encompassing reality in Jesus' life. Hans Küng has defined the kingdom as "God's creation healed." Another has seen it as "the energy of God realizing itself in human life." It is a fact that churches that talk the most about being saved from sin have the least to say about the kingdom of God.

Salvation is not an end in itself. God did not put us here to save us. Once our severed relationship with God is restored there is work to do. The kingdom is at hand. Our Communion liturgies celebrate what God has done for us. The balancing words we need to hear are what we may do for God. One cannot study Jesus' life without becoming struck by the energies he consistently committed to the kingdom.

A final benefit that issues from a lower Christology has to do with our ability to get along better with women and men of other religious traditions. God is the source of our redemption. The writer of the Letter of Jude closed his letter with an ascription of praise to "the only God our Savior." If God is one, we may be sure that God is at home in traditions not our own. The term "God" can be unifying. The name "Jesus" has proved to be divisive. Unless we are willing to summarily dismiss the faith claims of millions on millions of Jews, Hindus, Muslims, and Buddhists and consign them to outer darkness, we will have to concede that God conveys grace in many ways and forms.

In a moment of Christian triumphalism, the late William Temple wrote, "God may have other words for other worlds, but for this world the Word of God is Christ." But times have changed. It is not demonstrably clear today, if indeed it ever was, that Christians are richer in the fruits of the Spirit than are other people. If we start with dogma and theological postulates, we will never be in harmony with those whose beliefs are different. However, if we start with experiences of God and Spirit, we will find common ground and much to unite us. God is the constant wherever souls are lifted up in prayer. In one of the most regrettable and abused texts in the New Testament, Jesus is reported to have said, "I am the way, and the truth, and the life. No one comes to the Father except through me" (John 14:6). But, let it be noted, Jesus did not reverse the proposition and say, "The Father comes to no one save through me." God is not a prisoner of the incarnation. God's presence can be sensed immediately, that is, without mediation. The Divine can score a direct hit. As Thomas Müntzer, the rogue reformer, put it, "The people who wrote the Bible didn't have a Bible, and they did all right."

This is not a plea that we should be less Christian than we are now. Jesus is the one through whom we found God coming to us. It is, rather, a plea that we become more open to the way God works in the other religions of the world.

God is the Savior. The kingdom we serve is God's kingdom. The Spirit that we seek is God's Spirit. The world that we would heal is God's world. The good news that we believe and share is that God is for us. Even Paul, for all of his Christocentric musings, edged close to a unitarian point of view in his classic defense of the resurrection: "When all things are subjected to Christ, then the Son himself will also be subjected to the one who put all things in subjection under him, so that God may be all in all" (1 Cor. 15:28). The ultimate disclaimer may have come from Jesus himself in a text that very few have dared to expound: "Why do you call me good? No one is good but God alone" (Mark 10:18). Jesus believed in the goodness of God. We believe in him; now let us believe like him.

11

To Die and Rise Again:
Preaching the Gospel for Liberation

MARY LIN HUDSON

The words of God are words of liberation.
—David Buttrick, *A Captive Voice*

The rehabilitation of preaching has been a primary concern of homileticians during the last quarter of a century. Prominent among the voices for reform is David Buttick's call for the liberation of preaching from the idolatries of the church. He argues for a release of preaching from its present bondage to scripture, community, and culture in order for it to be free to serve God's redemptive purposes in the world. In other words, preaching itself must be liberated in order to participate in the liberation of God's creation.

"Preaching is 'word of God,' " Buttrick explains, "in that it participates in God's purpose, is initiated by Christ, and is supported by the Spirit with community in the world."[1] By continuing the preaching of Jesus that announced the arrival of the new reality of God in the midst of human life, preaching finds itself participating in God's redemptive work as it unfolds in the present. In this way, liberating preaching walks a path that was first traveled by Jesus. Informed by the narrative of Jesus that is remembered in proclamation, preaching gives up its life in expectation of its own resurrection in the midst of human community in the world.

The Language of Preaching

It is through the language of human speech that the liberating reality of God finds expression. By its very nature, however, language seems to impose restrictions on human freedom. Even in preaching (and perhaps especially in preaching) language seems to carry a proscriptive as well as prescriptive function. At the same time words fashion worlds of reality, they selectively shut out competing claims, relegating them to the realm of silence. Spoken word is never a benign force but always exerts a power both to shape and to destroy.

Nevertheless, Buttrick insists that the language of preaching is for liberation. If God's redemptive purpose is to bring about liberation or release from bondage, then the intended goal of preaching would be freedom, the state of release from confinement or restraint. That which is free would have the capacity to move toward fullest well-being. External controls would no longer interfere or regulate the actions of the liberated so that choices that are made would no longer be restricted to the limits imposed by some outside force. Instead, the desire and direction of choice would be shaped in such a way that nothing impedes the possibility of movement toward the full flourishing of life.[2]

How can the words of preaching participate in liberation? What kind of mysterious process takes the powerful, yet fragile, language of human design and transforms it into a living instrument of radical transformation and regeneration? Is there a distinguishable shape to this process that can offer itself as a model to inform the preaching of today and tomorrow?

The Nature of Jesus' Proclamation

Perhaps the experience of Jesus' proclamation of "good news" can offer insights into the nature of preaching for liberation. The message of Jesus' preaching may be summed up in one sentence: "The time is fulfilled, and the kingdom of God has come near; repent, and believe the good news" (Mark 1:15). Jesus announced the arrival of a new social reality that displaced competing political, social, economic, and religious systems of the day. The "kingdom" was both an eschatological reality, connected with the coming of a Messiah to usher in this new age, and a contemporary reality, available in the present to people of faith. Although it was not a new concept in the religious language of culture, Jesus' message did challenge the structures of thought and systems of power that shaped the reality of his world. The radical idea that this "new reality" was coming into being with its own transcendent authority instead of residing somewhere in the dreamy, distant future of Jewish hope sharply challenged those who found themselves overly invested in the present age. The prophetic message was intended to bring about radical transformation.[3]

Such a message of "new reality" can only be experienced as parable, an unfolding plot that unsettles our world in consciousness by inserting possibilities that move far beyond conventional understandings. By telling stories about losing coins, planting and harvesting seeds, investing

money, managing properties, baking bread and throwing parties, Jesus
found entrance into the common world of the audience, a world shaped
by conventional plots that reinforced cultural values of the age. Once
inside, however, the world was disrupted as the plot shifted to an unexpected ending, unsettling the listeners and surprising them with a different look at reality. Such a message called into question values, beliefs, and
motives, thus distancing the listener from the security of a predictable outcome. A crisis of meaning was created.

It is precisely in a moment of such crisis that liberation is possible. The
introduction of a radically different vision allows for the suspension of
beliefs and values that have dictated the choices of one's life. The
announcement of a completely new reality challenges the long-established
precedents that shape the listener's world, breaking their stranglehold and
creating the possibility for response. Such radical announcements come as
both promise and threat. They possess the power to shatter illusory worlds
and to supplant them with new possibilities. "New reality" sounds like
"hope" to those who are oppressed and in need of a radically changed
world. Those who are happy with the way things are, however, find themselves quite threatened by this subversive promise.[4]

Not only did the rhetorical shape of Jesus' message create a crisis of
meaning, but his personal presence was confrontational as well. His message and his identity were inextricably joined. Therefore, his ministry was
experienced in the same way as his message—as a parable. He came in
human form, a participant in the religious culture of his day, yet his ministry of eating and drinking with outcasts, conversing intelligently with
women, touching dead bodies, and violating Sabbath laws challenged
long-established traditions. His presence created a crisis of meaning, calling into question and, thus, suspending the authority of conventional
understandings of human experience. Tragically, the response of most
persons to this crisis was to attack and to eliminate its cause, rather than to
be transformed by it.[5]

So we see in the preaching of Jesus a paradox. The announced "good
news" created a crisis of meaning, which in turn led to the death of the
one who proclaimed it. The inauguration of new life necessarily sen-
tenced the life-giver to death because of the violent conflict that it generated. This paradox confused the disciples of Jesus. They believed that
both the astonishing message and the heroic messenger were given as
gifts to the world, possessing the special, divine power to rescue God's
people and restore God's rule. As disciples, their job was to set apart, to
honor, and to serve Jesus so that he could continue to preach the message
of God's new reality. No wonder they were confused when the conflict
with the powers and systems escalated to the point that Jesus' words

were silenced and the speaker crucified! How could "good news" lead to such tragedy?

The biblical witness suggests that Jesus understood the tragic nature of this mission from the beginning. The purpose of Jesus' incarnation and preaching was to allow the reality of God to come alive in the social world of the people who received the announcement. In order for that to happen, the word as it was originally proclaimed would have to die to itself in order to assume a new form of life in the hearts of the people. Until it died to itself, the word remained an objective reality to be debated, reacted against, and studied, rather than becoming the subject of people's lives.

Consider, for instance, the nature of Jesus' parables that demonstrate the way the kingdom of God comes to life in the world. In the parable of the mustard seed (Matt. 13:31–32), a huge shrub is the result of the planting of a very tiny seed. In the parable of the baker-woman (v. 33), huge loaves of bread arise from a small amount of yeast "hidden" in three measures of flour. In both of these parables, the results are extravagant and overwhelming. In one, the outcome stems from the initial "death" of an embarrassingly insignificant seed, which dies to its present form when planted; in the other, a bit of yeast must be "hidden" in flour, giving up its own form as the catalyst for transforming the flour into bread. A kind of paradoxical exchange takes place as one form relinquishes itself so that a new reality can arise to offer shelter and nourishment in a way that the original form could never provide.

In the parable of the sower (Matt. 13:3–9) and its interpretation (vv. 18–23), this paradox relates directly to the proclamation of the word. The seed sown on the path, on rocky soil, and among thorns did not have a chance to germinate properly, take root, or grow freely because of the restraint of outside forces preventing it from being reborn and flourishing. The seed that fell on good soil took root and grew, producing an abundance of grain that was beyond expectation. In all cases, regardless of outcome, the sowing of the seed necessarily meant that the seed was offered up in its original form in order for new life to arise and flourish.[6]

Attributing ultimate power to fragile, finite things such as a human person and a human word narrowed and restricted the way the disciples could experience the very reality that Jesus proclaimed. Their idolatry of the words and the preacher kept the "word" from taking root in their own lives. Instead they worked to preserve and defend the status of both Jesus and his announcement against attackers. As long as Jesus' words and ministry remained alive, the kingdom of God was objectified, thus preventing it from coming to life in the midst of their own community.

In a recent conversation, a friend was reflecting on her experience as a pastor. For eight years she preached thoughtful, passionate, prophetic sermons. For eight years she struggled to draw the congregation into some new kind of community of the Spirit based on the radical principles of justice, mercy, and freedom. During this time, the congregation flocked to the church, but they continued to do business in the old ways, resisting change and bypassing opportunities for open, fruitful dialogue as community. While supporting her prophetic ministry to the community and the world on their behalf, they targeted her with complaints about the message that was being delivered to them. It was only when she resigned and moved away that the congregation began talking honestly with each other and started to build a new community of trust and witness out of their own experience, rather than hers. "I used to wonder," she said, "what it meant to declare that 'Jesus died for our sins.' Now I have a better understanding. Jesus didn't have a choice. As long as he embodied the message, he remained the object of all of the disciples' fears and longings. Only when he died were the fears and longings transformed into faith in God. The miracle of resurrection was the resurrection of the community of faith."

The Transformative Power of Preaching

The gospel is preached for the sake of its transformation in the life of community. Thus, it continues the ministry of Jesus who lived and died so that people might become full participants in the new reality of God. In *The Passion for Life: A Messianic Lifestyle*, Jürgen Moltmann argues against viewing Jesus as any kind of folk hero or liberator. The work of Jesus was always to point away from himself toward God so that the people to whom he came would become the subjects of God's own history. "In Jesus," says Moltmann, "the people discover their own identity and worth of which no ruler can rob them. But neither can this identity be relinquished to a liberator."[7]

As long as people look beyond themselves for the source of their own liberation, they miss the reality of God's Spirit in their midst, the Spirit that could transform them into the new embodiment of God's reality in the world. They must learn to accept themselves as subjects, rather than objects, in light of the reality of Jesus.

In her discussion of women's experience of liberation, Elizabeth Johnson describes a process of contrast and conversion in which women turn away from a demeaning self-identity and turn toward new ownership of the female self as God's gift to creation.

> It is the kind of fruitful experience that transpires when persons bump up against the stubborn resistance of historical reality to what they sense to be true, good, and beautiful. When reality is thus "dis-illusioning," the contrast challenges people to a decision:

either close their minds and deny what they have experienced, or use it as a springboard to address and struggle with the causes of suffering.[8]

As the gospel is preached, the word confronts the world with a new interpretation of reality. This word "bumps up against" the culture and society of the present day, creating the crisis of meaning that opens up the possibility of liberation. This confrontive dimension is recognized by Christine Smith in her claim that preaching "shatters illusions and cracks open limited perspectives. . . . It is nothing less than the interpretation of our present world and an invitation to build a profoundly different new world."[9]

Preaching does more than offer contrast, however. It also confirms. Through the remembered narrative of the one who lived out this new reality of God, preaching presents a model of human flourishing that confirms the experience of persons who dare to live as subjects of God's new creation. As the contours of Jesus' life, ministry, death, and resurrection are re-presented through stories of faith, the shape of human flourishing is recognized and confirmed. Persons who long to live in freedom find the stories of Jesus encouraging and empowering. As they exercise the courage to live beyond the confines of cultural expectations, they find their own stories merging with Jesus' story. As they recall the meaning of Jesus' story for their lives, they experience solidarity with Jesus and with every other person who shares this identity. The particularities of gender, race, class, age, nationality, ability, or sexual orientation may shape differently the way they express their full humanity, but the shared story confirms their participation in the same reality of God. In solidarity, persons join together in resisting oppression and living more fully.[10]

Proclaiming the Gospel

Thus, proclamation not only participates in the conversion of those who believe, but confirms their experience, offers hope, and draws them into the solidarity of community. Yet what happens after the proclamation ceases? Silence. Silence is essential for the process of liberation to continue. As the voice of the word "dies" to its own form and agency, the ensuing silence creates the space for an echo of the word to resound in the memory of the listener. Like the silence that hovers after the turbulence of earthquake, wind, and fire, the stillness that follows on the heels of proclamation opens the possibility for a new sound to be heard. How can the word awaken in voices of the community of faith without it? Silence does not ensure resurrection of the word, but it does open up the possibility of it. Silence provides a dormant state in which the word may rest, take root in its new environment, and awaken to life in new forms—through the voices of the community.

The hymn writer Colin Gibson has captured this idea in the recently published song, "He Came Singing Love." The word "love" changes verse by verse to "faith," "hope," "peace," and the lines will accommodate any word that describes the reality of God's new order for creation. It is the structure of the poetry, however, that captures the parabolic nature of Jesus' ministry:

> He came singing love and he lived singing love;
>   he died, singing love.
> He arose in silence.
> For the love to go on we must make it our song;
>   you and I do the singing.[11]

Freedom cannot be imposed as an external force. That would violate freedom's nature. Instead, freedom is a condition that arises from within a person or community. It can develop only after the powers that restrict direction and choice are released. Therefore, the reality of Jesus cannot be forced onto humanity, but human community can find Christ's freedom taking shape within it. While the silence following proclamation provides room for Christ to emerge in a new form within community, the Spirit of Christ comes to life in the speech of the community as the word becomes embodied in its voice. Proclamation *does* participate in liberation, but it has to risk the silence of its own word in order for the gospel to continue in the freedom of community.

Isn't it amazing that a huge, leafy plant can grow from a tiny, yellow seed! Each form looks and feels so different. How could they possibly share the same life? Yet scientists can demonstrate that the genetic makeup of each is identical. The seed gives its life to the plant. In turn, the green, leafy plant must produce small, crusty seed in order for its genetic life to continue. In the same way, proclamation of the gospel must die to its original form as language and story and come to life in the actions and words of the faith community. As the community lives out the freedom of Christ, language and story will again find "voice" as the gospel is proclaimed. Without proclamation, the life of freedom could not continue. The cycle repeats itself.

Preachers who take seriously this paradoxical shape of liberation may find themselves standing in holy terror at the prospect of proclaiming the gospel. Preaching the joy of God means engendering scandal, anger, even violence. Conversely, the scandal, threat, and confrontation of the gospel make possible the joy of liberation. Caught in the middle is the preacher who, out of the joy of freedom, must forfeit comfort and security for the sake of continuing to proclaim the reality of God in the world. Preaching the gospel can be a risky business.

The preacher faces two important challenges. First, the preacher needs to release the word of proclamation so that it may take up residency within the life of community. Although the preacher's identity is invested in the language of proclamation, the preacher needs to be willing to forfeit ownership of it. Whenever the preacher is too closely attached to the word that is preached, the preacher and the message remain the objectified hope for liberation of the community. The message has little chance of taking root within the community itself.

A second challenge is for the preacher to allow herself or himself to be enlivened by the word as it arises from within community. Unless the preacher experiences the freedom of that new reality of God in community, he or she may find preaching a difficult and thankless task. Trying to preach within the confines of self-imposed restrictions or externally imposed regulations will eventually drain whatever vitality is left within the preacher. Burnout will soon be the result. At that point, proclamation may tend to weaken into a reflection of nothing more than the conventional wisdom of the day, or it may become packed with moralistic judgments that regulate and confine human behavior, treating human beings as objects of manipulation and rule. Preachers need the same solidarity in community that is proclaimed in gospel so that the freedom of Christ may grow within them.

It hasn't taken many years of teaching homiletics for me to realize how intimately wedded to the proclaimed word is the personal identity of the preacher. Critical evaluation of one's sermons may often trigger unexpected anxieties in even the most experienced preachers. How often do ministers measure their self-esteem by the praises of the congregation in response to their performance of proclamation and ministry! Yet the nature of liberation reveals that not only must we disengage from the word that we preach, we must also let it and the preacher in us die in order for the word to rise to new life in the hearts and voices of the faith community.

Perhaps the development of committees to assist the preacher in homiletical tasks can help ease the burden of proclamation that the preacher usually bears alone. However, the committee cannot claim ownership of the preached word any more than the preacher can. As Buttrick states, "We do not possess a word of God tucked away in our own psyches or hidden in the spirit (small s) of our congregations. No, the word of the gospel is emphatically God's word."[12]

In a sermon preached at Memphis Theological Seminary, Ronald Cole-Turner shared how difficult it was for him to accept other people's interpretations of his hymn, "Child of Blessing, Child of Promise." When he wrote it, he had in mind the joyous occasion of the baptism of his healthy, infant daughter and the celebration of her birth. As the hymn became widely published, he received letters telling stories of his hymn being sung in other settings. At the funeral of a child who died a painful death from cancer, the congregation sang,

> Child of joy, our dearest treasure,
>   God's you are, from God you came,
> Back to God we humbly give you:
>   Live as one who bears Christ's name.

In the classroom of a school for orphaned children, they learned words that were later repeated on the playground. They would swing back and forth singing, "Child of blessing, child of promise. . . ." With each story came his protest, "That's not what I meant when I wrote that hymn." But as he listened to these stories and others as they were told, the words took on new and different meanings. Because of these stories, he will never sing the hymn again in the same way that he once did. The words no longer belong to him, but have been handed back in a new form through the life of the community of faith.[13]

Preaching that follows the parabolic form of the gospel will offer itself in great thanksgiving and hope to the community of faith. In the Eucharist, mundane elements of bread and wine are offered to God in thanksgiving for God's redemptive actions in the world. Transformed by thanksgiving, they embody the meaning of the remembered narrative of Jesus Christ. Broken, shared, and consumed by the community of faith, the bread and wine take on new form in the actions and words of those who receive them, a continuation of God's redemptive action in the world. Even so, the common, fragile words of preaching are offered to God out of joyous gratitude for the redemptive action of God's reality coming into the world. This remembered narrative is transformed by the Spirit with community. The "Word" is broken into words, shared, and received by the community of faith, taking on a new form of life in the work and love of the ones who receive it.

Preaching continues the work of Jesus Christ as it gives up itself for the sake of resurrection within the life of community. In this way, preaching participates in God's liberation of the world.

NOTES

1. David Buttrick, *Homiletic: Moves and Structures* (Philadelphia: Fortress Press, 1987), 456. See "A Brief Theology of Preaching" in *Homiletic*, and *Preaching Jesus Christ* (Philadelphia: Fortress Press, 1988) for the development of his theology of preaching.

2. For a discussion of "freedom," see Edward Farley, *Good and Evil: Interpreting a Human Condition* (Minneapolis: Fortress Press, 1990).

3. Buttrick discusses the radical nature of Jesus' preaching in *Preaching Jesus Christ*, 33–44.

4. Ibid., 37–39.

5. Paul Ricoeur, "From Proclamation to Narrative," *Journal of Religion* 64:505–7.

6. Most scholars concentrate on the act of sowing or the size of the harvest, but give little consideration to the inherent process by which the seed comes to new life in the plant. For further discussion of these parables, see Jack D. Kingsbury, *The Parables of Jesus in Matthew 13* (London: SPCK, 1969); John R. Donahue, *The Gospel in Parable* (Philadelphia: Fortress Press, 1988); and Bernard Brandon Scott, *Hear Then the Parable* (Minneapolis: Fortress Press, 1989).

7. Jürgen Moltmann, *The Passion for Life: A Messianic Lifestyle* (Philadelphia: Fortress Press, 1978), 107.

8. Elizabeth A. Johnson, *She Who Is* (New York: Crossroad, 1992), 62–63.

9. Christine M. Smith, *Preaching as Weeping, Confession, and Resistance: Radical Responses to Radical Evil* (Louisville, Ky.: Westminster/John Knox Press, 1992), 2.

10. Elizabeth Johnson is particularly helpful in her discussion of "narrative remembering" and liberation in *She Who Is*, 63.

11. Colin Gibson, *He Came Singing Love* (Carol Stream, Ill.: Hope Publishing Co., 1994). Words © 1994 by Hope Publishing Co., Carol Stream, Il 60188. All rights reserved. Used by permissiom.

12. Buttrick, *A Captive Voice: The Liberation of Preaching* (Louisville, Ky.: Westminster John Knox Press, 1994), 52.

13. Ronald S. Cole-Turner, unpublished sermon, preached on October 11, 1995, for Memphis Theological Seminary's Fall Lectures. "Child of Blessing, Child of Promise," in *The Presbyterian Hymnal*, Hymn #498 (Louisville, Ky.: Westminster/John Knox Press, 1990). Copyright 1981 by Ronald S. Cole-Turner.

12

The Gospel as Empowered Speech for Proclamation and Persuasion

DONALD K. McKIM

David Buttrick's concern that the gospel be articulated has been central throughout all his works. His discipline is homiletics, his craft is preaching, but his vocation is always "servant of the Word." Buttrick's focus on the centrality of preaching and his resounding echo of Paul, "faith comes from what is heard" (Rom. 10:17), has strengthened, challenged, and energized many preachers and would-be preachers throughout the years. His stimulating homiletics classes, concern for students, and vigorous advocacy among colleagues have made him a treasured mentor and companion. His forthrightness, convictions, and acute intelligence make him a valued dialogue partner across many disciplines. He is tough-minded and tenderhearted—a rare and refreshing personality. His contributions to the church, liturgically and homiletically, have been many and significant. It is a joy to honor one who meant much to me as a professor at Pittsburgh Theological Seminary and who, as a guiding light, continues to point the way.

While David Buttrick is a master crafter of sermons and theoretical homiletician, he is also a fine theologian. His concern that a viable theology of preaching undergird the preacher is always present. Thus his *Homiletic: Moves and Structures* ends with the chapter, "A Brief Theology of Preaching."[1] There he wrestled with the question "Why do preachers preach?" and provides five theses to sketch his "brief theology."

In the following, I would like to look at the Christian gospel in relation to preaching and to offer a short description of what the gospel is for today. The thesis to be explicated is simply this: "The Gospel as Empowered Speech for Proclamation and Persuasion." The perspective is informed by the Reformed theological tradition, and much is drawn from Calvin. This is due not only to his importance for the tradition, but because I find his thought of enduring relevance. The purpose is to focus on the nature of the task before us in presenting the gospel while also recognizing the basis on which this presentation is carried out.

The Gospel

The gospel as "good news" took shape through the message and preaching of the early apostles. This gospel focused on Jesus Christ and what God had done in him. He is the culmination or fulfillment of God's promises to the covenant people of Israel as recorded throughout the Hebrew Scriptures. So early apostles preached, just as Jesus himself had done (Matt. 9:35). The message was "gospel" because it conveyed the promised "good news of great joy for all the people" (Luke 2:10).

The gospel as it took shape in the early church through ministries of preaching and teaching embraced many dimensions. Biblical images and metaphors capture aspects of who Jesus was and what he has done for the world. These emerged later into more complex theological statements, theories, and doctrines as the church continued its reflection on the gospel story. Jesus' own life and ministry, his death, resurrection, ascension, and anticipated second coming were seen in light of the scriptures of the people of Israel. What God did in Jesus Christ gave full expression to God's purposes as these were perceived through Israel's long history.

It is not then surprising to find that biblical images used to describe what early Christians experienced as God's astounding action in Jesus are related to images for experiences by foreparents in the Jewish faith as they perceived God's work in their history. Now in Jesus Christ, God's purposes are focused, intensified, and take on an ever more far-reaching character in that these purposes are now extended to the whole world.

The contours of early Christian experience have been identified by Edward Schillebeeckx, who expounds sixteen key New Testament concepts or images used to describe the Christian experience of "the decisive salvation in Jesus."[2] These concepts convey "what redemption through Christ Jesus is from and what it is for."[3] See the amazingly varied grace: salvation and redemption, freedom from servitude and slavery, liberation through purchase or for a ransom, reconciliation after a dispute, peace, expiation for sins, forgiveness of sins, justification and sanctification, legal aid, being redeemed for community, freed for Christian love, freed for freedom, renewal of humanity and the world, life in fullness, liberation as victory over alienating "demonic powers," glorification of the grace (*charis*) of God.[4] The gospel as the good news of Jesus Christ is a multifaceted message that meets persons in the midst of their needs, diverse as they are. What was not true then and is not true today is that the Christian gospel must be expressed in only one way, in only one vocabulary.

Those who present the gospel today, in preaching, teaching, and all other forms, must be open to the "varied grace" of the gospel. Cultural challenges to the gospel message abound on every side. A tunnel-visioned, single-note presentation of the gospel through a preestablished formula into which everyone's experience must be filtered is antithetical to the ways God works. What is needed is for preachers, teachers, and all who would communicate the "good news of great joy" to realize and convey the gospel in contemporary terms with meanings that are significant in our cultural contexts.

Similarly, the purposes for which the gospel is communicated are also diverse. They all revolve around God's purposes for the world and for establishing relationships within it. But the ways we understand what these purposes are and how they may be lived out among us will also, necessarily, be varied. For example, several quotations from John Calvin show how he recognized the multiple foci of gospel purposes:

> For where the Gospel is, there is the hope of everlasting salvation.[5]
> God has manifested life through His Word, or has manifested the Word of life through the preaching of the gospel.[6]
> For the whole purpose of the Gospel is that Christ be made ours, and that we be ingrafted into His body.[7]
> He [the apostle Paul] again refers to the purpose in preaching the Gospel which he mentioned at the beginning of the first chapter, viz. that God may lead all nations to the obedience of faith.[8]

"Everlasting salvation," "life through God's Word," "Christ be made ours and we be ingrafted into His body," "the obedience of faith"—all these are tied to the purposes of the gospel, yet each opens up wide arenas of theological understanding for the contours the gospel takes and how it shapes the lives of those who believe.[9]

The gospel message today must be known in all its fullness. Our studies—of scripture, the church, our culture, and the world—must lead us to creative ways of "en-fleshing" and "incarnating" the message of Jesus Christ. For as P. T. Forsyth noted, "The Gospel was there before the Bible, and it created the Bible, as it creates the true preacher and the true sermon everywhere. And it is for the sake and service of the Gospel that both Bible and preacher exist."[10] The varied gospel is at the center of the church's message.

Empowered Speech

Early Christian preachers were convinced that they did not preach the gospel on their own. As at Pentecost, the gospel Word is accompanied by God's Spirit as an effecting agent (Acts 4:31; 10:44). The Spirit accompanies believing what is heard (Gal. 3:2) and makes it operative.

The need for the Holy Spirit to activate and effectuate the gospel Word was a strong emphasis of the Protestant Reformers, especially Calvin. In commenting on Eph. 1:13, "In him you also, when you had heard the word of truth, the gospel of your salvation, and had believed in him, were marked with the seal of the promised Holy Spirit," Calvin wrote: "The foundation of faith would be frail and unsteady if it rested on human wisdom; and therefore, as preaching is the instrument of faith, so the Holy Spirit makes preaching efficacious";[11] for "only when God shines in us by the light of [God's] Spirit is there any profit from the Word."[12] Indeed, "without the illumination of the Holy Spirit, the Word can do nothing."[13]

The Holy Spirit thus empowers preached speech to enable it to accomplish God's purposes. The Spirit energizes and makes effectual that speech which is "gospel"—the message of Jesus Christ in all its varied forms (see 1 Thess. 1:5). The power of the gospel is the power of the Holy Spirit to make the gospel real to persons, whatever their situations. Through speech empowered by the Spirit, Jesus Christ himself is present within human consciousness. As Otto Weber put it, "The 'presence of Christ' made known in the Word through the Spirit is the yet-to-come, expected-and-always-to-be-expected 'presence'—*Veni, creator Spiritus* (Come, Creator Spirit)!"[14]

If so, there can be a fundamental theological courage in preaching. The "presence of the Word," God's Word in Jesus Christ as known through scripture, is real when human language and speech is used for communicating the gospel message. Human speech effects, preaching is a "performative action," when empowered by the Holy Spirit. The basic confidence is that God can do something in, with, and through gospel-message speech.

> [For] when, in the "apostolic succession" (*successio apostolica*), which is nothing other than the "succession of proclamation" (*successio praedicationis*), people are opened to the word, the Spirit is at work in that. The proclaimed Word does not just stand under the reservation of the Spirit's work, but is empowered by the affirmation given it in the Spirit (cf. for "binding and loosing" John 20:22f.; also 1 Cor. 5:4f.).[15]

To realize that theological courage belongs to the essence of the gospel as empowered speech can make every preaching event momentous. It is not that spectacular fireworks, conversions, or even outwardly visible results should occur. They may, or they may not. The theological courage and confidence that belongs to this view of the gospel, however, is the conviction that all "results" belong to the work of God's Spirit, since all that is salutary in preaching emerges from God's Spirit. The Spirit's work is mostly unspectacular by our standards. The formation of Christian character, the strengthening of faith, the clearer understanding of the gospel—these are elements of the Spirit's work that can come through the Spirit's "empowered speech." These are elements that ultimately belong to God's purposes for this world, the church, and individuals. Presenting the Christian gospel in language that can be empowered by the Holy Spirit is a Christian task that belongs to the essence of ministry and mission.[16] Christian confidence comes from the conviction that such work is God's work for the glorification of Jesus Christ and that this is a task that is meaningful to the maximum degree.[17] It was this courage that boosted the apostle Paul, in preaching and in all else: "You know that in the Lord your labor is not in vain" (1 Cor. 15:58). What else, after all, is really *worth* doing?

Proclamation

The gospel is empowered speech "for proclamation." The Spirit empowers speech for the purpose of proclamation. Early Christians had a message, an announcement, a proclamation to make as they preached the kerygma. God gave the strength and the gospel message (Rom. 16:25). Those who "gossiped the gospel" proclaimed it openly as accounts throughout the book of Acts show (e.g., Acts 5:42; 9:20; 16:10). The message impelled a communication. Those who collectively knew the life-changing reality of Jesus Christ could do nothing less than share this message and announce it to the world. This is the truth of Forsyth's observation that "preaching is thus the creation of the Gospel, and not our mere tribute to the Gospel."[18]

This proclamation of the Christian gospel by the church took many forms.[19] A major element, of course, was the oral proclamation of the gospel through empowered speech, in preaching. Here "proclamation" (*kerygma*) has the sense of a formal announcement, publicly made. Christian communities were gathered together by their response to the gospel word of proclamation.

The prominence of preaching was underlined by the sixteenth-century Protestant Reformers. As Weber has noted, for the Reformers, "the Community lives by the Word" and this Word is "understood by all the Reformers as primarily the proclaimed Word. None of the Reformers doubted that as such it was empowered."[20] Theologically, it is as the gospel is proclaimed that its fullness and power emerges, for "as concerns its essence the gospel is *kerygma*, message, and appeal in one (2 Cor. 5:20). Therefore, it must be proclaimed over and over again, and in that act it becomes what it is and wants to be."[21] The Spirit operates to empower speech in proclamation so that the reality of the Christian gospel can break loose in the world, for "the validity of the scriptural Word requires the 'living voice of the Gospel' (*viva vox evangelii*)."[22] Again, as Weber notes:

> Present-day proclamation is not a continuation of the Word passed on in Scripture, and it certainly is not its expansion. It actualizes the Word, which has already been spoken and heard, and makes room for it in us. That means that the Word is shown again and again to be relevant in proclamation.[23]

Thus the Word has its effect as it is proclaimed.

The types of effects proclamation yields vary indefinitely. Those who hear proclamation do so with ears variously attuned to the Spirit, or not. Positively, the empowered speech of proclamation engenders faith. As Calvin characteristically put it, "Faith does not depend on miracles or portents. It is the special gift of the Spirit and is born of the Word," for God's work is to draw humans to God and it is God's will "to work effectively" through the divine Word.[24] God "breathes faith into us only by the instrument of [God's] gospel, as Paul points out that 'faith comes from hearing'" (Rom. 10:17).[25] More succinctly, "Paul declares that faith is produced by preaching."[26]

Other theological effects are also engendered by the proclamation of the Word in the gospel. These include the illumination of the Holy Spirit, as "the Word is the instrument by which the Lord dispenses the illumination of his Spirit to believers";[27] "renewal";[28] "regeneration";[29] and "purification."[30] For, "there is such life energy in God's Word that it quickens the souls of all to whom God grants participation in it."[31] Negatively, the proclamation of the Word can "conduce to hardness of heart."[32]

Proclamation needs preachers. The wonder of it all is that God chooses to empower human speech by the Spirit and to use human proclaimers— shabby, sinful, and grubby as we are!—to be purveyors of the proclaimed Word. The theological courage for preaching, spoken of above, comes from the faith that God uses the gospel Word as empowered speech. The "terror and gladness"[33] of preaching is that God uses the likes of us to do the proclaiming.

Theologically, Calvin saw this as a wonderful example of God's "accommodation" or adjustment to human capacities; for "God accommodated to our limited capacity [*ad modulum nostrum attemperat*] every declaration which [God] makes of Himself."[34] God's revelation comes to humans in ways they can understand. God's use of humans as proclaimers of the gospel message, the Word, is an example of God's gracious concern or accommodation—of which the incarnation, God's becoming a human—is the supreme example. As Calvin put it, God "provides for our weakness in that [God] prefers to address us in human fashion through interpreters in order to draw us to himself, rather than to thunder at us and drive us away." It was a "singular privilege," Calvin said, that God "deigns to consecrate" the "mouths and tongues" of humans in order that God's "voice may resound in them."[35]

Recognizing the resounding importance of proclamation, the gracious privilege given to preachers to do the proclaiming is a further cause for joy. It is reassuring to realize that "the Word of God is never identical with a quality found in a person."[36] Forsyth was right when he commented that "the Church does not live by its preachers, but by its Word."[37] Despite human limits, failures, and sin, God uses preachers to proclaim. No human effort alone could ever be adequate. No human voice could "say it all." But as Calvin notes, it is "not that the voice coming from a [human's] mouth has so much efficacy in itself, but it is because Christ works in the heart by the Spirit; the voice itself is the instrument of cleansing."[38] The joy is that God is the "author of preaching" who joins the divine Spirit with it and "promises benefits from it."[39]

Persuasion

Ultimate reliance on Spirit-empowered speech that proclaims the gospel does not negate but engenders the most rigorous attention to the practice of preaching and, thus, the craft of preparing sermons. Historically, the discipline of homiletics has focused on this task. Theologically, while God through the Spirit is perfectly free to use any medium, any words, any deeds to communicate the divine self-revelation, the preaching event is a primary means by which God in Jesus Christ is communicated. Again from Calvin, commenting on the apostle Paul, "He calls the Gospel *the preaching of Jesus Christ*, since, the whole sum of it is contained in our knowledge of Christ";[40] for "the Gospel is properly the appointed preaching of Christ made manifest, in whom the promises themselves are revealed."[41] All that the gospel can mean occurs when Jesus Christ is preached.

The gospel is proclamation of Jesus Christ carried out persuasively; for, if the gospel is to be meaningful or "make sense," it must be proclaimed in ways that are "persuasive." This was the essence of Paul's words, "Therefore, knowing the fear of the Lord, we try to persuade others; but we ourselves are well known to God, and I hope that we are also well known to your consciences" (2 Cor. 5:11) as well as "So we are ambassadors for Christ, since God is making his appeal through us; we entreat you on behalf of Christ, be reconciled to God" (v. 20). The language of "persuasion" and "entreating" here indicates that the proclamation task is oriented toward a serious attempt at conveying the gospel in effective and functional ways. Engagement with an "audience" is crucial; proclamation and apologetic "strategies" must be employed.

Thus the gospel as empowered speech is for both proclamation and persuasion. The persuasive task of preaching is implicit in the crafting of sermons and thus in the discipline of homiletics. The history of preaching reveals varied uses of strategies in the ways sermons are conceived, the choice of words, the elements in the human makeup that are appealed to, and so on. To persuade through the use of language is a preaching goal, yet one that is carried out through a variety of linguistic means.

Classically, the art of rhetoric has been "the art of persuasion."[42] Thus, it is not surprising that, through the centuries, Christian preaching has been associated with rhetoric.[43] Despite attempts to avoid it, sermons preached by preachers are inevitably exercises in rhetoric. All sermons are "inescapably embodied and, thus rhetorical";[44] for "while preaching is unique, not least by being God's word, it is closely related to rhetoric as conversation or dialogue whose aim is persuasion or identification that seeks to enroll people in a way of life."[45]

Contemporary homileticians are helpfully focusing on rhetoric and rhetorical studies. This is occurring while the concept of rhetoric itself is expanding, as Craig Loscalzo notes, into arenas of "audience analysis, linguistic, gender-based communication, cultural biases in communication, as well as the more traditional purviews of speech studies."[46]

Persuasive preaching, then, will be intentional in its use of "rhetoric"—not for purposes of manipulation, of course. But rhetoric will be deliberate in the service of using all the gifts God has given us for the purposes of persuasion: persuasion of the reality and truth of the Christian gospel. David S. Cunningham has recently argued that "faithful persuasion" is an appropriate image for all theology:

> I want to claim that Christian theology is best understood as persuasive argument. . . . The goal of Christian theology, then, is *faithful persuasion*; to speak the word that theology must speak, in ways that are faithful to the God of Jesus Christ and persuasive to the world that God has always loved. This has been the goal of Christian theology since the days of one of its earliest practitioners, St. Paul. "Therefore, knowing the fear of the Lord, we try to persuade others" (2 Cor. 5:11).[47]

The study of rhetoric shows that there are varieties of rhetorical strategies and that communication for persuasion will be uniquely focused in relation to a number of social, gender, and cultural factors; thus, the need for smart, savvy preachers to find strategies of rhetoric and communication that are faithful to the Christian gospel and sensitive to the contexts and congregations where preaching takes place. The complexities of contemporary life call for the absolute best efforts we can give in finding means for "faithful persuasion."[48]

Ultimately, theologically, the work of "persuasion" belongs to the Holy Spirit. The Spirit can take what is said and enable effective "communication." Yet God calls the preacher to effort. If we take seriously the theological conviction that God uses humans for God's purposes and that the varied forms of the gospel elicit the need for diverse expressions of the gospel, then the tasks of developing the rhetorical strategies, crafting the sermon, and conveying the gospel faithfully are the inevitable responsibilities of the preacher. No cop-outs here. No shortcuts. No evasions. Preaching is hard work. As Wilson notes, "we put forward our best efforts toward faithful persuasion, and pray that in doing so we facilitate the clarity with which God's voice is heard."[49]

Preaching the Gospel Today

The gospel is empowered speech for proclamation and persuasion. To preach the gospel today is critically important as the means God uses for establishing faith and new life by the power of the Holy Spirit. The Word proclaimed "promotes the gospel as announcement of a radically new human situation inaugurated by God."[50] In so doing, the work of homiletics—as a persuasive project—attends to the means by which this gospel can be proclaimed persuasively, compellingly, and faithfully.

David Buttrick has said, "Perhaps the great calling of homiletics these days is the rearticulation of our faith. . . . Once more, we must be concerned to reformulate Christian faith, to find new metaphors and analogies to explain the gospel message."[51] His own work has helped point the way to these ends. Preaching the gospel is a theological action; it is also a profoundly human activity. This is both its gift and task. As we persuade and proclaim, trusting the Spirit to empower our speech, we can be grateful that God uses the preacher to announce "good news of a great joy." We can experience the "terror and gladness" of preaching with a profound awe. Our mission and ministries may embrace many areas, central to which will be communicating God's word. Forsyth's words point to the profundity of this work: "With preaching Christianity stands or falls because it is the declaration of a Gospel."[52]

NOTES

1. David Buttrick, "A Brief Theology of Preaching," in *Homiletic: Moves and Structures* (Philadelphia: Fortress Press, 1987), 449–59. Reprinted in *Major Themes in the Reformed Tradition*, ed. Donald K. McKim (Grand Rapids: Wm. B. Eerdmans Publishing Co., 1992), 318–25.

2. Edward Schillebeeckx, *Christ: The Experience of Jesus as Lord*, trans. John Bowden (New York: Crossroad, 1981), 463.

3. Ibid., 477.

4. See ibid., 477–512.

5. John Calvin, *Galatians, Ephesians, Philippians and Colossians*, Calvin's New Testament Commentaries, trans. T.H.L. Parker, ed. David W. Torrance and Thomas F. Torrance (Grand Rapids: Wm. B. Eerdmans Publishing Co., 1965), *Comm. Col.* 1:23. Further citations from Calvin's commentaries are from this translation series.

6. Calvin, *Comm. Tit.* 1:3.

7. Calvin, *Comm. 1 Cor.* 1:9.

8. Calvin, *Comm. Rom.* 16:21.

9. The citations here from Calvin, as from most theologians, could be multiplied, for example, the gospel may "radically reform our hearts as a seed of immortal life" (*Comm. 1 Pet.* 1:23); that "we have been cleansed of our sins by Christ's blood." See John Calvin, *Institutes of the Christian Religion*, Library of Christian Classics, trans. Ford Lewis Battles, ed., John T. McNeill (Philadelphia: Westminster Press, 1960), 4.15.4. Cf. T.H.L. Parker, *Calvin's Preaching* (Louisville, Ky.: Westminster/John Knox Press, 1992), chaps. 1–5.

10. P. T. Forsyth, *Positive Preaching and the Modern Mind*, 2nd ed. (Pittsburgh: Pickwick Press, 1981), 15.

11. Calvin, *Comm. Eph.* 1:13. The Holy Spirit is also the source of believers' certainty of the gospel as Word of God. Thus Calvin also wrote on this verse: "The true conviction which believers have of the Word of God, of their own salvation, and of all religion, does not spring from the feeling of the flesh, or from human and philosophical arguments, but from the sealing of the Spirit, who makes their consciences more certain and removes all doubt."

12. Calvin, *Comm. Rom.* 1:16.

13. Calvin, *Inst.* 3.2.33. Calvin went on to expand this when he wrote: "Indeed, the Word of God is like the sun, shining upon all those to whom it is proclaimed, but with no effect among the blind. Now, all of us are blind by nature in this respect. Accordingly, it cannot penetrate into our minds unless the Spirit, as the inner teacher, through his illumination makes entry for it" (3.2.34).

14. Otto Weber, *Foundations of Dogmatics*, trans. Darrell L. Guder, 2 vols. (Grand Rapids: Wm. B. Eerdmans Publishing Co., 1983), 2:517. Similarly, Buttrick writes that "preaching holds the living Christ before us as a contemporary, symbolic-reflective reality." *Preaching Jesus Christ: An Exercise in Homiletic Preaching* (Philadelphia: Fortress Press, 1988), 83.

15. Weber, *Foundations of Dogmatics*, 2:246.

16. The Confession of 1967 of the Presbyterian Church (U.S.A.) says that God instructs the "church and equips it for mission through preaching and teaching. By these, when they are carried on in fidelity to the Scriptures and dependence upon the Holy Spirit, the people hear the Word of God and accept and

follow Christ" (*The Book of Confessions* [Louisville, Ky.: Office of the General Assembly, 1991], 9.49).

17. As Buttrick puts it in terms of theology's relation to homiletics: "The primary task of ministry is *meaning*." See *A Captive Voice: The Liberation of Preaching* (Louisville Ky.: Westminster John Knox Press, 1994), 110.
18. Forsyth, *Positive Preaching and the Modern Mind*, 99.
19. David S. Cunningham points this out when he writes, "Christian proclamation is not limited to linguistic forms. Just as persuasion can take place without words, or through a combination of words and deeds, so too with proclamation. Thus, proclamation takes place, not only in the pulpit, but also at the altar; not only in acts of reading, but in acts of solidarity as well; not only in the Church, but throughout the world." *Faithful Persuasion: In Aid of a Rhetoric of Christian Theology* (Notre Dame, Ind.: University of Notre Dame Press, 1991), 202.
20. Weber, *Foundations of Dogmatics*, 2:516.
21. Hendrikus Berkhof, *Christian Faith*, trans. Sierd Woudstra, rev. ed. (Grand Rapids: Wm. B. Eerdmans Publishing Co., 1986), 361.
22. Weber, *Foundations of Dogmatics*, 1.191.
23. Ibid., 2:246.
24. Calvin, *Comm. Luke* 16:30.
25. Calvin, *Inst.* 4.1.5.
26. Calvin, *Comm. Rom.* 10:17. When Calvin lines out the traditional, scholastic causalities for salvation, he writes, "The mercy of God is the efficient cause, Christ with His blood the material cause, faith conceived by the Word the formal or instrumental cause, and the glory of both the divine justice and goodness the final cause." *Comm. Rom.* 3:24.
27. Calvin, *Inst.* 1.9.3.
28. Calvin, *Inst.* 2.5.5.
29. Calvin, *Comm. 1 Pet.* 1:23.
30. Calvin, *Comm. John* 15:3.
31. Calvin, *Inst.* 2.10.7.
32. Calvin, *Inst.* 3.24.13. Cf. the discussion in B. A. Gerrish, *Grace and Gratitude: The Eucharistic Theology of John Calvin* (Minneapolis: Fortress Press, 1993), 76ff. on "The Word as a Means of Grace." As Buttrick notes, "Even when preaching is rejected, it is nonetheless efficacious. Preaching will either soften or harden the heart, save or condemn" (*Encyclopedia of the Reformed Faith*, ed. Donald K. McKim [Louisville, Ky.: Westminster/John Knox Press, 1992], s.v. "Preaching, Theology of, ") 290. Hereafter cited as *ERF*.
33. Buttrick's phrase in "A Brief Theology of Preaching" in *Homiletic*, 459.
34. Calvin, *Comm. Rom.* 1:19. On accommodation and its importance, see Jack B. Rogers and Donald K. McKim, *The Authority and Interpretation of the Bible: An Historical Approach* (San Francisco: Harper & Row, 1979), passim and *ERF*, s.v. "Accommodation."
35. Calvin, *Inst.* 4.1.5.
36. Weber, *Foundations of Dogmatics*, 1:192.
37. Forsyth, *Positive Preaching and the Modern Mind*, 60.
38. Calvin, *Comm. John* 15:3. Calvin also writes on 1 Pet. 1:25: "It is indeed certain that those who plant and those who water, are nothing, but whenever God is pleased to bless their labour, [God] makes their doctrine efficacious by the power of His Spirit, and the Voice which is in itself mortal is an instrument of eternal life." *Comm. 1 Pet.* 1:25.

39. Calvin, *Inst.* 4.1.6.
40. Calvin, *Comm. Rom.* 16:21.
41. Calvin, *Comm. Rom.* 1:2.
42. Paul S. Wilson, *The Practice of Preaching* (Nashville: Abingdon Press, 1995), 63ff.; Cunningham, *Faithful Persuasion*, 38ff. Cunningham notes that Kenneth Burke pointed out that "the Greek word [for persuasion], *peithō*, comes from the same root as the Latin word for faith. Accordingly, Aristotle's term for rhetorical 'proof' is the related word, *pistis* . . . the word which, in Greek ecclesiastical literature, came to designate the highest order of Christian knowledge, 'faith' or 'belief' as contrasted with 'reason.' While the active form of *peithō* means to persuade, its middle and passive forms mean 'to obey.' " See Kenneth Burke, *A Rhetoric of Motives* (Berkeley: University of California Press, 1969), 52, cited in Cunningham, *Faithful Persuasion*, 39.
43. See *Concise Encyclopedia of Preaching*, ed. William H. Williman and Richard Lischer (Louisville, Ky.: Westminster John Knox Press, 1995), s.v. "Rhetoric" for a historical overview.
44. Thomas G. Long, "And How Shall They Hear? The Listener in Contemporary Preaching" in *Listening to the Word* (Nashville: Abingdon Press, 1993), 178.
45. Wilson, *Practice of Preaching*, 63–64. Cf. Buttrick's comment that "rhetoric is an ancient wisdom that undergirds all human conversation" and that "while rhetorical training could lead to insubstantial ornamentation or verbal pyrotechnics, for the most part rhetorical wisdom assisted preaching" (*Homiletic*, 40).
46. Craig A. Loscalzo, in *Concise Encyclopedia of Preaching*, 414.
47. Cunningham, *Faithful Persuasion*, 5. Cunningham also links theology and homiletics when he writes that "all Christian theology is proclamation. Homiletics and systematics differ from one another because of their audiences and the character by which they are authorized; but they are both acts of proclamation" (202). Buttrick has noted that "to preach the gospel is to do theology at a profound, if quite practical, level." See his *The Mystery and the Passion: A Homiletic Reading of the Gospel Traditions* (Minneapolis: Fortress Press, 1992), 11.
48. In addition to Buttrick's other contributions, previously mentioned, see his "On Doing Homiletics Today" in *Intersections: Post-Critical Studies in Preaching*, ed. Richard L. Eslinger (Grand Rapids: Wm. B. Eerdmans Publishing Co., 1994), 88–104.
49. Wilson, *Practice of Preaching*, 79. In Buttrick's words: "Preaching, therefore, is a spiritual discipline in which we offer our best words to Christ" (*Homiletic*, 452).
50. Buttrick's comment in his article on "Proclamation" in *Concise Encyclopedia of Preaching*, 385.
51. Buttrick, *A Captive Voice*, 73.
52. Forsyth, *Positive Preaching and the Modern Mind*, 5.

3. PREACHING AND SCRIPTURE

13

Biblical Studies and Preaching: A Growing Divide?

PAUL SCOTT WILSON

How are preachers, or those preparing for ordination, to regard biblical studies in relation to the pulpit? On the one hand, David Buttrick has rung a warning bell by being critical of biblical theology, laying at its door the loss of "our homiletical souls—prophetic silence, past-tense faith, and an enlarging tension between the Bible and the good news of the gospel message."[1] The future of homiletics, he proposes, is a recovery of rhetoric and theology,[2] for the primary task of the preacher must again be to dispense meaning.[3] The future is not in the direction of biblical historical criticism, for though preachers have benefited from it, it has had its "golden age."[4] The focus must be on helping preachers to move from the biblical text to the contemporary situation, and on recasting theology in the present.[5]

On the other hand, consensus among biblical scholars is that, even though efforts to discover a doctrinal center and uniform theology in the Bible were misguided, the biblical theology project is a worthy one. Gerhard F. Hasel, in contrast to Buttrick, claims that "the 'golden age' of Old Testament theology began in the 1930s and continues to the present."[6] Buttrick is among a number of scholars who are bold in their concern about the pulpit,[7] and the purpose of this chapter is to explore the validity of both the positive and negative claims for biblical studies as well as the possibility of future dialogue between biblical studies and homiletics. Several reasons for the current distance between the disciplines will be explored. First, each discipline has its own and not-always-compatible understanding concerning the theological curriculum. Second, in spite of the common regard for "what the text meant" and "what the text means," scholars in Bible and homiletics seem to mean different things by these terms. Third, the increased importance of being persuasive in preaching is altering the needs of preachers in relation to scholarship.

Interdisciplinary Attitudes

Biblical and pastoral disciplines represent distinct areas of the medieval theological quadrivium. Their natural differences are heightened by separate historical self-understandings, highlighted in part by Friedrich Schleiermacher, that can amount to different visions of theological education.

The Latin term *quadrivium* implies a meeting of four roads. In theology, these roads became Bible, systematic theology, history, and practical or pastoral theology. Historically, their meeting was in preaching, which theological education and the university itself initially existed to serve. Pastoral areas were understood as the application of Bible, theology, and history to the life and work of the church. In the German *Wissenschaft* model of theological education, common in Europe and evident in some schools like McGill University, Montreal, Quebec, pastoral matters are left to a separate, final practical year of training. In North America, the European model generally persists in attitude only, with pastoral courses often assumed to be the application and integration of what is taught elsewhere. The existence of pastoral departments inadvertently may have encouraged diminished attention to preaching in the teaching of other disciplines.[8]

Fragmentation of theological education has resulted in preaching no longer being the acknowledged center of theological education. Pastoral disciplines, slow to emerge as identifiable areas of academic integrity, have been more influenced than other disciplines by principles initially articulated by Schleiermacher.

In his *Brief Outline on the Study of Theology*, Schleiermacher proposed a revision of theological education with three equal areas of theological inquiry: philosophical theology (dealing with the essence of Christian faith, life, and ethics), historical theology (including church history, dogmatics, and biblical exegesis), and practical theology (including homiletics, liturgy, and principles of church leadership, service, and governance), which he called "the crown of theological study because it presupposes everything else."[9] His divisions, inadequate in several regards, not least in assessing the practical as mere technique,[10] failed to be adopted as a replacement to the quadrivium.

Three features of his program however are of abiding interest: (1) theological education springs from and exists in service to the life of the church;[11] (2) all three areas of theology relate to each other in a unified organic system;[12] and (3) an appropriate dialogical balance between empirical study and faith participation, or "scientific" and ecclesial interest, or theory and practice, or reflection and action, is essential for all church leaders.[13] Only by such connection to the life and leadership of the church do subjects in the theological curriculum, which could equally be taught in arts and science, become theological.[14]

Few would dispute Schleiermacher's first assumption: all theological disciplines assume that they exist in service to the life of the church, however broadly this is understood, whether it is directly tested or not. His other two assumptions operate at least to some degree in all departments, where, for instance, Marxist and liberation concerns surface, yet are common in pastoral departments, where theory and praxis rooted in the pastorate are dominant. Interdisciplinary discussion is essential for homiletics, for the obvious reason that preaching cannot be independent from the theological disciplines upon which it draws.

However, the traditional quadrivium allowed the Bible, theology, and history to be taught without practical regard for preaching or other matters of church life. The teaching of homiletics often fell to an available member of faculty or to an experienced preacher. In such circumstances, it was natural, perhaps, that conversation in the theological quadrivium would tend to be one way, *from* the cognate areas in which there is considerable interdisciplinary discussion *to* the pastoral areas, rather than back and forth. Collections of essays in biblical theology commonly refer to systematic theology and history, yet make no reference to preaching. Such lack of conversation may be one reason for Buttrick's lament concerning the help not given preachers by biblical scholars. Continuation of the silence can only contribute to the current problems of the church.

Biblical Theology
and the Pulpit

The silence of many biblical scholars concerning preaching and the church is difficult to comprehend if the agenda of biblical studies is not acknowledged. Biblical theology seeks to make the scriptures accessible to the church using the best scholarly resources. Homiletics seeks to render the Word of God in a manner that is faithful to the biblical witness, scholarship, and tradition, yet is specific to our time. Both disciplines are concerned with the meaning of the biblical text in its own context and with its meaning for today. Yet what each understands by these is different.

What the Text Meant

In biblical theology, "what the text meant" refers, naturally, to the historical reconstruction of the text, its setting, its social-cultural-political-religious background, and its history of scholarly problems and interpretations. In this century, a number of scholars have conceived of the possibility of a biblical interpretation that is largely objective, unaffected by one's faith tradition.[15] Debate raged over whether biblical theologians are to treat the Bible as scientifically as possible, in the same historical manner, for instance, as any other ancient text. The alternative is to treat the Bible as a document of faith, in which case certain prescriptive concerns become normative. Krister Stendahl argued, in a seminal essay, that the appropriate focus of biblical theology is on "what the text meant," that is, on the historical-critical descriptive method of reconstructing the biblical text in its own time and situation. To focus on "what the text means"[16] is normative and is the interpretive task, he argued, of the systematic theologian, not the biblical scholar. The general consensus today, of course, is against this separation of theology from what the text meant.

In homiletics, "what the text meant" can be similar: the recovery of the meaning of that text in its canonical biblical context through use of the best scholarly and critical resources of biblical theology. However, for obvious practical reasons imposed by the demands of the parish, this generally refers to a much abbreviated, more narrowly focused process: one specific meaning of the text in its own situation is the goal, chosen from several legitimate possibilities. This meaning is often referred to as *the central idea of the sermon* or *the sermon in a sentence*. Its advantage is not to oversimplify the text but rather to provide an accurate focus on it and to ensure simple, clear, and effective communication of the gospel to the congregation. In the sermon, this sentence will ideally be used to reconstruct the biblical text, context, and setting.

In the history of preaching, this central idea has often been either a single biblical verse or a doctrine found in it that, then, became the subject of the sermon. Homiletical development of this idea, traditionally, was in propositional-doctrinal format, although in recent decades, with the recovery of the pericope and the rediscovery of narrative in most disciplines, including biblical studies, retelling (to use Gerhard von Rad's term[17]) an aspect of the biblical story has become a common alternative. Reconstruction of a biblical text using either format in the sermon may achieve at least three goals: what the text actually said is established; the validity of the interpretation is evident; and the meaning is plainly understood and/or experienced in relation to the biblical setting.

One way of closing the distance between biblical studies and homiletics is to clarify different understandings of "what the text meant." Are differences merely to be attributed to different stages of the same process? What similarities are there between a preacher translating a text from its original language and reducing a text to a particular meaning? Are they two distinct kinds of hermeneutical activity? What is the dividing line between meaning for a biblical scholar and for a preacher? How does one articulate and defend the separateness of these activities?

What the Text Means

An even greater difference is evident between homiletics and biblical studies in the approach to "what the text means." In biblical theology, "what the text means" commonly has referred to the contemporary theological meaning of the text interpreted by either biblical scholars or systematic theologians.

In homiletics, this phrase usually refers to the specific meaning of the biblical text applied to the life of the congregation. This idea commonly identifies and addresses a contemporary need from a biblical and theological perspective. Said another way, it is not simply an extension of the biblical text. Stendahl suggested that "what the text meant" was an aspect of "original translation" whereas "what the text means" for the preacher is the life situation or *Sitz im Leben*.[18] Harry Emerson Fosdick, perhaps more helpfully, spoke of an *"object* to be achieved" as opposed to a *"subject* to be elucidated."[19] This contemporary idea is distinguished from the textual idea in a variety of paired terms that have emerged in homiletics since 1980: the "essence of the text in a sentence" and the "essence of the sermon in a sentence";[20] "what the text is saying" and "what the text is doing";[21] "the concern of the text" and "the concern of the sermon";[22] the "focus statement" and the "function statement";[23] the "controlling idea" and the "behavioral purpose."[24]

These terms have arisen to meet a need not being met by biblical scholars and theologians. How can preachers be guided in moving from biblical meanings to specific contemporary meanings? In other words, "what the text means" for the biblical scholar is not identical to "what the text means" for the preacher. The biblical scholar's commentary on the Bible leaves the preacher a long way from the pulpit. Preachers do not preach the commentaries, which is one reason *The New Interpreter's Bible* continues the practice of its predecessor in having a commentary section followed by a reflections section, offering "several trajectories of possible interpretation that connect with the situation of the contemporary listeners."[25] Even these trajectories are hit and miss, however, falling short of providing sound hermeneutical guidelines for homiletical accomplishment.

In homiletical theory that advocated an expository sermon format, contemporary possibilities for the biblical text were broadly covered by one word; what followed exegesis in the sermon was "application." The apparent simplicity of this essential move was deceptive. Recently application has been claimed as an essential part of the hermeneutical process.[26] It is identified and accomplished in various ways that help to indicate the complexity of the endeavor.

1. *Literal*. An understanding that the text means what it says bypasses the need to bridge a historical gap. Since the text means now what it meant then, ambiguity in the texts is effectively suppressed.[27]

2. *Synonym*. Brian Chapell claims that the Bible speaks directly to contemporary people. He assumes a common identity or synonymous relationship with the people in text.[28]

3. *Allegory*. In this, details of the text have one-to-one correspondence with events in our time, or with a typology brought to bear on the text. A recent book on preaching from Revelation was published to counter what its editors felt was possible misuse of apocalyptic allegory around the year 2000.[29]

4. *Analogy*. Stephen C. Farris advocates seeking some aspect of similarity in the biblical people or events, with people or events today, while allowing for many differences.[30]

5. *Metaphor*. Another approach, that for example of Eduard R. Riegert, describes as metaphor the tensive relationship between biblical text and stories from contemporary experience in the sermon; reality is imaginatively redescribed and new possibility becomes apparent.[31]

6. *Parable*. Some forms of narrative sermon intentionally mirror the open-ended parables of Jesus, inviting listeners to discern the connection with the biblical text or with their lives.[32]

7. *Image*. David Buttrick sees the text opening a field of meaning in the consciousness of the listener, like a camera that eventually allows the photographer to see more clearly what is being seen.[33] Alternatively, and experimentally, James A. Wallace advocates a Jungian approach, which anticipates biblical imagery addressing patterns in the human psyche.[34]

8. *Rhetoric*. Thomas G. Long suggests that the rhetorical function of literary forms of biblical texts can provide the bridge to today.[35]

9. *Metonymy*. Metonymy establishes linear relationships with ideas, events, or people in the biblical text on the basis of historical or theological causality or on the basis of contiguity (for example, a ritual mentioned in the biblical text leads the preacher to speak of church today).[36]

Not all biblical scholars or theologians have acknowledged the need for preachers to move from biblical meanings to specific contemporary meanings in the manner indicated. One reason has been the insufficient attention given to homiletics on the part of the church at large. Many scholars today were brought up with an understanding that a properly exegeted biblical text was itself the sermon, for it was already effectively addressing our time. Other scholars were taught that homiletics classes merely provided the right speaking or illustration of material. Others learned that preaching cannot be taught.

The appropriate contemporary meaning for many scholars was broad, general, conceptual, and theological in contrast to the historical meaning of the text. Von Rad, ahead of Hans Frei,[37] recognized the problem of reducing biblical texts to concepts and, thus, encouraged "retelling" the Old Testament text in the present time as the best means "actualizing"[38] or contemporizing it.[39] For Karl Barth, the Holy Spirit would convict the individual faithful listener of the specific meaning that text in the current day. Barth sought to avoid attention to rhetoric, reference to the self in the sermon, or to specific current events, for these were distractions from the task of proclaiming God's Word.[40] Scholars in homiletics are in general agreement concerning Barth's error. The preacher cannot assume to have a biblically literate or even interested congregation. The effect of Barth's understanding on a generation of preachers, says Buttrick, was disastrous:

> Barth in some ways all but destroyed preaching in the name of the Bible. He threw out sermon introductions because they might imply some sort of "point of contact," some natural affinity for the gospel in the human sphere; he lopped off conclusions because they might express works-righteousness. Above all, he denied social relevance: "The Preacher," he wrote, "must preach the Bible and *nothing* else." As a result, preaching became for Barth the reiteration of a biblical text . . . in which public events are excised from sermons.[41]

The problem Buttrick saw in Barth was a homiletic rooted in the objective/subjective split of the Enlightenment; it was "either objectively rational or subjectively romantic," when what was needed was a meeting of the two, as takes place, for instance, in human consciousness.[42]

Dissolution of "What the Text Meant" and "What the Text Means"

In recent years, the distinction in biblical theology between "what the text meant" and "what the text means" has been diminished. Many scholars, including R. E. Clements,[43] Paul D. Hanson,[44] Brevard S. Childs,[45] and

Walter Brueggemann,[46] in different ways argue that a rigid historical-critical descriptive approach overlooks the canon's function as revelation in the community of faith. In other words, the biblical texts can be interpreted correctly only by also considering the God to whom they point and the faith they nurture. Each of these approaches has positive implications for preaching. So general now is the rejection of the objective histori-cal-critical descriptive approach to the Old Testament that Hasel claims, "The Gabler-Wrede-Stendahl approach of 'what it meant' and 'what it means' has been seriously, if not irreparably, eroded, and may actually be rejected."[47]

What is replacing this distinction in biblical theology? Brevard Childs provides one important alternative in his agenda to recover the Bible as a document of faith. Twenty-five years ago he was already seeking to do away with what he called the "iron curtain" in biblical criticism between "what it meant" and "what it means."[48] He eventually proposed a union between the historical-descriptive task and the theological-constructive task, with priority and normative value given to the latter. The prehistory of the text was less important than the canonical forces that appropriated and shaped it as normative for the community of faith. The kerygmatic content of the New Testament could never be reduced to its history, just as the divine revelation of the Old Testament could never be separated from the form given it by Israel.[49] Theological responsibility lay "in following with precision the direction which is given by the shaping of the text itself, and to relate one's modern theological reflection to the unique dynamic which arises from the Bible's intertextuality."[50] For instance, how did the faith community's understanding of the identity of God or the Lordship of Jesus affect the final form of the canon?

Childs is reclaiming faith as a necessary tool for biblical theology, for in spite of the diversity of scripture and the limitations of history, "the true witness of the gospel can be heard in the sacred text through the continu-ing work of the Spirit. The New Testament is not a dead document need-ing to be purified, but a living voice waiting to be heard."[51] Moreover, all scripture points to Christ, and this "one scope of scripture" guides the interpretation of each passage.[52] This recovery of Reformed understand-ing of scripture has the resurrected Christ, not a particular theological doctrine, as the unifying center of the New Testament witness and the norm of biblical theology. "What the text meant" and "what the text means" are not radically different; they are united in the ongoing faith of the believing community.

Walter Brueggemann, one of a few biblical scholars who has devoted considerable writing to preaching,[53] provides another alternative to "what it meant." Old Testament faith may be articulated, he says, using a bipolar

dialectic: "in the fray" (e.g., Norman Gottwald) uses literary and sociological approaches to disclose "how we got the text"; whereas "above the
fray" (e.g., Brevard Childs) uses the final canonical form of the Bible to
determine "what the text is," that is, the text that matters theologically.[54]
Both are needed. Brueggemann's interest, significantly for preaching, is
not "with the process and character of the text, but with the process and
character of God met in the text."[55] A similar bipolar dialectic may be heard
in his words concerning the meaning of that text today: "in the fray" of
Israel's experience with structures and pain we find reflected the "ambiguity of our experiences"; "beyond the fray" of experience the faithful community discovers in the text "a normative standing place."[56] In other
words, transition to the present is made theologically. Brueggemann, like
Childs, assumes the constancy and oneness of God, in the midst of frac-
tured reality, ambiguity, and change.[57]

What is happening in the dissolution of "what the text meant" and
"what the text means" in biblical theology is the recovery of theology,
with God at the center, for the entire task of exegesis and interpretation.
This is an important help to preaching, which, following biblical criticism,
has become perhaps too focused on biblical history. Yet if "meant" and
"means" are to be dropped in biblical theology, they are of lasting importance in the preacher's hermeneutical endeavor to close the "two horizons," ancient and contemporary. It is still important to ask, At the end
point of biblical studies, are preachers much closer to the pulpit than in
previous eras? Academic pursuit cannot be reduced to pragmatic concerns, yet it is also less rich without them. Is the exegesis students are
taught most helpful for the pulpit? Are some courses, for example, those
on Q, best left for postgraduate studies, or do they assist students to
become better preachers?

There is another matter of concern. The Reformers could not conceive
of the Word of God separate from its correct interpretation in preaching.
Even as historical-descriptive approaches rendered the Bible theologically
mute, theological approaches to the canon are in danger of leaving the
pulpit mute concerning the Word of God. The silence of most scholars on
the subject of preaching may be an unexamined remnant from the former
science/faith split of exegesis/interpretation. This silence, nonetheless,
implies that primary access to the Word of God is other than in the church
at worship, which the scholar's desk is meant to assist. The history of the
community's reception of scripture in worship cannot meaningfully be
excluded from the exegetical enterprise any more than the contemporary
sermon can be considered as separate from a biblical text's contemporary
interpretation. Priority in scholarship still needs to be given to recovery of
the pulpit.

Changing Needs of the Pulpit

A final reason for the distance between biblical theology and homiletics is the changing needs of the pulpit brought on by sweeping changes in culture. Homiletics cannot avoid addressing facts like the decline in mainline church membership,[58] newcomers with little or no church background; many philosophies, religions, and groups competing for an individual's interest, loyalty, and time; mass media altering how people think and the rules for good communication; and erosion of the authority of institutions and their representatives, including preachers.

In such a climate, the sermon must be as persuasive as possible, hence the need for attention to appropriate rhetoric for the pulpit. The congregation needs to be given good reasons for accepting what is said. The preacher seeks to allow God and the Bible to set the agenda for preaching in relation to the local congregation, yet must be attentive to cultural factors that will facilitate or impair communication of the Word.

Here there is neither space nor need to detail what many scholars in homiletics have discussed elsewhere. A few of the crucial new demands on preachers may be mentioned to underscore challenges that preachers are having to face, without adjustments in the help they are receiving from biblical theologians: (1) Sermon time in the past century has generally dropped in Protestant churches from often over an hour to less than twenty minutes. Less time is available to do exegesis in the preacher's week, much less to present it in the sermon. Homiletical treatment of the Bible must be well focused and condensed in a clear, succinct fashion; (2) Sermons need to be less focused on information and lecturing and more focused on communication, for instance, paying attention to classical categories of pathos and ethos, in addition to logos, and to narrative and experience; (3) Sermons need to be more sensory, in particular more visual, as various media affect ways of contemporary thought. For instance, intertextual biblical material may be of less significance for the sermon than literary and sociological material that allows preachers visually to present biblical texts within the richness of their lived settings; (4) Finally, even as many preachers need to refocus on God, thus having God and humanity as their subject, many need to be attentive to the manner in which sermon form and sermon theology are related matters. Sermon form imposes a theology on the sermon in ways that affect biblical interpretation.[59] These kinds of matters can be shared interests of scholars in the quadrivium, in a manner envisioned by Schleiermacher, or they can be cause for ongoing division.

NOTES

1. David Buttrick, *A Captive Voice: The Liberation of Preaching* (Louisville, Ky.: Westminster John Knox Press, 1994), 12. See esp. 8–12, 62.
2. Ibid., 73–74.
3. Ibid., 110.
4. Ibid., 12.
5. Ibid., 89, 74.
6. Gerhard F. Hasel, *Old Testament Theology: Basic Issues in the Current Debate* (1972; rev. ed., Grand Rapids: Wm. B. Eerdmans Publishing Co., 1991), 26.
7. See, for instance, Walter Wink, *The Bible in Human Transformation: Toward a New Paradigm for Biblical Study* (Philadelphia: Fortress Press, 1974), 6, and Thomas C. Oden, *After Modernity . . . What? Agenda for Theology* (Grand Rapids: Zondervan Publishing House, 1990), 106–7. See also Stanley Hauerwas, *Unleashing the Scripture: Freeing the Bible from Captivity to America* (Nashville: Abingdon Press, 1993).
8. These and related points are argued in Paul S. Wilson, *The Practice of Preaching* (Nashville: Abingdon Press, 1995), 139–40, 155–56, 189–93.
9. Friedrich Schleiermacher, *Christian Caring: Selections from Practical Theology*, ed. James O. Duke and Howard Stone, trans. James O. Duke (Philadelphia: Fortress Press, 1988), 99.
10. One such area is practical theology. Faith, Schleiermacher says in *Christian Caring*, "constantly gives rise to activity" (91). Yet this activity does not lead all equally to pursue unity of the community, for "it is one thing to possess the spirit of Christianity inwardly and another thing to exhibit the common spirit outwardly in our actions" (91). Thus the aim of practical theology is "that of giving coherence to our activity and making it clear and deliberative" (100). In assessing this union of action and purpose, he understood practical theology as *technik* or rules of art that were separate from knowledge (92–93), yet equal to it, for only by this could leadership be produced.
11. See esp. Friedrich Schleiermacher, *Brief Outline on the Study of Theology*, trans. Terrence N. Nice (Richmond: John Knox Press, 1966), secs. 3 and 17.
12. See ibid., esp. secs. 6, 12, 16, 18, 25, 27.
13. See ibid., esp. secs. 9, 12, 14, 20, 26. Schleiermacher identifies elsewhere that "the term 'practical' is not altogether correct, for practical theology is not practice but the theory of practice. . . . If the true goal of theology is to carry out an activity, practical theology could be said to be theology proper and the other [theological] sciences, mere auxiliaries to it. But . . . the relationship among the disciplines is quite different—not one of subordination but rather more of equality" (*Christian Caring*, 89).
14. Schleiermacher, *Brief Outline*, 12. See also James O. Duke and Howard Stone, "An Orientation to Schleiermacher's Practical Theology," in Schleiermacher, *Christian Caring*, 19.
15. For instance, see Hasel's discussion of this in his *Old Testament Theology*, 30–38.
16. Krister Stendahl, "Biblical Theology, Contemporary," *Interpreter's Dictionary of the Bible*, 1, esp. 419–32 (Nashville: Abingdon Press, 1964); and "Method in the Study of Biblical Theology," in *The Bible in Modern Scholarship: Papers Read at the 100th Meeting of the Society for Biblical Literature*, ed. J. Phillip Hyatt (Nashville: Abingdon Press, 1965), 196–209.

17. Gerhard von Rad, *Old Testament Theology*, vol. 1: *The Theology of Israel's Historical Traditions*, trans. David M. G. Stalker (New York: Harper & Row, 1962), 121.
18. Stendahl, "Biblical Theology," 430.
19. Harry Emerson Fosdick, *The Living of These Days* (New York: Harper & Brothers, 1956), 99.
20. Harold T. Bryson and James C. Taylor, *Building Sermons to Meet People's Needs* (Nashville: Broadman Press, 1980), 52–68.
21. Fred B. Craddock, *Preaching* (Nashville: Abingdon Press, 1985), 123.
22. Paul S. Wilson, *Imagination of the Heart: New Understandings in Preaching* (Nashville: Abingdon Press, 1988), 70–72, 85–86.
23. Thomas G. Long, *The Witness of Preaching* (Louisville, Ky.: Westminster/John Knox Press, 1989), 86–91.
24. Henry H. Mitchell, *Celebration and Experience in Preaching* (Nashville: Abingdon Press, 1990), 52.
25. *The New Interpreter's Bible*, vol. 1 (Nashville: Abingdon Press, 1994), xviii.
26. Wilson, *Practice*, 125–94.
27. James Barr provides important insights to use of the literal in *The Bible in the Modern World* (London: SCM and Philadelphia: Trinity Press International, 1973, 1990), 168ff.
28. Brian Chapell, *Christ-Centered Preaching: Redeeming the Expository Sermon* (Nashville: Baker Books, 1994). See also a review by Wilson in *Homiletic* 20:1 (summer 1995): 11–14.
29. Cornish R. Rogers and Joseph R. Jeter, Jr., eds., *Preaching Through the Apocalypse: Sermons from Revelation* (St. Louis: Chalice Press, 1990).
30. Stephen C. Farris, "It's About Time," in *New Teaching, New Preaching*, ed. Peter G. White (Toronto: United Church Publishing House, 1991), 2–14.
31. Eduard R. Riegert, *Imaginative Shock: Preaching and Metaphor* (Burlington, ON: Trinity Press, 1990). See also Wilson, *Practice*, 238–63.
32. Writers on this are too numerous to catalog here, but an obvious place to start is Eugene L. Lowry, *How to Preach a Parable: Designs in Narrative Sermons* (Nashville: Abingdon Press, 1989).
33. David Buttrick, *Homiletic: Moves and Structures* (Philadelphia: Fortress Press, 1987), 294, 301. See also his "On Doing Homiletics Today," in *Intersections: Post-Critical Studies in Preaching*, ed. Richard L. Eslinger (Grand Rapids: Wm. B. Eerdmans Publishing Co., 1994), 88–104; esp. 104, where he calls for homiletics to "find a home in models of revelation that relate to images and symbols in social consciousness."
34. James A. Wallace, *Imaginal Preaching* (Mahwah, N.J.: Paulist Press, 1995).
35. Thomas G. Long, *Preaching and the Literary Forms of the Bible* (Philadelphia: Fortress Press, 1989).
36. Wilson, *Practice*, 220–37.
37. Hans Frei, *The Eclipse of Biblical Narrative* (New Haven, Conn.: Yale University Press, 1974).
38. Joseph W. Groves, *Actualization and Interpretation in the OT* (Atlanta: Scholars Press, 1987), 5–62. He identifies three types of actualization in Von Rad: literary (having to do with images), cultic, and chronological.
39. Von Rad, *Theology of Israel's Historical Traditions*, 121.
40. Typical of Barth's remarks is his admonition, "Avoid drawing special attention to particular events or commemorations." Karl Barth, *The Preaching of the Gospel*, trans. B. E. Hooke (Philadelphia: Westminster Press, 1963), 58–59.

41. Buttrick, *A Captive Voice*, 8. See also his "On Doing Homiletics Today," esp. 94.
42. Buttrick, "On Doing Homiletics Today," 104.
43. R. E. Clements, *Old Testament Theology: A Fresh Approach* (Atlanta: John Knox Press, 1978). He says, "If we restrict ourselves solely to reading the Old Testament as an ancient text, and endeavour to hear in it nothing that the ancient author could not have intended, then we should be denying something of the tradition which asserts that God has continued to speak to his people through it" (19).
44. Paul D. Hanson, *Dynamic Transcendence: The Correlation of Confessional Heritage and Contemporary Experience in a Biblical Model of Divine Activity* (Philadelphia: Fortress Press, 1978). The events of the Old Testament must be understood, he says, from within the framework of that faith community's dynamic vision of God's actions that continue to the present.
45. Brevard S. Childs, *Introduction to the Old Testament as Scripture* (Philadelphia: Fortress Press, 1979).
46. Walter Brueggemann, *Old Testament Theology: Essays on Structure, Theme and Text* (Minneapolis: Fortress Press, 1992).
47. Hasel, *Old Testament Theology*, 83.
48. Brevard S. Childs, *Biblical Theology in Crisis* (Philadelphia: Westminster Press, 1970), 141–42.
49. Brevard S. Childs, *Old Testament Theology in a Canonical Context* (Philadelphia: Fortress Press, 1986), 12.
50. Ibid., 154.
51. Brevard S. Childs, *Biblical Theology of the Old and New Testaments: Theological Reflection on the Christian Bible* (Minneapolis: Fortress Press, 1993), 215.
52. Ibid., 725.
53. In addition to his commentaries and other books, see esp. Walter Brueggemann, *Finally Comes the Poet: Daring Speech for Proclamation* (Minneapolis: Fortress Press, 1989). See also his "The Social Nature of the Biblical Text for Preaching," in *Preaching as a Social Act: Theology and Practice*, ed. Arthur van Seters (Nashville: Abingdon Press, 1988), 127–65.
54. Brueggemann, *Old Testament Theology*, 3–4.
55. Ibid., 4.
56. Ibid., 4–5.
57. Ibid., 43 and n. 29.
58. See John Killinger, *Preaching to a Church in Crisis: A Homiletic for the Last Days of the Mainline Church* (Lima, Ohio: CSS Publishing Co., 1995).
59. Wilson, *Practice*, 105ff.

14

Apocalyptic Vocation and Liberation: The Foolish Church in the World

L. SUSAN BOND

Apocalyptic makes most preachers uneasy. We shudder at the whiff of sulphur from a bottomless pit and run for shelter when squadrons of angels parachute from the clouds. Faith healings, storm stillings, miraculous resurrections! Not long ago, New Testament scholar Paul Minear wrote that some of the supernatural elements in the Gospel of John "repelled me more strongly than I have been ready to admit even to myself."[1] Theologians and biblical scholars can elaborate the religious culture that spun out fantastic stories, but the preacher is the one who faces the fidgety Sunday-morning crowd with the practical dilemma, How do we preach it? What on earth do we do with the walking dead, extraterrestrial visitors, and Godzilla-like sea monsters?

Apocalyptic Myth and the Self

Following Rudolf Bultmann and the New Hermeneutics, often we have assumed that the problem can be solved by substituting a modern worldview for the supernatural one. We have demythologized and then remythologized most of the New Testament into categories more comfortable to the twentieth-century mind. Bultmann's extentialist approach to interpreting mythological metaphors assumed that hermeneutical presuppositions were unavoidable but that the right presuppositions would yield authentic biblical meaning. He assumed that the Word of God "addresses man in his personal existence," giving "freedom from the world and from the sorrow and anxiety which overwhelm him when he forgets the beyond."[2]

The core meaning of biblical faith was addressed to a general human condition: the anxiety of the individual. This "life-relation" of anxiety toward the future and its misdirected grasping after worldly security was, for Bultmann, the fundamental human problem to which biblical faith provided an answer. The eschatological dimension of faith was in its rein-

terpretation of the individual's future in God. This was the deeper meaning of the mythological preaching of Jesus: to provide the individual with
the confidence to be open to God's future; "to be prepared for this future
which can come as a thief in the night when we do not expect it; to be prepared, because this future will be a judgment on all men who have bound
themselves to this world and are not free, not open to God's future."[3] The
solution to twentieth-century alienation was the individual's reunion with
God. Bultmann's approach was a theological update of the Platonic soul
with its worldly appetites,[4] a Greek psychology of love, that assumed a
human incompleteness, and Augustine's "restless heart," longing for rest
in God. The psychological approaches are alike in their assumption that
the primary reunion or reconciliation is an individual one, "each of us . . .
forever seeking the half that will tally with himself."[5] The individual finds
his or her lost half, the restless soul finds solace in God, the alienated person finds meaning in God's future.

Bultmann's approach has had a lasting grip on interpreting the wildly
mythological language of apocalyptic for a number of reasons. Of course,
it had the advantage of rationalizing the apparently irrational. But beyond
that, existentialist demythologizing, with its undertones of personal psychology, was a snug fit with two hundred years of highly individualized
personal piety in America. The rugged individualism of Paul Tillich's
"courage to be" smacks of the stoicism that already characterized much of
American frontier revivalism and its "personal relationship with Jesus
Christ."[6] By the middle of the twentieth century, most mainline preaching
served up a strange brew of Freudian therapy (another tripartite division
of the human psyche), pastoral counseling, existential personalism,
American individualism, and psychological revivalism. The effect was to
reduce the cosmic drama to an inner search for personal meaning. Healing
stories are treated more like self-help parables than glimpses of God's radical intentions for the world.

This type of demythologizing has stripped more than supernaturalism
from the tradition. It has also peeled away the prophetic, social, and political dimension of most Christian rhetoric, that is, all those elements that
power structures find so troubling. So even though we remember Ernst
Käsemann's sound bite that apocalyptic is the mother of all Christian theology, we are more likely to treat it like a loony cousin, slightly embar-
rassing and better kept at a safe distance.[7]

Bultmann, and the whole trajectory of existentialist scholarship, considered the metaphorical nature of apocalyptic as otherworldly to be
referring to something other than the social and historical realm, and
rejected it accordingly. Apocalyptic was understood to be unredeemably
escapist, in direct opposition to prophetic eschatology. The Käsemann-

Fuchs-Ebeling controversy of the late 1960s was grounded on just such an argument, with Ernst Fuchs and Gerhard Ebeling arguing that apocalyptic must be abandoned for a more realized existentialist eschatology. Ebeling's response to Käsemann's essay blasted its "dangerous tendency to construct history and to deal wholesale with it in a highly abstract way—in other words, actually to escape from history."[8] Taking history seriously was not "a thing we owe to apocalyptic."[9]

Apocalyptic Myth
and the Social World

But, the old assumptions that apocalyptic is concerned about justice in heaven and that prophecy is concerned about justice on earth are neither helpful nor accurate. Apocalyptic refers unabashedly to cosmic, social, and political realities. As a worldview or theological position, apocalyptic has an eschatological interest in the redemption of the world. Its audience is probably not the secular individual caught in personal anxiety but the faith community at odds with the secular world. The confessing community, not the fearless individual, is expected to be a glimpse of a new social order. Nothing less than the future redemption of the entire natural and social order hangs in the balance. The whole cosmos groans for rebirth. Apocalyptic seems to be more concerned with the reunion of creation and God than the reunion of individual selves with the Divine.

Paul Hanson's work on apocalyptic biblical literature deals extensively with the social dimensions of apocalyptic. His work allows a conversation among three distinct fields of scholarship: eschatological theology within the Judeo-Christian tradition, sociological analysis, and language/symbol theories. Hanson intends to "refocus the discussion of apocalypticism upon the ancient texts themselves and upon the sociological matrices within which those texts took form."[10] He assumes that the prophetic traditions of Israel and the apocalyptic mentality of the postexilic communities are part of a continuum. Apocalyptic eschatology "is the mode assumed by the prophetic tradition once it had been transferred to a new and radically altered setting in the post-exilic community."[11]

Hanson distinguishes prophetic eschatology and apocalyptic eschatology primarily by the degree to which each brand considers human agency possible.[12] In prophetic eschatology, human agency is considered the tool of divine plans, so prophetic activity is usually directly engaged in confrontation, criticism. Apocalyptic eschatology, says Hanson, is that which no longer considers human agency either possible or effective.[13] For this group, the eschatological vision is that which provides courage and hope for the faithful to endure oppression and suffering. Generally, Hanson characterizes prophetic eschatology as hopeful and optimistic about the possibilities for change through human agency, while apocalyptic movements are characterized theologically by an orientation toward cosmology, crisis, and two-age drama; they assume a more pessimistic and isolationist stance, "waiting for the divine judgement of God."[14]

Both brands consider their position to be critiques of their particular political and historical contexts, both appeal to God's purposes with regard to history, and both orient toward the future characterized by divine redemption. In general, the point of departure is the social reality of oppression or human evil. Both brands involve critique and judgment of society. Stephen O'Leary considers time, evil, and authority to be the three topoi of apocalyptic rhetoric.[15] But, questions of theodicy, the reality of human evil and human suffering, are fundamental to all types of theological eschatology. As Wendy Farley puts it, "the recognition of the phenomenon of radical suffering will affect the way Christian theology understands the nature of evil and, correlatively, the goodness and power of God."[16] Evil and suffering are human problems, manifest as social realities that limit life possibilities. Whether eschatology is of the prophetic or the apocalyptic type, it ultimately deals with the present social reality of evil and an imagined future where evil is absent.

While Hanson's field is Hebrew Bible, his work is significant for studies of New Testament apocalyptic. He connects prophecy with apocalyptic and establishes Jewish sources for the type of apocalyptic eschatology of the pre- and post-Easter church.

Historical scholarly debates had argued for the position that the type of apocalyptic language used in the early Christian communities was ultimately a history-denying, spiritualized experience, an eschatology that was "realized" within the believer or within the community. C. H. Dodd argued that Jesus' kingdom teachings referred to this type of realized spiritual community, and that the futuristic element didn't emerge until increasing frustration with delayed Parousia. Dodd suggested that both prophetic and apocalyptic eschatology are futuristically oriented "mistakes" of the early Christian community relative to Jesus' teachings. Bluntly, claimed Dodd, Jesus didn't teach about a tilt toward the future; his eschatology was fully realized.[17]

Dale Allison works out of a model similar to Hanson's and argues for the reversal of Dodd.[18] He claims that inaugurated eschatology was characteristic of the primitive church. Inaugurated eschatology is a process of redemption, with a beginning and a consummation, and an interim period of worldly struggle. He grounds much of his argument on the apocalyptic understanding of the general resurrection of the dead. The resurrection of Jesus terrified the early believers, since they understood it as the beginning of the general resurrection and a herald of the interim period of conflict. The conflict would not end until the general resurrection of the faithful was consummated. "The eschatological process was believed to have begun because certain eschatological promises had seemingly been fulfilled."[19] Christ's resurrection fulfilled a promise and was good news, since it signaled that the new creation had begun. It was terrifying news for the believers, since it meant that the period of trial and persecution was ahead of them. The symbol of the general resurrection of the faithful functioned as a vision of full reconciliation.

Allison's work is significant relative to Hanson's because he works with clusters of eschatological symbols and develops a future-oriented worldview that expresses itself in the language of historical crisis, physical suffering, and cosmic reversal. Allison, Hanson, and Minear support at the theological and semiotic level what Amos Wilder claims for the future tilt of New Testament rhetoric. In the "speech-acts" of the early church "[t]he believer did not hear it as a record of the past. With the brotherhood he found himself in the middle of the world-changing transaction of conflict, death and glory. . . . [F]or the Roman Church in a situation of persecution . . . [the rhetoric] presents the 'way' of Christ, the way of life in two successive phases which are yet telescoped."[20]

If we reconfigure Bultmann's assumptions into social categories, the eschatological dimension of faith is to provide the faith community with the confidence to be open to God's future. And the church can be faithful toward the purpose of reuniting the alienated world with God. As Edmund Husserl points out, time-consciousness happens and functions in the present. Amos Wilder, Minear, Dietrich Bonhoeffer, and others will argue that language about the past and about the future actually happen in the present. David Buttrick claims that our preaching invokes the presence of Christ. The Jesus of the past and the christological future take present shape in the faith-consciousness of the hearers. "Christian preaching paints images of expectation, indeed of salvation, so that the future of Jesus Christ can shape our common lives now."[21]

Apocalyptic Myth and Christian Vocation

But how does such an understanding shape our common lives now? How do concepts about the future shape the way social groups or moral communities function? We can shift from psychological theories to sociological theories, since we are concerned with preaching as a social act, addressed to a group, not to an individual psyche. Karl Mannheim's watershed work on the sociology of knowledge developed an analysis of the overarching myths by which societies stabilize and transform themselves. He distinguished between fictions (ideologies) and wish-dreams (utopias). Utopian ideas and ideologies differ primarily with regard to their relationship to the prevailing social order. Both ideologies and utopias are thought constructs that have a transcendent quality, but ideologies are "organically and harmoniously integrated into the world-view characteristic of the period (i.e., did not offer revolutionary possibilities)."[22] As mythical social constructs, both are similar to what Peter Berger has called "sacred canopies" and to what Berger and Thomas Luckmann call "symbolic universes."[23]

What Mannheim called utopias function, to some extent, as secular counterparts of theologically idealized future visions. Even though utopian visions are distortions, "incongruous with the state of reality" within which they occur, they also critique reality.[24] They depart from ideologies and are properly called utopian states of mind, which, "when they pass over into conduct, tend to shatter, either partially or wholly, the order of things prevailing at the time."[25] Utopian myths question the prevailing order. They provide legitimacy for either social revolution or liberal humanitarian evolution.[26]

Paul Ricoeur, in his *Lectures on Ideology and Utopia*, reclaims a more positive interpretation of ideologies as integrative social constructs. He agrees with Mannheim, though, that they legitimate existing institutions. Societies need the balance of utopias, which are "imaginative alternatives" that "open the possible" and offer a creative, future-oriented complement to the more conservative, integrative work of ideology.[27] "We may then place religion in a dialectical position between ideology and utopia. Religion functions as an ideology when it justifies the existing system of power, but it also functions as utopia to the extent that it is a motivation nourishing . . . critique."[28] Ricoeur distinguishes these religious functions in much the same way that cultural anthropologist Victor Turner distinguishes between ceremony, which reinforces the social order, and ritual, which can challenge social order.[29] Turner claims that ritual, with its more liminal and ambiguous nature, allows flexibility for redefining social roles.

Apocalyptic consciousness, or the apocalyptic mode of being presented in the New Testament, assumes that the visionary alternatives function within the community in the present. Although the language is about the future, it functions in the present for hope and for critique. Walter Brueggemann claims this type of alternative consciousness as fundamentally prophetic. Prophecy does not abandon the visionary future by a blind focus on the ground of present social action. And prophecy does not abandon the present by a squint into the mists of a heavenly hereafter. "The task of prophetic ministry is to nurture, nourish, and evoke a consciousness and perception alternative to the consciousness and perception of the dominant culture around us . . . with addressing . . . the dominant crisis that is enduring and resilient, of having our alternative vocation co-opted and domesticated."[30] Brueggemann allows that the alternative consciousness may address specific concrete issues, but that the real crisis is more enduring and runs beyond any specific issue. "Ad hoc liberals run from issue to issue without discerning the enduring domestication of vision in all of them."[31]

In contrast to the earlier assumed opposition between prophetic and apocalyptic eschatology, the two seem to be dimensions of the same phenomenon. An apocalyptic consciousness, the consciousness of an impossible possibility, is the foundation of prophetic activity. Prophetic activity that settles for practical or realistic goals always runs the risk of being co-opted. Such a compromise with or confirmation of actual social structures is precisely when a transformative vision shifts toward the ideological. History shows us that revolutionaries quickly become tyrants as soon as the power struggle ends. The same vision, alternative, or religious activity can function to confirm or transform. The caveat from Mannheim, Ricoeur, Brueggemann, and Turner is crucial. It is precisely the fantastic and improbable nature of visions that allows their transcendence and also allows for their critical possibilities.

Apocalyptic Myth
and Proclamation

But if apocalyptic eschatology is a theological perspective or worldview that takes the real world seriously, it is one frequently uttered in the poetic language of the surreal. The distinction is helpful to make, since the failure to make these distinctions has probably fomented much of the modern and postmodern rejection of New Testament apocalyptic. What is the relationship between the bizarre mythopoetic language of apocalyptic and the social reality (evil or idealized) to which to it points? Bluntly, can we maintain apocalyptic consciousness without apocalyptic language?

As a literary genre, apocalyptic involves poetic devices of a heavenly journey, battle scenes, cosmic catastrophe, and angelic supernatural spirit guides.[32] In the New Testament, the book of Revelation is the epitome of the genre. But the Gospels, Acts, and the Pauline letters also have apocalyptic flavor if not apocalyptic drama.[33] The ahistorical nature, the heavenly metaphors, and the cosmic sweep of apocalyptic suggest that the alternative to a world characterized by radical evil and sin is so beyond our real experience that only poetic language will suffice. Elements of apocalyptic worldview surface even in the language of texts we don't consider to be in the literary genre of apocalypse. Epiphanies, theophanies, transfigurations, angels, Satanic agents, nature miracles, and healing miracles are the nuts and bolts of most of the New Testament.

Minear points out that the most fundamental metaphors and images of the tradition, Baptism and the Lord's Supper, are grounded in apocalyptic understandings. Apocalyptic understandings provide the metaphorical clusters that defined daily Christian vocation, and Minear demands that the linguistic origins must be understood and respected for what they disclosed.[34] Baptism and the Lord's Supper marked this strange telescoping of time, where the believers were still in the world but already living in the promises of future vindication. As the saints press on toward their salvation, as disciples are thrown in jail, the proclamation of the church in word and sacrament assures the community that God is present to this drama in the mysterious presence of a dead/alive Savior.

Evoking this apocalyptic consciousness with respect to the metaphorical language of the tradition is central to the prophetic nature of Christian preaching.[35] Preaching is the task of making the highly symbolic and idealized future present to the imagination of a believing community, for the purpose of defining the worldly vocation of that community. Preaching is both hopeful and critical. As hope, Christian preaching proclaims that no matter how bad things are, God's redemptive presence can turn things around. As critique, Christian preaching proclaims that the sovereignty of Jesus the Christ strips ultimate authority from earthly lords. God's ultimate purpose for the world relativizes all other claims.

Rodney Kennedy's recent book on metaphor and rhetorical homiletics claims that apocalyptic consciousness is the essential rhetorical and metaphorical strategy necessary to Christian preaching.[36] He uses Ricoeur's definition of metaphor as epistemic. Metaphors produce new meaning and understanding by virtue of metaphorical tension.[37] Metaphors disclose the similarities in dissimilar concepts. Metaphor is not deviant language or mere ornamentation (to smack Plato around a little bit) but is, in fact, original language, prior to rational language. Metaphors do their work, they produce meaning, as Sallie McFague points out, "by using the similar to move into the unknown."[38] One word rubs up against another, involving tension of meaning. Again, in the words of McFague, metaphorical statements "always contain the whisper, 'it is and it is not.'"[39]

To say that time is money is to say that time is like money, in some ways, but is not exactly the same as money in all ways. Metaphors highlight or disclose meaning at the same time they minimize or veil other meanings. Metaphors cannot be literally interpreted or reduced and, so, defy the grasp of propositional statements. They do, however, cast shape, projecting horizons of meaning.[40] Ricoeur claims that they are types, both archetypical and prototypical, having an original or archetypal spark of meaning that is not exhausted at the original level. Metaphors also have a teleological burst toward the production of new meaning.[41] Metaphorical language is a boundary violator (to use a delightfully apocalyptic image) that creates thought in an indirect, open-ended, ambiguous, and revolutionary way. Metaphor redescribes reality. Metaphor, as primal speech or original language, calls worlds into being.

Rhetoric is a strategy for putting metaphor and its poor cousin, propositional language, together in persuasive discourse. Rhetoric involves the invention of strategy. As discourse rhetoric exists in the twilight zone of what is contingent but uncertain. Rhetoric cannot prove or disprove, but is epistemic or, to use a perfectly good religious word, a revelatory discourse that produces action-directed meaning.[42] Rhetorical discourse can either argue somewhat inductively toward a preferred structure of reality or it can assume a structure of reality and argue from it. Rhetoric produces meaning by the use of metaphorical language, put together in such a way to flow from or point to a structure of reality.[43] To paraphrase Kennedy, rhetoric is the strategic use of metaphors to construct an alternative reality or to assume that reality from the outset and then examine its dimensions.

Kennedy's rhetorical/metaphorical homiletic uses apocalyptic consciousness as the key. Apocalyptic consciousness redescribes reality by reference to an impossible or unimaginable possibility. Preaching describes the world as it is, whispering "it is," and redescribes a new world whispering "it is not yet." The new world is one radically permeated by the presence of the vision of God's purpose for the world. Preaching evokes apocalyptic consciousness by offering an alternative vision that offers hope to the oppressed and a critique of the oppressors.

As such, preaching is a rhetoric of folly,[44] including hope for things unseen and a rebuke for the powers and principalities of this world. A rhetoric of folly involves that strange dialectic of power through weakness, strength through vulnerability,[45] and victory through failure.

The central metaphors of the cross and resurrection are social. As metaphorical identity for a community, they go up against the success and death metaphors of dominant culture. For the Christian community, success is understood as cross-bearing and challenges the cultural norms of conformity, self-indulgence, and greed. The community of believers fulfills its vocation by pouring itself out for the world. Resurrection is also a social metaphor. Rather than individual rebirth or new beginning, the church becomes the community already living "in the world" but not "of the world." As the Pauline writer has it, God has chosen what is weak and foolish, by worldly standards, to shame what the world considers powerful. "God chose what is low and despised in the world, things that are not, to reduce to nothing things that are" (1 Cor. 1:28).

As a rhetoric of hope, Christian preaching forms the alternative consciousness of those the world considers low and despised, so that they may persist in the face of apparent worldly failure. Liberation theologians, African American theologians, and feminist theologians see the power of apocalyptic consciousness for resistance and for challenging those in power. At the rhetorical level, liberation preachers construct identification with those who have been faithful unto death, those who have risked everything and have already begun living new lives in the resurrection hope of a new creation. Those who are slaves and servants of Christ have no earthly masters, nothing can scare them into silence or inactivity. The oppressed who have put on Christ have nothing to fear. Radical obedience becomes radical liberation. By his death, we are set free.

Apocalyptic Myth:
Vocation as Ecclesiology

Now, there are certainly reasons to question whether early Christian communities were in real or actual situations of persecution or relative deprivation. Here theology's captivity to historical criticism can do some disservice. Although the historical situation of the early church is certainly relevant, it may not be the primary hermeneutical approach. The "rhetorical situation" of the New Testament is one of perceived otherness, of a philosophical and ethical distance so radical as to be described metaphorically as warfare. Certainly there are contemporary Christian communities not under physical persecution, but which are, nonetheless, aware that their common vocation sets them against the values of the world. We do not want to valorize a "Christ against culture" mentality that physically disassociates from the secular world, but a transformative stance of thoroughgoing sacrificial engagement in the world. I prefer to imagine the common vocation as the kenotic or "inside-out" church, rather than the isolationist sanctuary model of much sectarianism.

In her commentary on the book of Revelation, Elisabeth Schüssler Fiorenza points out that the rhetorical strategy of the book is to evoke the consciousness of Christ's immediate presence. Its symbolic discourse aims at engendering staying power (resistance) by promising that the audience will participate in the future eschatological reversal of history.[46] The resurrection hope of a just world is what she identifies as a prototype of reversal that serves to critique even the sexist language and the hierarchical models of the New Testament itself. We can almost hear Ernst Käsemann chuckling in the background: "Apocalyptic is the *mother* of all Christian theology."

White feminists are not the only ones to see the liberating power of apocalyptic. Allan Boesak's treatment of apocalyptic is consistent with the rhetoric of hope and rebuke when he claims that anything that trivializes political powers is powerful in its own right and makes claims that the dominant culture interprets as treason. Boesak's own work *Comfort and Protest: Reflections on the Apocalypse of John of Patmos* was written less than ten years ago, while he was imprisoned in Pretoria. During his solitary confinement, he read Bonhoeffer and noted the key struggle between the myth of human progress and the sovereignty of God. For him, the apocalyptic book serves as "underground letters to a persecuted church" and echoes the assumption that Christian faith can best be interpreted and critiqued from the margins.[47]

Calling for Christian martyrdom and perseverance, Boesak focuses much of his book on the Woman, the Dragon, and the Child of Revelation, and considers these prototypical resurrection and generative images. This birth image becomes a glorious defiance of death by a faithful pregnant woman, where Eros, life, and hope come together in one metaphor. For scholars who want to argue that the violence, eroticism, and gender language of apocalyptic is essentially sadomasochistic, Boesak and Schüssler Fiorenza offer an alternative reading. Apocalyptic is revolutionary when heard from the bottom.

Other liberationists have claimed the revolutionary power of apocalyptic. Within the African American community, Gayraud Wilmore claims that this eschatological perspective has long been at the heart of African American preaching.[48] The earliest slave rebellions were led by preachers who claimed apocalyptic visions. Their apocalyptic consciousness continued through the tradition, carried out in Martin Luther King's apocalyptic "I Have a Dream" speech and the impossible foolish language of a future "Beloved Community." Even Malcolm X spoke the apocalyptic language of divine retribution and reversal. His critique of American society was couched in the metaphors of warfare and divine election, and his labeling of white Americans as "Blue-eyed Devils" is classic apocalyptic rhetoric.

So, can apocalyptic consciousness as a rhetoric of hope be liberating in all situations? Can preachers just preach "God is on your side, hang in there" to any community of believers? Probably not. In a world full of Newt Gingriches, sprawling Disney mergers, and first world military egomania, the word that Christ is Sovereign is not good news, but a downright rebuke. As Karl Mannheim pointed out, utopian visions are too easily co-opted by those who are already in power. A rhetoric of hope or ultimate victory becomes demonic when it slides off the lips of those who speak from within ideological positions of authority. In the 1980s we heard a senile, benevolent American President invoking the image of Armageddon in order to justify increased military offensives in the Middle East. Whenever apocalyptic language or metaphors are used to justify aggression or to prop up a particular group (even a church or denomination), such discourse betrays the basic apocalyptic consciousness that relativizes all human constructs.

The rhetoric of folly helps us with its paradoxical understanding of power manifested as weakness, strength manifested as vulnerability, and wisdom manifested as folly. The purpose of the rhetoric of folly is to trivialize worldly power structures, not to support them. Apocalyptic rhetoric of hope and resistance in the service of the status quo elevates greed to a virtue and violence to a sacrament. Along with Kennedy, Schüssler Fiorenza and others caution against using apocalyptic in the hopeful sense. As one preacher notes, "to preach in an untranslated apocalyptic voice to Christians who retain some actual power in the society is to risk irrelevance at best and to encourage faithless passivity at worst."[49] Feminist Tina Pippin fears that the passion for a martyr's death and the use of war metaphors is unredeemably a lust for literal destruction and not just poetic trivializing.[50] Schüssler Fiorenza puts it best, "Whenever Christians join the power structures of their own society and seek to stabilize or protect them, the same rhetorical world of vision serves to sacralize dominant authorities and preach revenge against their enemies."[51]

The preacher of the rhetoric of folly must be in solidarity with the oppressed and must be willing to risk censure, rejection, and loss of status. Preaching the apocalyptic vision undercuts the myth of human progress that is at the heart of nineteenth-century liberalism and the social gospel. But, preaching the cross and resurrection as a community model, we will also be undercutting the psychological myth of the individual, the myth of self-actualization, and the myth of personal decision. If we preach a vision of social transformation and expect a self-denying kenotic community, we will be going up against some of the most cherished American cultural ideals.

We must be ready to take risks, that is, to be cross bearers, since the radicality of the rhetoric will turn the powerful against us with a vengeance. A rhetoric of folly will trivialize the values that adhere to contemporary Christian privilege—naming them as the powers and principalities—and will slay them with nothing more or less than a word. Preaching the apocalyptic vision to those in relative power must always employ the rhetoric of folly as an honest critique. Without necessarily chastising or condemning, the rhetoric of folly puts things in perspective, that is, upside-down. The rhetoric of folly laughs at worldly power and invites the hearers to laugh at themselves, reevaluating their worldly wisdom as folly. And it leads first to repentance and, then, to the self-sacrifice of resistance to those worldly powers.

Tempted as we may be to shame and crush, we wield a rhetoric of folly that transforms by grace. We will also have to remember that, even within the metaphorical battlefield where good and evil clash, God is the one who eliminates evil. The faithful martyrs do not engage in battle except as innocent victims. Lambs led to slaughter, they sing hosannas and get their heads chopped off. And, of course, Christ as the victorious hero wields a sword made only from the Word. When the battle is at its pitch, the Savior of the universe faces evil armed with nothing more than a sermon. So, the faithful do not ask the question How will we win? but will see that the ultimate victors are the losers of history.

So, preaching is ultimately rhetorical and metaphorical and apocalyptic. Like Dietrich Bonhoeffer, we will want to violate the boundaries of ordinary secular language and transfigure it.[52] Like a body being resurrected, ordinary language can become the familiar starting point that leads us into mystery. "The word of the sermon has, and is, the presence of Christ . . . the Word of God has really entered into the humiliation of the word of [humans]."[53] Preaching is where the foundation for a new world is laid; "the proclaimed word is not a medium of expression for something else as if something lies behind it, but rather it is the very Christ, walking through the congregation as the Word."[54]

As such, Christian preaching, whether we preach to social losers or social winners, is, by definition, an exercise in the rhetoric of folly. We become metaphors ourselves, foolishly proclaiming a world where losers are winners and winners are losers. After all, the final apocalyptic vision is not the battlefield but the New Jerusalem, where evil has been run out of town on a rail.

But, look, the churches and the preachers are absent, too. The ultimate rhetoric of folly assumes that our own "success" will look like failure by worldly standards. The "inside-out" church will not be popular with the church-growth movement. A preacher confronted with this kenotic model complained, "If I preach that, my struggling little church will die." Exactly. Perhaps the successful model of the church is one that foolishly dies for the world. If so, let us sing hosannas and laugh in the very face of death.

NOTES

1. Paul S. Minear, *John, the Martyr's Gospel* (New York: Pilgrim Press, 1984), ix.
2. Rudolf Bultmann, *Jesus Christ and Mythology* (New York: Charles Scribner's Sons, 1958), 40.
3. Ibid., 31–32.
4. Plato, *The Republic*, 431a.
5. This is Aristophanes' anthropology of love, in Plato's *Symposium*, 191e.
6. Phillip Rieff's *The Triumph of the Therapeutic* (New York: Harper & Row, 1966) and Robert Bellah's now-familiar *Habits of the Heart* (New York: Harper &

Row, 1985) offer different perspectives on this American ethos. Harold Bloom's recent book,*The American Religion* (New York: Simon & Schuster, 1992), extends his discussion of American gnosticism.

7. Ernst Käsemann, "The Beginnings of Christian Theology," in *Journal for Theology and the Church*, vol. 6: *Apocalypticism* (New York: Herder & Herder, 1969), 40.

8. Gerhard Ebeling, "The Ground of Christian Theology," in *Journal for Theology and the Church*, vol. 6: *Apocalypticism* (New York: Herder & Herder, 1969), 65.

9. Ibid.

10. Paul Hanson, *The Dawn of Apocalyptic* (Philadelphia: Fortress Press, 1979), 1.

11. Ibid., 10.

12. Ibid., 11–12.

13. Paul S. Minear will argue that apocalyptic eschatology is not hopeless but rather a manifestation of exceeding hope. See his *Christian Hope and the Second Coming* (Philadelphia: Westminster Press, 1965), and also his *New Testament Apocalyptic* (Nashville: Abingdon Press, 1981). For a somewhat different perspective on the same themes, see Minear, *Christians and the New Creation: Genesis Motifs in the New Testament* (Louisville, Ky.: Westminster John Knox Press, 1994).

14. Some of these are also genre-marks of apocalyptic, but apocalyptic metaphors and understandings can be distinguished even in works that are not of the apocalyptic genre.

15. Stephen O'Leary, *Arguing the Apocalypse: A Theory of Millennial Rhetoric* (New York: Oxford University Press, 1994).

16. Wendy Farley, *Tragic Vision and Divine Compassion: A Contemporary Theodicy* (Louisville, Ky.: Westminster/John Knox Press, 1990), 40. See also Paul Ricoeur, *The Symbolism of Evil*; Peter L. Berger, *The Sacred Canopy: Elements of a Sociological Theory of Religion* (Garden City, N.Y.: Doubleday & Co., 1969).

17. C. H. Dodd, *The Apostolic Preaching and Its Developments* (Chicago: Willett, Clark & Co., 1937).

18. Dale C. Allison, *The End of the Ages Has Come* (Edinburgh: T. & T. Clark, 1987).

19. Ibid., 3.

20. Amos Wilder, *Early Christian Rhetoric* (Cambridge, Mass.: Harvard University Press, 1978), 29.

21. David G. Buttrick, *Preaching Jesus Christ: An Exercise in Homiletic Theology* (Philadelphia: Fortress Press, 1988), 83.

22. Karl Mannheim, *Ideology and Utopia: An Introduction to the Sociology of Knowledge* (New York: Harcourt, Brace & Co., 1936), 193.

23. Berger, *The Sacred Canopy*, and Peter L. Berger and Thomas Luckmann, *The Social Construction of Reality* (Garden City, N.Y.: Doubleday & Co., 1967).

24. Mannheim, *Ideology and Utopia*, 98ff.

25. Ibid., 192.

26. Ibid., 211–25.

27. Paul Ricoeur, *Lectures on Ideology and Utopia* (New York: Columbia University Press, 1986), 182.

28. Ibid., 231.

29. Victor Turner, *The Forest of Symbols* (Ithaca, N.Y.: Cornell University Press, 1967), 95.

30. Walter Brueggemann, *The Prophetic Imagination* (Philadelphia: Fortress Press, 1978), 13.

31. Ibid.

32. Hanson, *Dawn of Apocalyptic*, 430.

33. See J. Christiaan Beker, *Paul the Apostle: The Triumph of God* (Philadelphia: Fortress Press; Edinburgh: T. & T. Clark, 1980), and *Paul's Apocalyptic Gospel: The Coming Triumph of God* (Philadelphia: Fortress Press, 1982); Paul S. Minear, *New Testament Apocalyptic* (Nashville: Abingdon Press, 1981); Daniel Patte, *Preaching Paul* (Philadelphia: Fortress Press, 1984).
34. Minear, *New Testament Apocalyptic*, 61.
35. An understanding of worship symbols and context is an integral part of homiletic strategy. The same apocalyptic metaphorical patterns fund preaching and ritual activity.
36. Rodney Kennedy, *The Creative Power of Metaphor: A Rhetorical Homiletics* (Lanham, Md: University Press of America, 1994).
37. Ibid., 4–5.
38. Sallie McFague, *Metaphorical Theology: Models of God in Religious Language* (Philadelphia: Fortress Press, 1982), 36.
39. Ibid., 13.
40. This argument leans toward Hans-Georg Gadamer and away from Jürgen Habermas without making the full Heideggerian leap toward an ontological claim. For this "experientialist" position, see the work of George Lakoff and Mark Johnson, *Metaphors We Live By* (Chicago: University of Chicago Press, 1980). They claim that this position avoids the "myth of subjectivity" and the "myth of objectivity."
41. Paul Ricoeur, *The Conflict of Interpretations* (Evanston, Ill.: Northwestern University Press, 1974), 22–23.
42. Kennedy, *Creative Power of Metaphor*, 5. He cites Robert L. Scott, "On Viewing Rhetoric as Epistemic," *Central States Speech Journal* 18 (February 1967): 9–17. See also Scott's follow-up essay, "On Viewing Rhetoric as Epistemic: Ten Years Later," in *Methods of Rhetorical Criticism*, ed. Bernard L. Brock, Robert L. Scott, and James W. Cheseboro (Detroit: Wayne State University Press, 1990).
43. Chaim Perelman, *The Realm of Rhetoric* (Notre Dame, Ind.: University of Notre Dame Press, 1982).
44. Kennedy, *Creative Power of Metaphor*, 44–45.
45. Ibid., 45.
46. Elisabeth Schüssler Fiorenza, *Revelation: Vision of a Just World* (Minneapolis: Fortress Press, 1991), 129.
47. Allan A. Boesak, *Comfort and Protest: Reflections on the Apocalypse of John of Patmos* (Philadelphia: Westminster Press, 1987).
48. Gayraud S. Wilmore, *Last Things First* (Philadelphia: Westminster Press, 1982).
49. Thomas Long, "The Preacher and the Beast," in *Intersections: Post-Critical Studies in Preaching*, ed. Richard L. Eslinger (Grand Rapids: Wm. B. Eerdmans Publishing Co., 1994), 20.
50. Tina Pippin, *Death and Desire: The Rhetoric of Gender in the Apocalypse of John* (Louisville, Ky.: Westminster/John Knox Press, 1992).
51. Schüssler Fiorenza, *Revelation*, 139.
52. Dietrich Bonhoeffer, *Wordly Preaching: Lectures on Preaching*, ed. Clyde Fant (Nashville: Thomas Nelson, 1975).
53. Ibid., 21.
54. Ibid., 126.

15

Toward a New Paradigm for Preaching

EDWARD FARLEY

Several years ago, I began what has turned out to be a two-part exploration on the possibility of nonbiblicist preaching. The first essay criticized the "bridge" paradigm that still prevails in pulpits and in homiletic theory, according to which that-which-is-preached is a content located in biblical passages.[1] Since there is no necessary reason why a biblical passage has as such a preachable content and because such content is only rarely what we call the gospel, this paradigm sticks the preacher with an impossible task. The sermon that results more often than not sounds like it has traveled from the passage to a specific situation, but it has been forced to bypass strict exegesis and to invent an applicable content. Though it seems to foster "biblical preaching," this paradigm forces the preacher to distort and even ignore the Bible insofar as the Bible is not an aggregate of thousands of authoritative and preachable passages. Ironically, the bridge paradigm preempts a preaching of the gospel and the world of the gospel. And surely we are summoned to preach the gospel, not the Bible. But this statement raises a host of new questions. If the Bible is not that-which-is-preached, does the preacher then simply turn away from the Bible in order to preach? And if not, if preaching does take place in some relation to or use of the Bible, what precisely is that? How can we go about preaching if we abandon the quasi-fundamentalist idea of a Bible carved up into discrete and authoritative passages? What follows here is little more than a preliminary suggestion of another way to think about scripture, the gospel, and preaching in relation to one another.

Liturgy as the Locus of Preaching

First, we must review what we are talking about when we use the term "preaching." Lacking that clarification, we may facilely presume that the preaching that now takes place in churches is simply an imitation of what

Hebrew prophets, Jesus, and the apostles were doing. It should be evident that contemporary preaching, however much it may share certain features with what these ancient figures did, is by no means a mere continuation of their activity. Hebrew prophets were more or less cultically independent figures who opposed, in both speaking and writing, the political and religious life of their day. John the Baptist and Jesus were also cultically independent and itinerant figures who confronted the public and religious life of their time. The Christian movement spread initially by way of itinerant figures who told what happened to Jesus and at Pentecost. Their concern was less the public life of a specific people as the availability of salvation through the crucified and soon-to-appear crucified Messiah. But with certain exceptions, itinerancy, confronting a people's public life, and the announcement of a new salvific figure do not constitute the typical situation of contemporary preaching. Preaching now takes place in a particular, repeated, liturgical, and congregational setting. Members (for the most part) of a weekly gathered congregation is its expected audience. Preaching, thus, is an event in the ritual life of congregations. While there are differences between Roman Catholic, Protestant, and sect-type churches, they all assume that this weekly event of worship and preaching has something to do with the way redemption takes place and the way congregations are empowered. The preaching that is the subject of this chapter is then, this regularized, rhetorical event in the setting of congregational worship.

Preaching as a Discourse of Redemption

How did this situation come to be? I ask the question not in a historical but in a theological way. How is it that this weekly rhetorical-interpretative event became part of the congregational life of the Christian movement? What is the "idea" of preaching as something spawned in the Christian movement? We rarely find preaching in the corporate rituals of other religious faiths. Why is it so prominent in Christian liturgy? The Christian way of understanding redemptive transformation gives us our first clue. Both Jewish and Christian faiths thematize individual and social moral corruption, manifest in malice, dishonesty, coldheartedness, alienation from others, and social oppression. All of these things are tangled up with and are borne by human discourse. In and through language, we render the other marginal, invisible, or such an absolute threat that anything we do to that other is justified. In and through language, we lie, deceive ourselves, insult, and reduce the beauty and mystery of nature to what is utile. Sedimentations and prevailing metaphors of language give human evil an enduring and structural status. The language of oppression, of reductive behavior, of various idolatries settles on societies and on individual consciousness like a pall. Redemptive transformation will surely not take place if it bypasses the way our language whitewashes our institutions and guides our exploitive agendas. Redemption, then, is not just a way of doing but a way of discoursing, which means a way of speaking, listening, interpreting, addressing, remembering, and narrating. Thus, to say the human being can be redemptively transformed is also to say its discourse must be altered. But corrupted and corrupting discourse recede only before a powerful and modifying discourse: a new master narrative, deep symbolisms, and altered practices of speaking and listening. Human beings negotiate the world by way of a flow of interpretation. If redemption is to affect this negotiation, it must reach the human being's linguistic and interpretive life. Because transformation takes place, at least in part, through the transformation of discourse, interpretation has a central role in various ways the traditions of faith are mediated.

To argue for the importance of interpretation in redemptive transformation is not necessarily to show why *preaching* is a central act of a worshiping congregation. A community's *teaching* can be the way it engages in the modification of corrupting discourse. But we should not be too quick to make teaching and preaching two utterly different things. If preaching is in some way a narration, interpretation, or parable, it surely is a form of teaching. But what form? It is the teaching that takes place in and is appropriate to the liturgical setting of worship. But how does worship render teaching into the form of preaching? Here we must recall that worship takes place in and reflects the aims of a community of redemption. When "believers" gather for worship, they do not leave behind concerns about oppressive institutions, corrupted relations, or individual hopes for transformation. The God they worship is known in the first place primarily in connection to these things. Worship, accordingly, places before God the specific situations of human tragedy, corruption, and hope. Redemption, thus, is the environment of worship. The worshiper's posture is thus one of listening for what disrupts the hold of evil and offers hope for change. The posture (aim) of those who lead worship is to do and say things pertinent to this listening and to this expectation. In worship, the *teaching* and interpretation expected by listeners and leaders must both disrupt and give hope to their specific situation. And this is just what teaching as *preaching* is. In the preaching that takes place in the ritual setting of the congregation, situation, disruption, and redemptive hope all come together in a discourse of interpretation. To listen to such preaching is to place one's self, family, nation, environment, and relations before God in repentance and hope.

The World of Gospel
as What We Preach

What is it that, when interpreted, disrupts and gives hope? What in other words is it that is preached? Jesus preached the good news of the impending kingdom (reign) of God. When the crucified and resurrected Jesus became himself the decisive agent of salvation (that is, the impending kingdom of God), his followers preached the good news (gospel) that salvation was available through him. Gospel then arises as a christological twist on the message of the impending kingdom. The center of this message is that through Jesus, evil and corruption can give way to redemption. Such is gospel as it is given succinct expression by Paul and other New Testament writers.

When we start to unpack this succinct summary, when we subject it to close scrutiny, we find at work in its phrases ("through Jesus," "salvation," "evil") a whole world of interrelated symbols. In this symbolic world of gospel are the mysteries of God's activity in the world, mysteries of creation, world-openness to grace, the world's corruptibility, the tragedy, evil, and openness to grace of all that is historical. Thus, when we say that the what-is-preached is gospel, we are unable to restrict that to a single motif such as incarnation, atoning death, or resurrection. To proclaim salvation available through Jesus is to stand before and be opened onto the various mysteries that attend salvation. What-is-preached, then, is the world of the gospel. Gathering that world together and giving it a certain unity is the dialectic of corruption and redemption. Thus, the formal structure of preaching the world of the gospel is this dialectic of critique and hope.

To say that what-is-preached is the world of the gospel has a negative and positive implication. If we say that what-is-preached is the *world* of the gospel, we refuse to reduce or narrow gospel to a single text, set of texts, or even theme. For instance, the world of the gospel is not reducible simply to the event of Jesus as attested in the four Gospels. Nor can we narrow gospel to what we find in the books of the New Testament. For these writings presuppose and draw on a whole world of symbols that come from the faith of Israel and are to be found in the Hebrew Bible. Creation, social evil, Torah, justice, theodicy, future hope, and judgment are also part of the world of the gospel. Nor can we say that the two-Testament canon exhausts the world of the gospel. For innumerable postcanonical texts associated with various times and places of the Christian movement engage, articulate, illumine, and even develop the world of the gospel. This whole line of questioning is flawed insofar as it would discover which collection of texts coincides with or yields the world of the gospel. For the world of the gospel as the mysteries with which we have to do when we participate in redemption is, itself, not a text or collection of texts.

The positive implication has to do with the temporal dimension of the world of the gospel. One reason the world of the gospel cannot itself be an authoritative text is that it, like the kingdom of God (or as the christological definition of the kingdom of God) is always contemporary. The mysteries of redemption are not simply events, persons, or "truths" of some past time but bespeak how God, world, and history are related to each other in the present. This is not to say that the world of the gospel is unrelated to the past or the future. Since the divine redemptive activity is at work in all historical times, and since this activity found expression in the singers, prophets, and historians of Israel, the contemporary world of the gospel grows out of the traditioned past. Without this continuity, the world of the gospel in the present would have no perceivable content. It would be without voice, song, tradition, metaphor, and narrative. Further, the contemporary world of the gospel has to do with redemption as a way of existing toward the future, an existence in the mode of hope. But the realities or powers at work in the world of the gospel (God, evil, creation, redemption) are ever present. This is why preaching the world of the gospel can never be simply a recitation of the past, a mere interpretation of a past authoritative discourse. The *what* of preaching is not the concrete but now past situation of Isaiah or Paul but rather the concrete situation of the present. The God of this preaching is not stuck in the past, simply to be remembered.

It is because what-is-preached is the contemporaneous world of the gospel that preaching is not simply applied exegesis. Once preachers realize that what-is-preached is the world of the gospel, once that world of interconnected mysteries is opened up, they face a *theological* task. For that is just what theology in the setting of a living religious community is, a becoming aware of, a thinking directed to, the mysteries that attend that community's experience of evil and redemption. As a theological task of interpreting the mysteries of faith, preaching is cut loose from all formulaic self-definitions and easily described step-by-step methods. Thus the world of preaching is not the safe and efficient world of applying verses and passages but the more muddy, unsafe, and uncertain world of interpreting the mysteries of faith. Insofar as the *what* of preaching is the world of the gospel, preaching is not supplied with a clear doctrinal, ethical, or exegetical given. Rather, its given is the very mystery of God's (present) activity in the situations of the world.

But surely we misread the situation of preaching if we think that the world of the gospel is the *product* of inquiry, thinking, or theological interpretation. The world of the gospel, that is, the mysteries of redemption, is present and to some degree manifest insofar as redemption actually takes place. Thus, the world of the gospel is always already a structuring content in the community of faith, partially expressed in the community's liturgies, stories, doctrines, and even in its "collective unconsciousness." To participate in a community of faith is to participate in and to some degree be aware of the world of the gospel. Accordingly, preachers, church leaders, and theologians do not deliver the world of the gospel to the community of faith. Finding it already there, they render it into forms of self-reflection, remembrance, new interpretation, spiritual discipline, and education.

Scripture and Preaching

If *what*-is-preached is not a text (and therefore scripture) but the world of the gospel, what relation does preaching have to texts, especially the text we call scripture? Here the situation gets even muddier, frustrating those who need an exact and specific formula for using scripture (as texts) to discern the world of the gospel. What in the first place do we mean by "scripture"? To speak of "scripture" and not just the Bible is to grant to a set of writings some sort of preeminence in the community in which it is used. It is to affirm in some sense that the community is "subject to," or "lives from" this set of writings.

Existing from scripture, a community values and tries to preserve its continuity with its own past; for the writings called scripture record over a rather long period of time the way a people has existed together and before God. The contemporary community of faith in some sense lives from and is subject to this record. Fundamentalism is one way of understanding this being "subject to." According to fundamentalism, *scripture* is a collection of writings in which each passage, even verse, is a preachable and necessarily believable divinely revealed truth. In fundamentalism, the world of the gospel *is* the texts of scripture. If we reject this way of understanding how we live from scripture and at the same time retain the idea of scripture, we embrace some distinction between scripture and the world of the gospel. This distinction carries with it the additional distinction between the historical-hermeneutical study of the "world of the text" (Ricoeur) and the theological task of understanding the world of the gospel.

That the community of faith is subject to the world of the gospel goes without saying. It is after all constituted by that world. If the community is also subject to scripture, this implies some relation between scripture (and its textual worlds) and the world of the gospel. What is that relation?

Scripture and the World of the Gospel

I said previously that the world of the gospel has obtained historical expression in the writings of Israel and early Christianity. This discursive embodiment of the world of the gospel, that is, scripture, can be normative for the present community in two ways.

First, redemption is never merely general. As historically particular, it finds expression in such texts as the moral criticisms of Israelite society and cultus by the prophets and the *agape* motif in Paul or John. And a particular paradigm of redemption is in close company with a particular kind of community of redemption. For example, the community that arose with the event of the crucified Jesus proposed no specific ethnic people as its carrier, hence in a certain sense was a universal community of faith. This particularity of kind, expressed in the written accounts of the faith community, serves as a norm for any future community of faith that would continue to be that type of community. In this sense the contemporary community of faith is ever subject to or ever exists from the scriptures.

Second, insofar as the past community of faith is a community of redemption, it will in some ways relate to, embody, and discursively express the world of the gospel; thus, God, evil, hope, creation, law, freedom, and so on. In this sense, scripture records in a historical way thematics of the world of the gospel.

But if there is no pre-given formula that enables us to know precisely when and whether a writing has given an account of the world of the gospel, how does this constitute a way the community of faith is "subject to" scripture? At this point we can only say that if the contemporary community is also a community of redemption, thus engaged with the world of the gospel, it has a way of recognizing the thematics or mysteries of that world in the texts of the ancient community. But there is nothing wooden, automatic, or fixed about this situation. We cannot say that a contemporary community of faith simply determines out of its own thematics how or whether an ancient writing is engaged with the world of the gospel. On the contrary, the contemporary community may have suppressed dimensions of that world that the ancient texts help it to recover. This can take place because the world of the gospel is a horizon of mystery, not a given set of fixed contents. To be a redemptive community at all is to exist on that horizon, and this existence is the ground of the ability to recognize, learn from, and be corrected by the world of the gospel in the ancient literature.

But the relation of the contemporary community to the world of the gospel discerned in scripture is never a mere conformity. Even if the community attempted to imitate the past community, it would necessarily fail since its historical situation contains too many new elements. And when it does attempt such a conformation, it suppresses both its own situationality and the possibilities of new creative responses to such. The community's relation to the epochs, texts, and communities of its past is less a conformity as a participation in a tradition and a criticial reinterpretation.

The Role of Scripture in Preaching

I come finally to the specific subject of this chapter, the place of scripture in a postbiblicist paradigm of preaching. If the world of the gospel is *what* is preached, if that world is constituted by the mysteries with which a community of redemption has to do, and if these mysteries had an earlier formulation in the narratives of scripture, what then is the place of scripture in preaching? Here it would serve us to recollect what makes up the biblicist paradigm for which we seek an alternative. According to the bridge paradigm, preaching's *to-which* is some appropriate body of listeners, usually a gathered congregation, and its *in-the-light-of-which* is the situation in which the listeners live and struggle. Further, *that-which-is preached* is the Bible, or, more specifically, some applicable truth present in a selected passage of the Bible.

In the bridge paradigm, the task that preaching sets for the preacher is the preparation of a rhetorical unit (a sermon) that connects the passage and its applicable truth to the situation. The fundamentalist element in this paradigm is the assumption that any passage of scripture *necessarily* contains a "true," authoritative, and, thus, preachable content.[2] If we reject this assumption, we have no alternative but to search for an alternate paradigm. This chapter does little more than suggest some items of that alternative paradigm.

In the new paradigm, *what-is-preached* shifts from the Bible or a passage of the Bible to the gospel and elements of the world of the gospel. Further, something new is added to the paradigm, that *through-which* preaching takes place. This through-which is a critical, historical-hermeneutical, and theological response to the world of the gospel as retrieved from scripture. Let me elaborate.

In the new paradigm, the problem and task of preaching does not begin when the preacher sets forth to write or prepare for a sermon. That version of the problem of preaching virtually reduces it to a problem of technique.[3] Taking place in a specific congregation, a sermon inevitably reflects the way the preacher is part of and responsive to the congregation's situation. Further, sermons also take place against the background of who the preacher is and what the preacher does over the long haul to function adequately as a leader (minister, priest) of a congregation. If ministers understand themselves primarily as managers of an institution, if they know management theory and technique and are indifferent to the world of the gospel and to theological thinking, this indifference will surely show up in the way preaching is understood and therefore in specific sermons. The sermon, therefore, begins to be written as the self-understanding of the preacher forms, in the way the preacher relates to (ignores, studies, values) the church's history, tradition, and theology, and the sense in which the preacher subjects scripture to critical study.

In the new paradigm for preaching, the preacher is ever preparing for preaching in at least three ongoing interpretive activities: critical-historical studies of scripture, theological thinking, and situational analyses. Of these three, recent theological education has especially privileged the third item. Thus, by way of psychology, politics, literature, and the like, preaching can be assured of cultural and situational relevance. The bridge paradigm privileges the first item, biblical study, but tends to restrict it to exegesis of passages of the Bible.

In the alternative paradigm, the study of scripture must mean a study by means of whatever tools are appropriate of scripture simply as it presents itself. And surely scripture as a set of writings presents more to us than an aggregate of passages. That is less a presentation of scripture as something fostered onto scripture. But as a set of writings scripture presents to us authors (and questions of authorship), ancient historical situations and ways of reading them, events and questions of their historicality, literary structures and devices, basic metaphors, narratives, editorial and authorial viewpoints, sociological structures (e.g., priestly castes, ruling bodies, rich and poor), personal pieties (e.g., Psalms), radical political critiques. A preacher can easily miss most of this by asking how one can "apply" the message of a selected passage. A genuine engagement with scripture as a set of ancient writings surely will confront these many things and more. But when that study is part of the background of preaching, it has a guiding aim.

Intriguing as the narratives, sociological structures, and literary devices are, they are not as such the final end of the preacher's study of scripture. For the preacher would identify in the narratives, metaphors, and authorial viewpoints the world of the gospel; that is, the way the ancient communities of faith articulated their engagement with the mysteries of faith. Yet even when that is identified, it does not in that form (e.g., apocalyptic in Matthew) become that-which-is-preached.

It is at this point that biblical study joins with a second activity that makes up the background and genesis of preaching. This activity is the thinking that subjects the historically transmitted motifs of the world of the gospel to critical and truth-oriented reflection. For instance, the *agape* motif of the Fourth Gospel seems to express something about the world of the gospel. But how does this motif fare if we could understand its intrinsic character, the possibility that it expresses something real and actual, its relation to other forms of love, and the sphere it occupies (the interhuman? the human psyche?)? Only when the retrieved motif is subjected to this kind of thinking can it be something that is proclaimed. And when this step is omitted (as it is in the bridge paradigm), it becomes abstract and vague, and remains an ancient word that we simply insert into our situation. Accordingly, preaching in the bridge paradigm tries to make up for the vagueness of ancient but "authoritative" notions by fleshing them out with modern illustrations. This is why human autonomy and not scripture or the world of the gospel predominates the bridge paradigm.

The third ongoing activity that serves as the background from which the sermon originates is situational analysis. This too is an enterprise of ongoing study and discernment, not the instant analysis that a specific sermon calls for. It ranges from attempts to understand the larger movements of culture (e.g., the postmodern, therapeutic subcultures, late capitalism) to the specific dynamics of the congregation.

Conclusion

In the new paradigm, the world of the gospel (what-is-preached) is set forth in relation to a situation (the in-the-light-of-which) from ongoing studies of and critical reflection on the world of scripture (the through-which). The formal or essential task of preaching is the disruption of the world of the congregation under the hopeful expectation of redemption. That is to say, something about the world of the gospel is brought to bear on the situation of the congregation by way of this dialectic of exposure (repentance) and new possibility (redemption). Preaching in this sense is only partly retrieval, only partly a movement from the texts of the community's past. Since the world of the gospel means the mysteries that attend redemptive process, it is never a fixed content. If history itself is a succession of new situations, if human societies, individuals, and congregations never simply repeat the past, then the disruptions and redemptions of the world of the gospel ever evoke new discourses, new thematics, even new insights into the world of scripture. And if the world of the gospel embraces the mysteries of God's working, then it will always transcend and even be normative toward specific passages of scripture. This transcendent character of the world of the gospel is the reason why the church can expose, judge, and move beyond the xenophobias, homophobias, and sexisms of the ancient community and its scripture.

In a postbiblicist paradigm of preaching, scripture is the through-which of the sermon not simply in the form of isolated passages. While the passage may serve to explore something in the world of the gospel, more often than not, because of its isolation, it turns the preacher away from the world of the gospel. Scripture as a set of writings is multidimensional, hence editorial viewpoints, lists, letters, stories, poems, arguments, and theological viewpoints may all carry and express the world of the gospel.

Accordingly, in the new paradigm for preaching, the tyranny of the passage over the sermon will give way to a multivalent use of scripture.

I realize that this chapter is frustratingly vague concerning the specific way scripture functions in preaching. This vagueness is only partly due to the unfinished and programmatic character of this exploration of a new paradigm. There is something about the situation of preaching itself that resists overprecise specification of method and technique. It is of course our temptation and need to resolve the situation of preaching into a step-by-step method whose product is a clearly written composition. And for those who need certainty, utter clarity, or simplicity, this new paradigm will be insufficient. Paradoxically, however, and in spite of the fact that it contains the possibility of opposing certain texts of scripture, the new paradigm may in fact be more "biblical" than the bridge paradigm with its apparent commitment to authoritative passages.

NOTES

1. See Edward Farley, "Preaching the Bible and Preaching the Gospel," *Theology Today* 51:1 (April 1994):90–104.
2. A certain irony is present in the many nonfundamentalists who are passionately committed to lectionary preaching. To divide the Bible into passages, each of which contains something that is "preachable," must ignore two centuries of historical ways of interpreting the Bible and rests on the fundamentalist notion that any and all ways of slicing up the Bible contain something that is true and preachable.
3. My impression—and that is all it is—is that many present-day ministers as well as programs in which preaching is taught reduce the problem of preaching to sermon preparation. Accordingly, what would help them to be better preachers are more homiletic courses, studies in the rhetoric and techniques of sermon writing. I have no inclination to challenge the importance of the homiletic literature that does in fact help the preacher specifically to write the sermon. But preaching fails (is dull, trivial, superficial, moralistic, incoherent, sentimental, etc.) not simply at the point where the sermon is written down but at the point of the preacher's total reflective, experiential, and intellectual life. In many cases the problem of preaching falls primarily here, at the point of the preacher's ongoing interpretive struggle (or lack of it) with the world of the gospel. If this is the case, many ministers would be helped to be better preachers by a set of studies such as the theme of justice in the Hebrew prophets, New Testament eschatology, the neoclassical critique of the classical theology of God, or feminist articulations of the symbolics of God.

16

Why Preach from Passages in the Bible?

RONALD J. ALLEN

I have long been drawn to David Buttrick's work in preaching. Buttrick is always provocative and frequently insightful. Further, Buttrick is often somewhat iconoclastic. As a child of the 1960s, I identify with iconoclasm. The latter quality arrests my attention in this chapter. For Buttrick and his colleague at the Divinity School of Vanderbilt University, Edward Farley, call into question a commonplace assumption of contemporary preaching. They argue that it is not necessary for a pastor to preach on a specific biblical passage in order to preach a Christian sermon. In fact they contend that preaching a pericope sometimes works against the gospel. Indeed, Farley declares that the pattern of building a bridge from an ancient text to the contemporary world is a failed paradigm.[1]

In this chapter, I first review (and supplement) the Buttrick-Farley argument. To a significant degree, I join their discontent. But, with them, I still see an important place for interpreting passages in regular parish preaching.[2] I offer a cursory rationale for commending this honored pattern. Further, I rethink the relationship of text, preacher, and congregation: the bridge paradigm gives way to conversation and mutual critical correlation as ways to bring together gospel, Bible, pastor, and Christian community. Finally, I enumerate several positive values that can accrue to the preacher and the congregation as a result of interacting with specific biblical passages.

The Buttrick-Farley Reservations Concerning Preaching on Biblical Passages

I begin with a caveat: The positions of Buttrick and Farley should not be casually equated; their analyses of these issues have different nuances.[3] Farley is more acid in his critique of pericope preaching. Nonetheless, these colleagues share a common core that allows me to discuss them in conjunction.

The Buttrick-Farley hypothesis is based on a simple but significant premise: The purpose of preaching is first and foremost to announce the gospel and its implications for the contemporary world.[4] (In this context, "gospel" refers not to a literary genre—e.g., Matthew, Mark, Luke, or John—but to a concise expression of the core of the Christian faith.) The exact theological content of gospel can be formulated in different ways. But, in general, the gospel is the good news of God's redemptive presence and purposes in the world.

The fundamental intention of the sermon is not to preach the Bible or specific biblical passages. The Bible is intended to be a witness (or, better, a collection of witnesses) to the gospel. However, some parts of the Bible do not articulate the gospel. In fact, some passages are anti-gospel. Buttrick recalls a visiting scholar of the First Testament lecturing on how to preach Ps. 137:9: "Happy shall they be who take your little ones and dash them against the rock!"

> The lecture was witty, quite brilliant, and full of homiletic insight. But when it was over, the first question from the audience was devastating. The question was, Why bother? Why would preachers bother to preach a baby-bashing text when they could be declaring the good news of the gospel? Is the whole Bible a book that must be preached simply because it is the Bible and somebody has labeled it as the Word of God? Do we preach to study particular biblical passages, or is preaching a theological endeavor that seeks to make sense of life now in view of God's graciousness in Jesus Christ?[5]

Farley summarizes: the gospel message is not *necessarily* contained in every biblical text.[6] Some passages in the Bible do contain the gospel, but some do not. Occasional texts, in fact, oppose the gospel.

The bridge paradigm assumes that the sermon must build a bridge from the ancient text to the contemporary congregation, that is, the preacher must find a positive point of connection between the biblical passage and the situation of today's listeners. In view of the mixed theological content of biblical texts, the unremitting use of the bridge paradigm can leave the witness of the sermon in a compromised position.

> Because the passage is a delimited piece in a larger writing and because there is no guaranteed verbal inerrancy about the writing at any level, there may be no X (preachable truth) in the passage. Or the content of the passage may be something one should preach against. Or the passage may have a moralizable content, something that lends itself to a "lesson for life." To the degree that there is nothing preachable in the text, the preacher who still must find a way from the text to the sermon must invent X. Something

> about the text is latched onto as that which is preached: a word, a phrase, an action, the text as narrative. Whatever this is, it must be made into a lesson for life. Since what most biblical passages are up to, judged on strict exegetical grounds, is not to provide such lessons, the preacher must wring an X out of the exegeted passage. The passage then is not so much "preached on" as something that provides a jumping off place for the sermon.[7]

The preacher who assumes the bridge paradigm week after week eventually misrepresents, misuses, or trivializes the content of a biblical text or the gospel itself.

In my judgment, Buttrick and Farley correctly assess the purpose of preaching and its relationship to the gospel, and to the Bible. They stand on patterns of preaching in the period of the Second Testament itself.[8] The earliest Christian preachers did not preach texts; they preached Christ, though they often used biblical texts (or allusions) to help clarify the significance of Christ. Buttrick and Farley also stand on the Reformation principle that the gospel itself is the highest authority in the church.[9] The authority of the gospel supersedes that of the Bible.[10]

Preaching from singular biblical texts can be problematic in other ways. It is notoriously easy for preachers to read our own biases and prejudices into texts. In the last thirty years, biblical scholars have emphasized the plurality and diversity within the books of the Bible. Unless the preacher has a clear theological method to mediate among different points of view in the Bible, the sermon is left at the mercy of the theology of the text of the week. In a few instances, the preacher could even preach contradictions from week to week.

Further, if sermons focus only on individual snippets of scripture, the congregation may never get a sense of the sweep of the whole story. The congregation receives bits and pieces of the Bible in isolation without understanding how they relate to one another, to the documents in which they are found, to the broader sweep of the Bible, or to Christian theology beyond the Bible. When preaching from an isolated text, the preacher's theological vision may adjust itself to the size of the text. In some cases, the preacher's vision may enlarge in accordance with the larger vision of the text. But often, the preacher's perspective will shrink to that of the text. Preachers can focus so much on details of historical and literary interpretation that the sermon becomes a boring lecture that never helps the community discern God's presence and purposes today. Indeed, some preachers think that recovering some original meaning of the text (if that is possible) is to discover the contemporary significance of the passage. Some preachers so focus on a single element within a text that the text itself (as a context) is lost.

When preachers choose their own Bible passages as the basis for sermons, they tend to be selective. Preachers often choose texts with which they are familiar or that appear to go along with their preexisting thinking. They tend to avoid texts that are difficult, or that move the preachers outside their habitual patterns of thought.

The use of a lectionary broadens most preachers' homiletical repertoires, but lectionaries, too, are limited and biased in their assignment of Bible passages. In fact, lectionary preaching receives some of Buttrick's most trenchant critique.[11] Like much biblically based preaching, lectionaries tend to slice and dice the Bible. More, Buttrick complains that (whether intended or not) preachers who use a lectionary tend to speak relatively little about significant public issues that cry for Christian interpretation.[12] A preacher may mention such an issue, but usually only in passing or as an illustration. Lectionary-based sermons are often mesmerized by explaining the text and seldom analyze current personal and social phenomena in detail. Such analysis does not come to expression in other arenas of Christian life. Hence, the community is left without significant Christian reflection on matters that weigh heavily on the consciousness of the contemporary world.

At any rate, the Bible does not address the full range of concerns that face today's Christian community. It is not always possible to find a satisfactory analogy (or other mode of relationship) between the Bible and today's concerns. And, at times, the congregation is confronted with a problem whose immediacy or complexity requires direct immediate or extended attention. In such cases, a preacher may find it too cumbersome, time-consuming, and distracting in the sermon to develop the exegetical depth necessary to handle a text with integrity and to address the need. Sermon time may be better spent bringing the gospel itself to bear on the situation at hand. Indeed, individual biblical texts may not provide sufficient Christian wisdom to interpret the need.

However, none of these problems render the practice of preaching from passages *inherently* unsatisfactory. Many Sundays, it is not only possible but desirable to preach the gospel using a biblical passage as a basis for a congregation's encounter with the gospel.

A Brief Rationale for Preaching from Passages in the Bible[13]

Farley and Buttrick join the wide stream of Christian theologians in thinking that a knowledge of the Bible is essential for the Christian community and that the Bible plays important roles in Christian preaching. Farley asks, "Does this mean that preaching cannot and should not be done in connection with the Bible? I would hope not. First, it seems evident that to struggle with the world of the gospel in its mystery and reality is to be launched into the world of the Bible. Second, the Bible can surely be used to set forth something in the world of the gospel."[14] Buttrick amplifies, "While scripture is not the whole story of Christ and the church, it is the constitutive story, the story of the 'church' in Israel transformed by Jesus Christ, and, therefore, crucial to the question of identity."[15] The Bible contains primal witnesses which join the larger conversation in the Christian community whose purpose is to name the presence, purposes, and power of God in the world, and to help the congregation respond faithfully.[16]

The church needs to know both the content of the Bible and how to interpret it so that the church and the Bible can have an appropriate relationship, and so that the Bible can make its optimum contribution to conversation in the Christian community that aims to help the community recognize and respond to God.

Preaching cannot bear sole responsibility in the Christian community for helping the community learn the content of the Bible or how to interpret it. These agenda need to be a part of the whole system of congregational life. But sermons can help the congregation learn essential aspects of the content of the Bible and its interpretation. Some sermons can help the congregation get a sense of the overarching story told in the Bible and, hence, can help the congregation develop a framework within which to place individual books, characters, events, pericopes. Preaching can help the congregation trace themes (words, concepts, images, motifs, events, characters) through the biblical corpus, noting how themes are enlarged, refined, debated, and transformed as they make their way from one biblical book or author to another.[17] From time to time, sermons can focus on issues and methods in biblical interpretation itself.

Preaching from specific passages can also acquaint the congregation with the content (and methods of interpretation) of the Bible. Through texts the Christian community encounters the particularity of Christian witness. Often this encounter is vivid and memorable, thus giving the text (and its interpretation) an opportunity to become a part of the community's everyday consciousness. Indeed, texts can become images by which the Christian community understands God, faith, and Christian life and witness.

Conversation as a Way of Rethinking the Relationship of the Preacher and the Text

The pastor can preach the gospel without working with a biblical text.[18] But when the preacher deals with a text, it is important for the minister to have a clear understanding of the relationship of the preacher (and the congregation) with the text. As noted earlier, Buttrick and Farley say that the preacher does not "preach the text." Alternatively, L. Susan May, Buttrick's colleague in the Divinity School of Vanderbilt University, proposes that the minister preach "through" the text.[19] Calvin Butts, pastor of the Abyssinian Baptist Church in Harlem, preaches "from" a text.[20] David Jacobsen, one of Buttrick's students, envisions preaching "with" a text.[21] According to these latter designations, the text makes an important contribution to the sermon, but it is not the imperial ruler of the homiletical realm.

Recent theology offers conversation as a model to supplant the bridge paradigm as a way of conceiving the relationship between the gospel, a text, a preacher, and a congregation.[22] The conversational model is premised on the notion that all the partners have their own integrity. A text, as an other, can be a conversation partner.[23] The first task of a conversation is to clarify the viewpoints (and the unsettled points) of each of the partners. The next task is to compare and contrast the various viewpoints, identifying strengths and weaknesses. The conversation partners assess which contributions are the most attractive for the future life of the conversation and the community.[24] Often, the process of conversation itself generates fresh alternatives that become a part of the conversational mix.

In David Tracy's eloquent language, "The movement in conversation is questioning itself. Neither my present opinions on the question nor the text's original response to the question but the question itself must control every conversation." Conversation is not an examination or a debate. "It is questioning itself. It is a willingness to follow the question wherever it may go. It is dialogue."[25]

Conversation among gospel, preacher, text, and congregation results in a theology (and a homiletic) of mutual critical correlation.[26] In the process of conversation, the preacher correlates gospel (and its historic witnesses, such as scripture, statements of Christian doctrine, Christian practices) with the experience of the contemporary congregation and the world. At the same time, the preacher explores ways in which the experience of the contemporary congregation and world may cause the preacher (and the church) to rethink its understanding of the gospel and Christian tradition. In the process of mutual critical correlation, the congregation's understanding and evaluation of particular biblical passages, of Christian doctrines, of ecclesiastical practices, and of the gospel itself, may be transformed.

In the paradigm of conversation and mutual critical correlation, the preacher does not simply build a bridge from a biblical text to the contemporary congregation. The preacher asks, What is the witness of the text? Does this witness seem adequate to the gospel? If so, how can it help the congregation critique, supplement, enlarge, refocus (or otherwise enhance) its perception and behavior? What questions does the text put to me, to the Christian community, to the larger world? If the text does not seem to make an adequate witness, the preacher asks, What is an appropriate relationship between today's Christian community and the text? What does the congregation learn from our *encounter* with the text that is of value to the contemporary Christian community?

The preacher hopes that the conversation can lead the community to a fresh (or renewed) awareness of the divine presence and purposes. Even a problematic text, such as Ps. 137:8–9, can become an occasion when the congregation reflects on what it most deeply believes about the nature of God, and God's purposes for the world. The viewpoint of the text pushes the preacher and the congregation to clarify their beliefs.

Conversation with a text can lead the preacher and the community to a number of possible relationships with the passage.[27] The preacher may altogether agree with the text. The sermon might move directly from the message of the text to the message for the congregation. The preacher might agree with aspects of the text's theology, ethical prescription, or worldview but disagree with other aspects. The preacher may find that some difficulties in a text can be critiqued in the light of other elements in the text itself. The preacher may need to correct the witness of a text. The text may be so problematic that the minister is compelled to preach against it (or against some aspect of it). A text's problems in theology, ethical life, or worldview may suggest matters that are similarly problematic in the congregation's theology, ethical life, or worldview. The pastor may be able to draw an analogy between the world of the text and today's world. The text may be a case study from which the pastor can extrapolate principles or attitudes that can be applied to the different case of the congregation. From time to time a bridge will be an ideal model for relating a particular text to a particular community. There are multiple possibilities for locating the relationship between the passage and the people.

These perspectives reframe critical questions that are often used to help evaluate sermons. A primary question is no longer, Was the preacher true to the text? A more penetrating question is, Was the preacher true to the gospel? If the pastor preached through or from a text, then a correlate question needs to be asked: Did the preacher honor the integrity of the text in its historical, cultural, literary, and theological contexts (insofar as these can be identified)?

Values of Preaching from Passages

Preaching from specific passages can offer several significant values to the preacher and the community. I now enumerate some of the most important.

Working from a text allows pastor and people to explore that particular segment of the Bible in depth. The massive size of the Bible, and its diversity (theological, literary, and cultural), make it difficult for preacher or congregation to think and speak in terms of "the" Bible. The Christian community tends to enter the world of the Bible through distinct passages. While the congregation needs to grasp the overarching biblical story, they also need to know its individual chapters.

The sermon implicitly models patterns of engaging a text exegetically and hermeneutically; the sermon's value as a model of encounter with a biblical passage will increase as the preacher thinks conscientiously about how it can so function in the congregation. In order to avoid the atomization of the Bible, and some of the other problems associated with preaching from specific passages (as enumerated in the first section of this chapter), the preacher ought to help the congregation locate the text in the larger biblical, historical, cultural, and theological realms.[28]

As noted above, particular passages furnish (or contribute to) many of the Christian community's ideas and images for God, the world, and Christian life and witness.[29] The congregation's appreciation of these symbols (and the community's ability to evaluate them critically) is enhanced as the people become acquainted with the contexts in which they came to expression. These symbols make their way into sermons, systematic theology, ethical reflection, and the liturgy.

Often the language that began in the Bible takes on a life of its own outside of scripture. Frequently (though not always), as this language moves away from the Bible and into the mainstream of the church, it loses some of its vividness and force. It can even become domesticated or repressive. Attending to individual biblical passages in which the speech of the church came to birth can often bring the language to new life or can help the community assess the strengths and weaknesses of its ways of naming God, the world. The sermon is a useful vehicle for helping the church reflect critically on its speech.

A pericope typically came to expression in response to particular circumstances. A pericope thus represents a community's attempt to interpret a life situation in the light of the gospel (or some aspect of God's relationship with the world). Recent trends in biblical scholarship have exposed profound difficulties in reconstructing many of these situations with precision. Even when a historical situation can be posited as the background to which a text is addressed, the meaning of the text for that setting may not exhaust the meaning(s) a text may have for today's communities. Scholars today speak of texts having a surplus of meaning, or polyvalence; many texts have more possibilities for meaning than can be isolated in any single situation. Indeed, sensitive preachers often find that texts can speak eloquently to contemporary situations far removed in time, place, and circumstance from their original settings.

Nonetheless, the fact that a text arose in a particular context reminds the pastor that the sermon should interpret *specific* aspects of the world (and the congregation's world in particular). I mention this because a fair amount of today's preaching is generic; it does not illumine particular aspects of the congregation's situation or worldview. Preaching from particular texts should encourage the preacher to particularize the gospel.

Buttrick has cast a remarkably withering glance at the informal alliance between the therapeutic disciplines and theology.[30] Consequently, I hesitate to cite positively one of the most influential members of the therapeutic culture. But, Carl Rogers makes a point that is applicable: that which is most particular is most universal (at least in Euro-American culture).[31] When we encounter a particular person, a particular story, a particular situation, we identify with some element of it and refract it through our own experience. Much the same is true of particular passages from the Bible. As the congregation encounters the particularity of a passage (its setting, images, movement, characters), we relate the passage to our own community and situations. The specifics of the congregation's encounter with the passage have a good opportunity of affecting the community in some depth. Of course, the sermon that comes from the gospel itself (and not from a text) can lead the congregation to a similar point.

If the selection of specific texts in a preaching season is sufficiently broad, the sermons help the congregation get a sense of the diversity of the biblical corpus. And if preachers follow the interpretations of the texts (and the doctrines, themes, and images suggested by them) into the history and theology of the church, the sermons help the congregation become aware of the diversity of the church's doctrine and tradition. In a setting that is increasingly postmodern, this emphasis on pluralism and diversity will be welcomed by many. "The" Christian tradition is not a monolith but a great chorus of witnesses. Awareness of the multitude of Christian voices enhances the congregation's options for identifying possible Christian options for interpreting life. And it helps the congregation focus on the limits of diversity and toleration in the Christian community.[32] What, really, is acceptable as genuine Christian understanding and behavior? What is not acceptable? Ironically, then, exposure to the pluralism of the Bible and the Christian tradition ought to encourage the congregation to ponder the normative aspects of Christian faith, identity, community, and practice.

Preaching from a pericope is often a help when the preacher must preach against some aspect of the text, the Bible, or Christian tradition. Working from a text gives the preacher a particular setting from which to expose the inadequate, even oppressive or destructive aspects of the text (or of dimensions of Christian witness or life that are related to the text but that go beyond it). When critiquing Christian thought or practice from a passage, the preacher does not appear to be making a scattershot attack on a vague principle or behavior, but patently confronts specific indiscretions in the Christian house.

A particular passage can give the preacher a starting point for sermon preparation. This benefit is especially true for lectionary-based preachers and for preachers who freely preselect their texts for significant periods of time.[33] Having a place to start helps focus the preacher's time and energy. I know pastors who flop like fish out of water searching for topics (or even texts). They twist one way and then another as they contemplate various foci for the sermon. Before they know it, Wednesday (or Thursday, or even Friday) has come, and they are not settled on a direction for the sermon. The need to interpret a text immediately focuses the preacher's agenda. The particularity of the text ought to help the hermeneutically sensitive preacher think of particular theological connections to the life of the congregation.

Of course, a text may not necessarily provide the best starting point for a particular sermon. A preacher who is artificially loyal to the lectionary or to a preselected text may thus be distracted from bringing the gospel to bear on the community in the most luminous way. Or, a preacher may slip into a mode in which fascination with the archaeology of the text supersedes theological pertinence. Buttrick laments that lectionary preaching tends to shy away from thorough conversation about public issues. But these deficiencies are not inherent with the textual or lectionary systems.[34]

Conclusion

Both Edward Farley and David Buttrick acknowledge that preaching is in a time of transition.[35] Future paradigms for preaching are not fully developed. Over the next generation, pastors will likely explore a plurality of ways of voicing the gospel in and out of the church. We may well discover that no single paradigm will do. The multiplicity of settings, of ways by which human beings process communications, of needs, may lead us to see that the preacher needs to be able to speak in a plurality of modes. Whatever the case, Farley and Buttrick point to the most essential piece of the preaching life: a critical theological consciousness that allows the preacher to reflect critically on possibilities for preaching. I am confident that some of the future preaching of the church will center on the exposition of biblical texts; such cases call for the pastor's best theological acumen. Buttrick and Farley are marvelous conversation partners in helping identify the elements necessary for a mature theological consciousness.

NOTES

1. Edward Farley, "Preaching the Bible and Preaching the Gospel," *Theology Today* 51:1 (April 1994):93–95. Farley's observations are rooted in his highly developed analysis of authority in the church. See further his *Ecclesial Reflection: The Anatomy of Theological Method* (Philadelphia: Fortress Press, 1982); idem and Peter Hodgson, "Scripture and Tradition," in *Christian Theology: An Introduction to Its Traditions and Tasks*, rev. and enl., ed. Peter C. Hodgson and Robert H. King (Philadelphia: Fortress Press, 1985), 61–87.

2. Farley and Buttrick do not completely jettison the possibility of preaching on biblical passages. See Farley, "Preaching the Bible," 103; David Buttrick, *A Captive Voice: The Liberation of Preaching* (Louisville, Ky.: Westminster John Knox Press, 1994), 15–21, 30, 83–99; idem, *Homiletic: Moves and Structures* (Philadelphia: Fortress Press, 1987), 263–81, 301–3, 333–404.

3. I suppose that Farley locates some of Buttrick's earlier work in the failed paradigm. For when Farley mentions exceptions to the bridge paradigm, he names only Buttrick's recent *A Captive Voice* (Farley, "Preaching the Bible," 98, n. 8). In any event, as indicated in notes 12 and 13, both Buttrick and Farley continue to see positive values in bringing the Bible into the sermon.

4. Farley, "Preaching the Bible," 93; Buttrick, *A Captive Voice*, 11–13, passim.

5. Buttrick, *A Captive Voice*, 11.

6. Farley, "Preaching the Bible," 95.

7. Ibid., 96–97.

8. Farley, "Preaching the Bible," 93–94; Buttrick regards the preaching of Jesus as a model for the preacher (*A Captive Voice*, 49–52). The disciplines of canonical criticism and tradition criticism help us see that similar phenomena were at work in the period of the First Testament: the Jewish community interpreted and reinterpreted its sacred texts and its situations in the light of its core vision of God and of God's purposes in the world. Also, they sometimes reinterpreted aspects of the core vision in the light of changing perceptions of their circumstances. Similar processes are at work in the vast body of literature grouped loosely under the heading of Midrash.

9. Buttrick, *A Captive Voice*, 23–29.

10. My sympathies with this approach are a matter of record in Ronald J. Allen, "Preaching against the Text," *Encounter* 48 (1987):105–16; idem and Clark M. Williamson, *Interpreting Difficult Texts: Anti-Judaism and Christian Preaching* (Philadelphia: Trinity Press International and London: SCM Press, 1989), 6–8, 73–74, 84–85; idem, *The Teaching Minister* (Louisville, Ky.: Westminster/John Knox Press, 1991), 75–82; idem, *A Credible and Timely Word: Process Theology and Preaching* (St. Louis: Chalice Press, 1992), 71–129; Ronald J. Allen, *Preaching the Topical Sermon* (Louisville, Ky.: Westminster/John Knox Press, 1992), 1–10, 19–35, 54–57.

11. Buttrick, *A Captive Voice*, 7, 9, 15–16, 19.

12. Ibid., 9–12.

13. I am embarrassingly aware that this "rationale" is all too brief. However, space precludes a more developed argument.

14. Farley, "Preaching the Bible," 103, who continues, "But note the order here. The sermon is first of all a preaching of the gospel, not a preaching of a passage."

15. Buttrick, *Homiletic*, 232. Cf. idem, *A Captive Voice*, 16–32. Buttrick proposes three structures for preaching in *Homiletic*: in the modes of immediacy, reflec-

tivity, and praxis. The first two of these aim to help the congregation encounter the theological structure of biblical *texts* in consciousness. Furthermore, Buttrick continues to write for lectionary-based preaching helps, e.g., *Proclamation 5–Easter: Interpreting the Lessons of the Church Year* (Minneapolis: Fortress Press, 1993).

16. On naming as a function of preaching and of scripture, see Buttrick, *Homiletic*, 5–20, esp. 17–20.

17. Ronald J. Allen, "Preaching on a Theme from the Bible," *Pulpit Digest* 75:526 (1994):78–86.

18. For models for doing so, see Buttrick, *Homiletic*, 405–45, and Allen, *Preaching the Topical Sermon*.

19. L. Susan May, "Unraveling the Canon," *Perspectives* 9:1 (1994):24.

20. James W. Wall, "A Joint Venture," *The Christian Century* 111 (1994):771–72.

21. Personal correspondence. This note gives me the opportunity to thank David Jacobsen for a helpful critical reading of an earlier draft of this chapter.

22. The seminal work is Hans-Georg Gadamer, *Truth and Method*, trans. Garrett Barden and John Cumming (New York: Seabury Press, 1975), esp. 323–24, 357–66. For discussion of preaching from the standpoint of conversation, see John McClure, *The Roundtable Pulpit* (Nashville: Abingdon Press, 1995), as well as William E. Dorman and Ronald J. Allen, "Preaching as Hospitality," *Quarterly Review* 14 (1994):295–310.

23. On this quality of texts, see Steven Kepnes, *The Text as Thou* (Bloomington, Ind.: Indiana University Press, 1992).

24. David Tracy outlines five steps in the conversational hermeneutical process: retrieval, critique, suspicion, explanation, understanding in his "Theological Method," in *Christian Theology*, 56–57. These "steps" do not necessarily occur sequentially.

25. David Tracy, *Plurality and Ambiguity* (San Francisco: Harper & Row, 1987), 18.

26. The foundational works are still David Tracy, *Blessed Rage for Order: The New Pluralism in Theology* (New York: Seabury Press, 1975); idem, *The Analogical Imagination: Christian Theology and the Culture of Pluralism* (New York: Crossroad, 1981); idem, "Theological Method," 35–60, esp. 52–59; idem, "Hermeneutical Reflections in the New Paradigm," in *Paradigm Change in Theology*, ed. Hans Kueng and David Tracy, trans. Margaret Koehl (Edinburgh: T. & T. Clark, 1989), 334–62.

27. For typologies of possible relationships between biblical texts and contemporary Christian communities, see Williamson and Allen, *A Credible and Timely Word*, 111–22, and Tracy, "Theological Method," 56–57; Dorman and Allen, "Preaching as Hospitality."

28. If it would be awkward to provide such orientation in the sermon itself, the preacher could bring it in a brief teaching moment at the time of the scripture reading or through a note printed in the worship bulletin.

29. David Buttrick's discussion of the nature and function of language and images is especially instructive. Note *Homiletic*, 5–20, 173–85, 187–98. For an extended, critical study of a symbol, see his *Preaching Jesus Christ: An Exercise in Homiletic Theology* (Philadelphia: Fortress Press, 1988).

30. For example, Buttrick, *A Captive Voice*, 2, 12, 13, 19, 46–47, 52, 72, 77, 81, 103–5, 108; idem, *Homiletic*, 31, 266, 273–274, 398, 407; idem, *Preaching Jesus Christ*, 69–85.

31. Carl Rogers, *A Way of Being* (Boston: Houghton Mifflin Co., 1980), 8.

32. For an insightful discussion of this phenomenon, see Michael K. Kinnamon, *Truth and Community: Diversity and Its Limits in the Ecumenical Movement* (Grand Rapids: Wm. B. Eerdmans Publishing Co., 1988).
33. For instance, many pastors find it helpful to plan their preaching texts for a quarter, a half year, or even a year at a time.
34. For a systematic review of the strengths and weaknesses of the lectionary, see Ronald J. Allen, "Preaching and the Christian Year," in *Handbook of Contemporary Preaching*, ed. Michael Duiduit (Nashville: Broadman Press, 1992), 236–46.
35. Farley, "Preaching the Bible," 100; Buttrick, *A Captive Voice*, 100–13.

Selected Bibliography of Works by David G. Buttrick

Books

"The Figure of Charles: A Study of the Theology and Fiction of Charles Williams." Union Theological Seminary, New York, 1951.

Service for the Lord's Day [Writer/Editor]. Philadelphia: Westminster Press, 1964.

Book of Common Worship—Provisional Services. [Writer/Editor]. Philadelphia: Westminster Press, 1966.

The Worshipbook—Services [Writer/Editor]. Philadelphia: Westminster Press, 1970.

Jesus and Man's Hope [Editor]. Pittsburgh: Pittsburgh Theological Seminary, 1970.

Proclamation 2—Pentecost B. With Donald H. Juel. Philadelphia: Fortress Press, 1980.

Proclamation 3—Epiphany. Philadelphia: Fortress Press, 1985.

Homiletic: Moves and Structures. Philadelphia: Fortress Press, 1987.

Preaching Jesus Christ: An Exercise in Homiletic Theology. Philadelphia: Fortress Press, 1988.

Proclamation 4—Pentecost 3. Philadelphia: Fortress Press, 1989.

The Mystery and the Passion: A Homiletic Reading of the Gospel Traditions. Minneapolis: Fortress Press, 1992.

Proclamation 5—Easter. Minneapolis: Fortress Press, 1993.

A Captive Voice: The Liberation of Preaching. Louisville, Ky.: Westminster John Knox Press, 1994.

Chapters in Books

"Renewal of Worship—A Source of Unity?" In *Ecumenism, the Spirit, and Worship*, edited by Leonard Swidler. Pittsburgh: Duquesne University Press, 1967.

"A Sketchbook: Preaching and Worship." In *Preaching and Worship*, edited by L. Kennel. Academy of Homiletics, 1980.

"Preaching on the Family." In *Preaching In and Out of Season*, edited by Thomas G. Long and Neely Dixon McCarter. Louisville, Ky.: Westminster/John Knox Press, 1990.

"Preaching, Hermeneutics and Liberation." In *Standing with the Poor: Theological Reflections on Economic Reality*, edited by Paul P. Parker. Cleveland: Pilgrim Press, 1992.

"Who's Listening?" In *Listening to the Word: Essays in Honor of Fred B. Craddock*, edited by Thomas G. Long and Gail R. O'Day. Nashville: Abingdon, Press, 1993.

"On Doing Homiletics Today." In *Intersections: Post-Critical Studies in Preaching*, edited by Richard L. Eslinger. Grand Rapids: Wm. B. Eerdmans Publishing Co., 1994.

"The Use of the Bible in Preaching." In *The New Interpreter's Bible*, vol. 1, 188–99. Nashville: Abingdon, Press, 1994.

"Laughing with the Gospel." In *Sharing Heaven's Music: Essays on Christian Preaching in Honor of James Earl Massey*, edited by Barry L. Callen. Nashville: Abingdon Press, 1995.

"Speaking Between Times." In *Theology and the Interhuman*, edited by Robert R. Williams. New York: Trinity Press International, 1995.

"Teaching Preachers to Preach." In *Preaching on the Brink*, edited by Martha Simmons. Nashville: Abingdon Press, 1996.

Articles

Our Act of Worship. A Living Faith Pamphlet. Philadelphia: Westminster Press, 1962.

Holy Communion. A Living Faith Pamphlet. Philadelphia: Westminster Press, 1964.

"An Act of Contrition." *Monday Morning*, May 6, 1968. Subsequently excerpted in *The New York Times*, May 17, 1968; *Newsweek*, May 27, 1968.

"The Problem with 'Situation Ethics.'" Special Publication, North Area Council of Churches, Pittsburgh, Pa., September 1969.

"A Revision of *The Worshipbook*." *Reformed Liturgy & Music* 9 (fall 1974).

"Preaching on the Resurrection." *Religion in Life*, Autumn 1976.

"Gestures toward a New Homiletic." Paper for the Theological Association of Mid-America. 1978.

"Marriage and the Marriage Service." *Reformed Liturgy & Music* 14 (winter 1980).

"Preaching and Interpretation." *Interpretation*, January 1981.

"On Liturgical Language." *Reformed Liturgy & Music* 15 (spring 1981).

"A Sketchbook: Preaching and Worship." *Reformed Liturgy & Music* 16, no. 1 (winter 1982).

"On Preaching a Parable: The Problem of Homiletic Method." *Reformed Liturgy & Music* 17, no. 1 (winter 1983).

"Let's Dream a Peaceable Kingdom," *The 7th Angel* 12, no. 2 (March 15, 1984).

"P. T. Forsyth—The Man, The Preacher's Theologian, Prophet for the Twentieth Century" [A Review-Article]. *Princeton Seminary Bulletin*, November 1985.

"Homiletic Resources for the Easter Season." *Quarterly Review* 6, no. 1 (spring 1986).

"Preaching in an Unbrave New World." *The Spire* 13, no. 1 (summer/fall, 1988).

"On Preaching from Romans 9—11." *Ex Auditu* 4 (1989): 113–122.

"Preaching and the Passion Narratives." *Reformed Liturgy & Music* 24, no. 1 (winter 1990): 6–10.

"Liturgy, Reformed." In *Encyclopedia of the Reformed Faith*, edited by Donald K. McKim, 220–23. Louisville, Ky.: Westminster/John Knox Press, 1992.

"Preaching, Theology of." In *Encyclopedia of the Reformed Faith*, edited by Donald K. McKim, 289–91. Louisville, Ky.: Westminster/John Knox Press, 1992.

"Preaching Between the Times." *Newsletter* [College of Preachers] 33, no. 4 (spring/summer 1993): 1–12.

"Preaching the Lectionary: Two Cheers and Some Questions." *Reformed Liturgy & Music* 28, no. 2 (spring 1994): 77–81.

"Preaching and the Search for Meaning." *Pulpit Digest*, May/June 1995, 73–81.

"Presbyterian and Reformed Worship in America." In *Dictionary of the Presbyterian and Reformed Tradition in America*, edited by Darryl G. Hart and Mark Noll. Downers Grove, Ill.: Intervarsity Press, 1996.